# Ninja Foodi 2-Basket Air Fryer Cookbook for Beginners

## 365 Affordable and Crispy Recipes for Your Whole Family to Master Double Zone Air Fryer

Jamie Graham

# Table of Contents

## Fish And Seafood Recipes ........ 69



## Vegetables And Sides Recipes ........ 85



## Desserts Recipes ........ 97

# Introduction

Life is too busy today, and there is no time to cook for a long day. If you want to eat delicious and healthy meals, the Ninja Foodi Dual Zone Air Fryer solves your problem. The Ninja Foodi Dual Zone Air Fryer is a new arrival amongst diversified air fryers. Now, you can cook a large amount of food because it has two baskets. You can cook two different food items with two same or different settings. It is different from a single basket air fryer. This appliance targets people who want to enjoy delicious and healthy but less fatty meals with a crispy texture. The Ninja Foodi Dual Zone Air Fryer is an excellent appliance to fulfill all the cooking needs. You can create excellent restaurant-style meals in your kitchen with the Ninja Foodi Dual Zone Air Fryer.

No doubt, the Ninja Foodi Dual Zone Air Fryer plays a vital role in making healthy and delicious foods. You don't need to stand in your kitchen cooking food for a long time. The benefits of this appliance are that it is easily washable and requires less oil to cook food. The Ninja Foodi Dual Zone Air Fryer works on dual zone technology. It allows you to prepare double dishes at the same time with two different cooking baskets and temperatures. If you have a big family, then you can cook food for them at the same time. The cooking zones have a separate temperature controller and cyclonic fan that spread heat evenly into the cooking baskets. The Ninja Foodi Dual Zone Air Fryer cooks your favorite food in less oil. It gives you crispy food without changing the taste and texture.

You can create different dishes for any occasion or picnic. The Ninja Foodi Dual Zone Air Fryer has useful cooking functions, such as max crisp, air fry, roast, reheat, dehydrate, and bake. All valuable functions are present in one appliance. You don't need to purchase separate appliances for baking or dehydrating food. You can roast chicken, beef, and fish using this appliance. Bake the cake, muffins, cupcakes, pancakes using bake cooking functions.

This Ninja Foodi Dual Zone Air Fryer cookbook will introduce you to the features and benefits of this revolutionary appliance. Apart from that, the functions of the Ninja Foodi Dual Zone Air Fryer are discussed in this cookbook, helping you unleash its full potential. And, of course, I'll introduce you to a wide variety of recipes so you can use it every day. The air fryer is pretty simple to use. Once you understand the Ninja Foodi Dual Zone Air Fryer, you can prepare delicious food for your family and friends without any hesitation. Cook food with the Ninja Foodi Dual Zone Air Fryer!

# Getting Started with the Ninja Foodi Dual Zone Air Fryer

## What is the Ninja Foodi Dual Zone Air Fryer

The new Ninja Foodi Dual Zone Air Fryer has a DUAL-ZONE technology that includes a smart finish button that cooks two food items in two different ways at the same time. It has a MATCH button that cooks food by copying the setting across both zones.

If you are always worried about the lack of time to prepare two different meals or a large number of meals in a single go, then this appliance is a must to have. It can hold plenty of food that can feed a large family.

## The Features and Benefits of the Ninja Foodi Dual Zone Air Fryers

The Ninja Foodi Dual Zone Air Fryer is one of the innovative product designs manufactured. If you are looking for a perfect air fryer for your family, then the Ninja Foodi Dual Zone Air Fryer is one of the best options available for you. Some of the important features and benefits of the Ninja Foodi Dual Zone Air Fryer are mentioned as follows.

**1. 8-Quart Capacity XL**

The enormous 8-quart capacity, which can be divided into two sections, provides ample area for cooking both large and small amounts of food. This oven can cook 2 pounds of fries and 2 pounds of wings and drumettes.

**2. Multifunctional Air Fryer**

The Ninja Foodi Dual Zone Air Fryer comes with 6 preset functions. These easily customizable functions include max crisp, air fry, roast, bake, reheat and dehydrate. You never need to buy separate appliances for a single cooking function.

**3. Safer Than Deep Fryer**

Traditional deep frying method involves a large container full of sizzling oil. This can increase the safety risk of splashing hot oil over the skin. While the Ninja Foodi Dual Zone Air Fryer is close from all the sides when getting hot, there is no risk of

splashing, spilling or accidental burn during the cooking process.

4. **Smart Finish**

This culinary marvel can intelligently sync the cook timings of both cooking zones, allowing you to prepare multiple items at the same time while maintaining the same finish time.

So, here's how it's done! When you put various foods in the baskets, each one takes a different amount of time to cook. When you use the smart cooking feature and start the operation, the basket with the longer cooking time will run first, while the other basket will remain on hold until the other chamber reaches the same cooking duration. Both sides finish cooking at the same time in this manner.

5. **Match Cook**

This air fryer's total 8 quartz capacity is divided into two 4-quart air fryer baskets, allowing you to cook various foods and the same dish in both baskets at the same time. You can utilize the same cooking mode for both baskets and utilize the XL capacity with the match cook technology.

6. **Reduce the Risk of Acrylamide Formation**

Deep frying is one of the high heat cooking methods in which harmful acrylamide is formed. It is one of the causes of developing some cancer like ovarian, endometrial, oesophageal and breast cancer. On the other side, this air fryer cooks your food into very little oil and fat by circulating hot air around the food. This process lowers the risk of acrylamide formation.

7. **Use Less Oil and Fats**

The cooking basket of the oven comes with ceramic non-stick coatings and allows you to prepare your favorite food using up to 75 to 80 % less fat and oils than the traditional deep frying method.

8. **Wide Temperature Range**

The Ninja Foodi Dual Zone Air Fryer offers a range of 105 °F to 400 °F temperature. The lower temperature range is suitable for dehydrating your favorite fruits, vegetable, and meat slices, and the higher temperature range allows you to cook thick cuts of meat.

9. **Easy to Clean**

The interior of this air fryer is made up of a non-stick coating so that you can clean it easily. The cooking tray comes in metallic and dishwasher safe, but you can easily clean it by hand if you want to.

## Tips for Cooking Success

Remember these nifty tips whenever you are cooking with your new air fryer.

1. Pressing the Start/Pause button while using the Smart Finish will pause the cooking process on both zones. Press the same button to resume cooking.
2. If at any time you need to pause the cooking process in one of the baskets, first select the zone, then the Start/Pause button.
3. To stop or end the cooking process, select the zone, then set the time to zero using the arrow down button. The display should show End after a few seconds, and the cooking process in this zone will stop.
4. You can adjust the temperature and time in each zone at any time during the cooking process. Select the zone, then adjust the setting using the arrow buttons.
5. Place a single layer of food and avoid stacking whenever possible.
6. To get the best results, toss or shake the food at least twice within the cooking cycle, especially for foods that overlap, like French fries. This will produce a more even cooking throughout.
7. When cooking fresh vegetables, add at least one tablespoon of cooking oil. More oil can be added to create a crispier texture.
8. Use the crisper plates when you want your food to become crunchy. Note that the crisper plates will slightly elevate your food to allow hot air to permeate the bottom and result in a crispier texture.
9. Follow the correct breading technique for wet battered food. Coat the food with flour first, then with egg, and finally with bread crumbs. Press the crumbs into the food to avoid it from flying around when air frying.
10. It is best to regularly check the progress to avoid overcooking.
11. A food-safe temperature must be reached to avoid any foodborne illness. Use a thermometer to check for doneness, especially when cooking raw meat. Instant-read thermometers are your best choice for this. Once cooking time is up or when the desired browning is achieved, promptly remove the food from the unit.
12. Do not use metal cutleries or tools that can damage the non-stick coating. Dump the food directly on a plate or use silicon-tipped tongs.
13. Small bits of food may be blown away while cooking. You can avoid this by securing pieces of food with toothpicks.
14. To cook recipes intended for traditional ovens, simply reduce the temperature by 25 ° F and regularly check for doneness.
15. Do not let food touch the heating elements.
16. Never overload the baskets. Not only will this result in uneven cooking, but it may also cause the appliance to malfunction as well.

## Main Functions of the Ninja Foodi Dual Zone Air Fryers

The Ninja Foodi Dual Zone Air Fryer has six cooking functions: max crisp, air fry, roast, reheat, dehydrate and bake. This appliance has a large capacity. You can prepare food for your big family. If you want to bake a cake with the Ninja Foodi Dual Zone Air Fryer, you can select "bake" cooking mode.

1. **Max Crisp**

This cooking function is perfect for frozen foods such as chicken nuggets and French fries etc. Using this function, you will get crispy and tender food. With less time, you will get crispy and tender food.

2. **Air Fry**

This cooking function will allow you to cook food with less oil and fat than other cooking methods. Using this function, you will get crunchy and crispy food from the outside and juicy and tender food from the inside. You can prepare chicken, beef, lamb, pork, and seafood using this cooking option.

**3. Roast**
Now, you didn't need an oven to roast food. The Ninja Foodi Dual Zone Air Fryer has useful cooking function, "roast". With this function, you can roast chicken, lamb, seafood, and vegetable dishes. It is one of the dry cooking methods that give you a nice brown texture to the food and increase the flavor of your foods.

**4. Reheat**
The reheat function can quickly warm your food without changing its texture and flavor if you have leftover food. Now, you didn't need to place food onto the stovetop for reheating.

**5. Dehydrate**
This cooking function is used to dehydrate fruits, meat, and vegetables. Using this cooking method, you can preserve food for a long time. It takes hours to dehydrate the food but gives you a delicious and crispy texture.

**6. Bake**
This cooking method allows you to bake cakes, muffins, cupcakes, and any other dessert on any occasion or regular day. You didn't need an oven to bake the food. The Ninja Foodi Dual Zone Air Fryer has a baking option for baking your food with delicious texture.

## Maintaining and Cleaning the Appliance

**1. Maintaining**

- It is very important to check that the voltage indication is corresponding to the main voltage from the switch.
- Do not immerse the appliance in water.
- Keep the cord away from the hot area.
- Do not touch the outer surface of the air fryer hen using for cooking purposes.
- Put the appliance on a horizontal and flat surface.
- Unplug the appliance after use.

**2. Cleaning**

- First, unplug the power cord of the air fryer.
- Make sure the appliance is cooled before cleaning.
- The air fryer should be cleaning after every use.
- To clean the outer surface, use a damp towel.
- Clean the inside of the air fryer with a nonabrasive sponge.

- The accessories of the air fryer are dishwasher safe, but to extend the life of the drawers, it's recommended to wash them manually.

## Tips for Cooking Success

Remember these nifty tips whenever you are cooking with your new air fryer.

1. Pressing the Start/Pause button while using the Smart Finish will pause the cooking process on both zones. Press the same button to resume cooking.
2. If at any time you need to pause the cooking process in one of the baskets, first select the zone, then the Start/Pause button.
3. To stop or end the cooking process, select the zone, then set the time to zero using the arrow down button. The display should show End after a few seconds, and the cooking process in this zone will stop.
4. You can adjust the temperature and time in each zone at any time during the cooking process. Select the zone, then adjust the setting using the arrow buttons.
5. Place a single layer of food and avoid stacking whenever possible.
6. To get the best results, toss or shake the food at least twice within the cooking cycle, especially for foods that overlap, like French fries. This will produce a more even cooking through out.

7. \ hen cooking fresh vegetables, add at least one tablespoon of cooking oil. More oil can be added to create a crispier texture.
8. Use the crisper plates when you want your food to become crunchy. Note that the crisper plates will slightly elevate your food to allow hot air to permeate the bottom and result in a crispier texture.
9. Follow the correct breading technique for wet battered food. Coat the food with flour first, then with egg, and finally with bread crumbs. Press the crumbs into the food to avoid it from flying around when air frying.
10. It is best to regularly check the progress to avoid overcooking.
11. A food-safe temperature must be reached to avoid any foodborne illness. Use a thermometer to check for doneness, especially when cooking raw meat. Instant-read thermometers are your best choice for this. Once cooking time is up or when the desired browning is achieved, promptly remove the food from the unit.
12. Do not use metal cutleries or tools that can damage the non-stick coating. Dump the food directly on a plate or use silicon-tipped tongs.
13. Small bits of food may be blown away while cooking. You can avoid this by securing pieces of food with toothpicks.
14. To cook recipes intended for traditional ovens, simply reduce the temperature by 25 °F and regularly check for doneness.
15. Do not let food touch the heating elements.
16. Never overload the baskets. Not only will this result in uneven cooking, but it may also cause the appliance to malfunction as well.

# Measurement Conversions

## BASIC KITCHEN CONVERSIONS & EQUIVALENTS

**DRY MEASUREMENTS CONVERSION CHART**

3 TEASPOONS = 1 TABLESPOON = 1/16 CUP
6 TEASPOONS = 2 TABLESPOONS = 1/8 CUP
12 TEASPOONS = 4 TABLESPOONS = 1/4 CUP
24 TEASPOONS = 8 TABLESPOONS = 1/2 CUP
36 TEASPOONS = 12 TABLESPOONS = 3/4 CUP
48 TEASPOONS = 16 TABLESPOONS = 1 CUP

**METRIC TO US COOKING CONVER SIONS**

**OVEN TEMPERATURES**

120 °C = 250 °F
160 °C = 320 °F
180° C = 360 °F
205 °C = 400 °F
220 °C = 425 °F

**LIQUID MEASUREMENTS CONVERSION CHART**

8 FLUID OUNCES = 1 CUP = 1/2 PINT = 1/4 QUART
16 FLUID OUNCES = 2 CUPS = 1 PINT = 1/2 QUART
32 FLUID OUNCES = 4 CUPS = 2 PINTS = 1 QUART = 1/4 GALLON
128 FLUID OUNCES = 16 CUPS = 8 PINTS = 4 QUARTS = 1 GALLON

**BAKING IN GRAMS**

1 CUP FLOUR = 140 GRAMS
1 CUP SUGAR = 150 GRAMS
1 CUP POWDERED SUGAR = 160 GRAMS
1 CUP HEAVY CREAM = 235 GRAMS

**VOLUME**

1 MILLILITER = 1/5 TEASPOON
5 ML = 1 TEASPOON
15 ML = 1 TABLESPOON
240 ML = 1 CUP OR 8 FLUID OUNCES
1 LITER = 34 FL. OUNCES

**WEIGHT**

1 GRAM = .035 OUNCES
100 GRAMS = 3.5 OUNCES
500 GRAMS = 1.1 POUNDS
1 KILOGRAM = 35 OUNCES

**US TO METRIC COOKING CONVERSIONS**

1/5 TSP = 1 ML
1 TSP = 5 ML
1 TBSP = 15 ML
1 FL OUNCE = 30 ML
1 CUP = 237 ML
1 PINT (2 CUPS) = 473 ML
1 QUART (4 CUPS) = .95 LITER
1 GALLON (16 CUPS) = 3.8 LITERS
1 OZ = 28 GRAMS
1 POUND = 454 GRAMS

**BUTTER**

1 CUP BUTTER = 2 STICKS = 8 OUNCES = 230 GRAMS = 8 TABLESPOONS

**WHAT DOES 1 CUP EQUAL**

1 CUP = 8 FLUID OUNCES
1 CUP = 16 TABLESPOONS
1 CUP = 48 TEASPOONS
1 CUP = 1/2 PINT
1 CUP = 1/4 QUART
1 CUP = 1/16 GALLON
1 CUP = 240 ML

**BAKING PAN CONVERSIONS**

1 CUP ALL-PURPOSE FLOUR = 4.5 OZ
1 CUP ROLLED OATS = 3 OZ 1 LARGE EGG = 1.7 OZ
1 CUP BUTTER = 8 OZ 1 CUP MILK = 8 OZ
1 CUP HEAVY CREAM = 8.4 OZ
1 CUP GRANULATED SUGAR = 7.1 OZ
1 CUP PACKED BROWN SUGAR = 7.75 OZ
1 CUP VEGETABLE OIL = 7.7 OZ
1 CUP UNSIFTED POWDERED SUGAR = 4.4 OZ

**BAKING PAN CONVERSIONS**

9-INCH ROUND CAKE PAN = 12 CUPS
10-INCH TUBE PAN =16 CUPS
11-INCH BUNDT PAN = 12 CUPS
9-INCH SPRINGFORM PAN = 10 CUPS
9 X 5 INCH LOAF PAN = 8 CUPS
9-INCH SQUARE PAN = 8 CUPS

# Snacks And Appetizers Recipes

## Fried Cheese

Servings: 4
Cooking Time: 12 Minutes
**Ingredients:**
- 1 Mozzarella cheese block, cut into sticks
- 2 teaspoons olive oil

**Directions:**
1. Divide the cheese slices into the Ninja Foodi 2 Baskets Air Fryer baskets.
2. Drizzle olive oil over the cheese slices.
3. Return the air fryer basket 1 to Zone 1, and basket 2 to Zone 2 of the Ninja Foodi 2-Basket Air Fryer.
4. Choose the "Air Fry" mode for Zone 1 and set the temperature to 360 degrees F (180°C) and 12 minutes of cooking time.
5. Flip the cheese slices once cooked halfway through.
6. Serve.

**Nutrition:**
- (Per serving) Calories 186 | Fat 3g |Sodium 223mg | Carbs 31g | Fiber 8.7g | Sugar 5.5g | Protein 9.7g

## Parmesan Crush Chicken

Servings:4
Cooking Time:18
**Ingredients:**
- 4 chicken breasts
- 1 cup parmesan cheese
- 1 cup bread crumb
- 2 eggs, whisked
- Salt, to taste
- Oil spray, for greasing

**Directions:**
1. Whisk egg in a large bowl and set aside.
2. Season the chicken breast with salt and then put it in egg wash.
3. Next, dredge it in breadcrumb then parmesan cheese.
4. Line both the basket of the air fryer with parchment paper.
5. Divided the breast pieces between the backsets, and oil spray the breast pieces.
6. Set zone 1 basket to air fry mode at 350 degrees F(175°C) for 18 minutes.
7. Select the MATCH button for the zone 2 basket.
8. Once it's done, serve.

**Nutrition:**
- (Per serving) Calories574 | Fat25g | Sodium848 mg | Carbs 21.4g | Fiber 1.2g| Sugar 1.8g | Protein 64.4g

## Chili-lime Crispy Chickpeas Pizza-seasoned Crispy Chickpeas

Servings:6
Cooking Time: 20 Minutes
**Ingredients:**
- FOR THE CHILI-LIME CHICKPEAS
- 1½ cups canned chickpeas, rinsed and drained
- ¼ cup fresh lime juice
- 1 tablespoon olive oil
- 1½ teaspoons chili powder
- ½ teaspoon kosher salt
- FOR THE PIZZA-SEASONED CHICKPEAS
- 1½ cups canned chickpeas, rinsed and drained
- 1 tablespoon olive oil
- 1 tablespoon grated Parmesan cheese
- ½ teaspoon dried basil
- ½ teaspoon dried oregano
- ½ teaspoon kosher salt
- ¼ teaspoon onion powder
- ¼ teaspoon garlic powder
- ¼ teaspoon fennel seeds
- ¼ teaspoon dried thyme
- ¼ teaspoon red pepper flakes (optional)

**Directions:**
1. To prep the chili-lime chickpeas: In a small bowl, mix the chickpeas, lime juice, olive oil, chili powder, and salt until the chickpeas are well coated.
2. To prep the pizza-seasoned chickpeas: In a small bowl, mix the chickpeas, olive oil, Parmesan, basil, oregano, salt, onion powder, garlic powder, fennel, thyme, and red pepper flakes (if using) until the chickpeas are well coated.
3. To cook the chickpeas: Install a crisper plate in each of the two baskets. Place the chili-lime chickpeas in the Zone 1 basket and insert the basket in the unit. Place the pizza-seasoned chickpeas in the Zone 2 basket and insert the basket in the unit.
4. Select Zone 1, select AIR FRY, set the temperature to 375°F (190°C), and set the time to 20 minutes. Select MATCH COOK to match Zone 2 settings to Zone 1.
5. Press START/PAUSE to begin cooking.
6. When both timers read 10 minutes, press START/PAUSE. Remove both baskets and give each basket a shake to redistribute the chickpeas. Reinsert both baskets and press START/PAUSE to resume cooking.
7. When both timers read 5 minutes, press START/PAUSE. Remove both baskets and give each basket a good shake again. Reinsert both baskets and press START/PAUSE to resume cooking.
8. When cooking is complete, the chickpeas will be crisp and golden brown. Serve warm or at room temperature.

**Nutrition:**
- (Per serving) Calories: 145; Total fat: 6.5g; Saturated fat: 0.5g; Carbohydrates: 17g; Fiber: 4.5g; Protein: 5g; Sodium: 348mg

## Cheddar Quiche

Servings:2
Cooking Time:12
**Ingredients:**
- 4 eggs, organic
- 1-1/4 cup heavy cream
- Salt, pinch
- ½ cup broccoli florets
- ½ cup cheddar cheese, shredded and for sprinkling

**Directions:**
1. Take a Pyrex pitcher and crack two eggs in it.
2. And fill it with heavy cream, about half the way up.
3. Add in the salt and then add in the broccoli and pour this into two quiche dishes, and top it with shredded cheddar cheese.

4. Now divide it between both zones of baskets.
5. For zone 1, set the time to 10-12 minutes at 325 degrees F(160°C) .
6. Select the MATCH button for the zone 2 basket.
7. Once done, serve hot.

**Nutrition:**

- (Per serving) Calories 454| Fat40g | Sodium 406mg | Carbs 4.2g | Fiber 0.6g| Sugar1.3 g | Protein 20g

## Goat Cheese And Garlic Crostini & Sweet Bacon Potato Crunchies

Servings: 8
Cooking Time: 7 Minutes

**Ingredients:**

- Goat Cheese and Garlic Crostini:
- 1 wholemeal baguette
- 60 ml olive oil
- 2 garlic cloves, minced
- 113 g goat cheese
- 2 tablespoons fresh basil, minced
- Sweet Bacon Potato Crunchies:
- 24 frozen potato crunchies
- 6 slices cooked bacon
- 2 tablespoons maple syrup
- 240 ml shredded Cheddar cheese

**Directions:**

1. Make the Goat Cheese and Garlic Crostini :
2. Preheat the air fryer to 190ºC.
3. Cut the baguette into ½-inch-thick slices.
4. In a small bowl, mix together the olive oil and garlic, then brush it over one side of each slice of bread.
5. Place the olive-oil-coated bread in a single layer in the zone 1 air fryer basket and bake for 5 minutes.
6. Meanwhile, in a small bowl, mix together the goat cheese and basil.
7. Remove the toast from the air fryer, then spread a thin layer of the goat cheese mixture over the top of each piece and serve.
8. Make the Sweet Bacon Potato Crunchies :
9. Preheat the air fryer to 205ºC.
10. Put the potato crunchies in the zone 2 air fryer basket. Air fry for 10 minutes, shaking the basket halfway through the cooking time.
11. Meanwhile, cut the bacon into 1-inch pieces.
12. Remove the potato crunchies from the air fryer basket and put into a baking pan. Top with the bacon and drizzle with the maple syrup. Air fry for 5 minutes, or until the crunchies and bacon are crisp.
13. Top with the cheese and air fry for 2 minutes, or until the cheese is melted.
14. Serve hot.

## Cinnamon Sugar Chickpeas

Servings: 4
Cooking Time: 15 Minutes

**Ingredients:**

- 2 cups chickpeas, drained
- Spray oil
- 1 tablespoon coconut sugar
- ½ teaspoon cinnamon
- Serving
- 57g cheddar cheese, cubed
- ¼ cup raw almonds
- 85g jerky, sliced

**Directions:**

1. Toss chickpeas with coconut sugar, cinnamon and oil in a bowl.
2. Divide the chickpeas into the Ninja Foodi 2 Baskets Air Fryer baskets.
3. Drizzle cheddar cheese, almonds and jerky on top.
4. Return the air fryer basket 1 to Zone 1, and basket 2 to Zone 2 of the Ninja Foodi 2-Basket Air Fryer.
5. Choose the "Air Fry" mode for Zone 1 at 380 degrees F(195°C) and 15 minutes of cooking time.
6. Select the "MATCH COOK" option to copy the settings for Zone 2.
7. Initiate cooking by pressing the START/PAUSE BUTTON.
8. Toss the chickpeas once cooked halfway through.
9. Serve warm.

**Nutrition:**

- (Per serving) Calories 103 | Fat 8.4g |Sodium 117mg | Carbs 3.5g | Fiber 0.9g | Sugar 1.5g | Protein 5.1g

## Veggie Shrimp Toast

Servings: 4
Cooking Time: 3 To 6 Minutes

**Ingredients:**

- 8 large raw shrimp, peeled and finely chopped
- 1 egg white
- 2 garlic cloves, minced
- 3 tablespoons minced red pepper
- 1 medium celery stalk, minced
- 2 tablespoons cornflour
- ¼ teaspoon Chinese five-spice powder
- 3 slices firm thin-sliced no-salt wholemeal bread

**Directions:**

1. Preheat the air fryer to 175ºC.
2. In a small bowl, stir together the shrimp, egg white, garlic, red pepper, celery, cornflour, and five-spice powder. Top each slice of bread with one-third of the shrimp mixture, spreading it evenly to the edges. With a sharp knife, cut each slice of bread into 4 strips.
3. Place the shrimp toasts in the two air fryer baskets in a single layer. Air fry for 3 to 6 minutes, until crisp and golden brown.
4. Serve hot.

## Crispy Popcorn Shrimp

Servings: 4
Cooking Time: 6 Minutes

**Ingredients:**

- 170g shrimp, peeled and diced
- ½ cup breadcrumbs
- Salt and black pepper to taste
- 2 eggs, beaten

**Directions:**

1. Mix breadcrumbs with black pepper and salt in a bowl.
2. Dip the shrimp pieces in the eggs and coat each with breadcrumbs.
3. Divide the shrimp popcorn into the 2 Air Fryer baskets.
4. Return the air fryer basket 1 to Zone 1, and basket 2 to Zone 2 of the Ninja Foodi 2-Basket Air Fryer.
5. Choose the "Air Fry" mode for Zone 1 at 400 degrees F(205°C) and 6 minutes of cooking time.
6. Select the "MATCH COOK" option to copy the settings for Zone 2.
7. Initiate cooking by pressing the START/PAUSE BUTTON.
8. Serve warm.

**Nutrition:**

- (Per serving) Calories 180 | Fat 3.2g |Sodium 133mg | Carbs 32g | Fiber 1.1g | Sugar 1.8g | Protein 9g

## Kale Potato Nuggets

Servings: 4
Cooking Time: 15minutes
**Ingredients:**
- 279g potatoes, chopped, boiled & mashed
- 268g kale, chopped
- 1 garlic clove, minced
- 30ml milk
- Pepper
- Salt

**Directions:**
1. In a bowl, mix potatoes, kale, milk, garlic, pepper, and salt until well combined.
2. Insert a crisper plate in the Ninja Foodi air fryer baskets.
3. Make small balls from the potato mixture and place them both baskets.
4. Select zone 1 then select "air fry" mode and set the temperature to 390 degrees F(200°C) for 15 minutes. Press "match" to match zone 2 settings to zone 1. Press "start/stop" to begin. Turn halfway through.

**Nutrition:**
- (Per serving) Calories 90 | Fat 0.2g |Sodium 76mg | Carbs 19.4g | Fiber 2.8g | Sugar 1.2g | Protein 3.6g

## Pretzels Hot Dog

Servings: 8
Cooking Time: 15 Minutes
**Ingredients:**
- 180ml warm water
- 2¼ teaspoons instant yeast
- 1 teaspoon sugar
- 2 teaspoons olive oil
- 250g plain flour
- ½ teaspoon salt
- 1 large egg
- 1 tablespoon water
- 8 hot dogs

**Directions:**
1. Combine warm water, yeast, sugar, and olive oil in a large mixing basin to make the dough.
2. Stir everything together and leave aside for about 5 minutes.
3. Mix in roughly 125g flour and a pinch of salt. Add 125g of flour at a time until the dough comes together into a ball and pulls away from the bowl's sides.
4. On a floured board, pour the dough. Knead the dough for 3 to 5 minutes, adding extra flour until it is no longer sticky.
5. Cut the dough into eight pieces.
6. Roll the dough between your hands, and roll each piece into an 20 cm to 25 cm rope.
7. Pat, the hot dogs, dry with paper towels to make wrapping the dough around them easier.
8. Begin wrapping the dough around one end of each hot dog in a spiral. To seal the ends, pinch them together.
9. In a small mixing dish, whisk together an egg and a tablespoon of water. Coat the dough in egg wash from all sides.
10. Press your chosen zone - "Zone 1" or "Zone 2" and then rotate the knob to select "Air Fryer".
11. Set the temperature to 200 degrees C, and then set the time for 5 minutes to preheat.
12. After preheating, arrange pretzels into the basket of each zone.
13. Slide the baskets into Air Fryer and set the time for 8 minutes.
14. After cooking time is completed, place on a wire rack for a few minutes, then transfer onto serving plates and serve.

## Stuffed Bell Peppers

Servings:3
Cooking Time:16
**Ingredients:**
- 6 large bell peppers
- 1-1/2 cup cooked rice
- 2 cups cheddar cheese

**Directions:**
1. Cut the bell peppers in half lengthwise and remove all the seeds.
2. Fill the cavity of each bell pepper with cooked rice.
3. Divide the bell peppers amongst the two zones of the air fryer basket.
4. Set the time for zone 1 for 200 degrees F (95°C) for 10 minutes.
5. Select MATCH button of zone 2 basket.
6. Afterward, take out the baskets and sprinkle cheese on top.
7. Set the time for zone 1 for 200 degrees F(95°C) for 6 minutes.
8. Select MATCH button of zone 2 basket.
9. Once it's done, serve.

**Nutrition:**
- (Per serving) Calories 605| Fat 26g | Sodium477 mg | Carbs68.3 g | Fiber4 g| Sugar 12.5g | Protein25.6 g

## Strawberries And Walnuts Muffins

Servings:2
Cooking Time:15
**Ingredients:**
- Salt, pinch
- 2 eggs, whisked
- 1/3 cup maple syrup
- 1/3 cup coconut oil
- 4 tablespoons of water
- 1 teaspoon of orange zest
- ¼ teaspoon of vanilla extract
- ½ teaspoon of baking powder
- 1 cup all-purpose flour
- 1 cup strawberries, finely chopped
- 1/3 cup walnuts, chopped and roasted

**Directions:**
1. Take one cup size of 4 ramekins that are oven safe.
2. Layer it with muffin paper.
3. In a bowl and add egg, maple syrup, oil, water, vanilla extract, and orange zest.
4. Whisk it all very well
5. In a separate bowl, mix flour, baking powder, and salt.
6. Now add dry ingredients slowly to wet ingredients.
7. Now pour this batter into ramekins and top it with strawberries and walnuts.
8. Now divide it between both zones and set the time for zone 1 basket to 15 minutes at 350 degrees F(175°C) .
9. Select the MATCH button for the zone 2 basket.
10. Check if not done let it AIR FRY FOR one more minute.
11. Once done, serve.

**Nutrition:**
- (Per serving) Calories 897| Fat 53.9g | Sodium 148mg | Carbs 92g | Fiber 4.7g| Sugar35.6 g | Protein 17.5g

## Fried Pickles

Servings: 4
Cooking Time: 15 Minutes
**Ingredients:**
- 2 cups sliced dill pickles
- 1 cup flour
- 1 tablespoon garlic powder
- 1 tablespoon Cajun spice
- ½ tablespoon cayenne pepper
- Olive Oil or cooking spray

**Directions:**
1. Mix together the flour and spices in a bowl.

2. Coat the sliced pickles with the flour mixture.
3. Place a crisper plate in each drawer. Put the pickles in a single layer in each drawer. Insert the drawers into the unit.
4. Select zone 1, then AIR FRY, then set the temperature to 400 degrees F/ 205 degrees C with a 15-minute timer. To match zone 2 settings to zone 1, choose MATCH. To begin, select START/STOP.

**Nutrition:**

- (Per serving) Calories 161 | Fat 4.1g | Sodium 975mg | Carbs 27.5g | Fiber 2.2g | Sugar 1.5g | Protein 4g

## Jalapeño Popper Chicken

Servings: 4
Cooking Time: 50 Minutes

**Ingredients:**

- 2 ounces cream cheese, softened
- ¼ cup shredded cheddar cheese
- ¼ cup shredded mozzarella cheese
- ¼ teaspoon garlic powder
- 4 small jalapeño peppers, seeds removed and diced
- Kosher salt, as desired
- Ground black pepper, as desired
- 4 organic boneless, skinless chicken breasts
- 8 slices bacon

**Directions:**

1. Cream together the cream cheese, cheddar cheese, mozzarella cheese, garlic powder, and jalapeño in a mixing bowl. Add salt and pepper to taste.
2. Make a deep pocket in the center of each chicken breast, but be cautious not to cut all the way through.
3. Fill each chicken breast's pocket with the cream cheese mixture.
4. Wrap two strips of bacon around each chicken breast and attach them with toothpicks.
5. Place a crisper plate in each drawer. Put the chicken breasts in the drawers. Place both drawers in the unit.
6. Select zone 1, then AIR FRY, and set the temperature to 350 degrees F/ 175 degrees C with a 30-minute timer. To match zone 2 and zone 1 settings, select MATCH. To begin cooking, press the START/STOP button.
7. When cooking is complete, remove the chicken breasts and allow them to rest for 5 minutes before serving

**Nutrition:**

- (Per serving) Calories 507 | Fat 27.5g | Sodium 1432mg | Carbs 2.3g | Fiber 0.6g | Sugar 0.6g | Protein 58.2g

## Lemony Endive In Curried Yoghurt

Servings: 6
Cooking Time: 10 Minutes

**Ingredients:**

- 6 heads endive
- 120 ml plain and fat-free yoghurt
- 3 tablespoons lemon juice
- 1 teaspoon garlic powder
- ½ teaspoon curry powder
- Salt and ground black pepper, to taste

**Directions:**

1. Wash the endives and slice them in half lengthwise.
2. In a bowl, mix together the yoghurt, lemon juice, garlic powder, curry powder, salt and pepper.
3. Brush the endive halves with the marinade, coating them completely. Allow to sit for at least 30 minutes or up to 24 hours.
4. Preheat the air fryer to 160°C.
5. Put the endives in the two air fryer baskets and air fry for 10 minutes.
6. Serve hot.

## Shrimp Pirogues

Servings: 8
Cooking Time: 4 To 5 Minutes

**Ingredients:**

- 340 g small, peeled, and deveined raw shrimp
- 85 g soft white cheese, room temperature
- 2 tablespoons natural yoghurt
- 1 teaspoon lemon juice
- 1 teaspoon dried dill weed, crushed
- Salt, to taste
- 4 small hothouse cucumbers, each approximately 6 inches long

**Directions:**

1. Pour 4 tablespoons water in bottom of air fryer drawer.
2. Place shrimp in air fryer basket in single layer and air fry at 200ºC for 4 to 5 minutes, just until done. Watch carefully because shrimp cooks quickly, and overcooking makes it tough.
3. Chop shrimp into small pieces, no larger than ½ inch. Refrigerate while mixing the remaining ingredients.
4. With a fork, mash and whip the soft white cheese until smooth.
5. Stir in the yoghurt and beat until smooth. Stir in lemon juice, dill weed, and chopped shrimp.
6. Taste for seasoning. If needed, add ¼ to ½ teaspoon salt to suit your taste.
7. Store in refrigerator until serving time.
8. When ready to serve, wash and dry cucumbers and split them lengthwise. Scoop out the seeds and turn cucumbers upside down on paper towels to drain for 10 minutes.
9. Just before filling, wipe centres of cucumbers dry. Spoon the shrimp mixture into the pirogues and cut in half crosswise. Serve immediately.

## Avocado Fries With Sriracha Dip

Servings: 4
Cooking Time: 6 Minutes

**Ingredients:**

- Avocado Fries
- 4 avocados, peeled and cut into sticks
- ¾ cup panko breadcrumbs
- ¼ cup flour
- 2 eggs, beaten
- ½ teaspoon garlic powder
- ½ teaspoon salt
- SRIRACHA-RANCH SAUCE
- ¼ cup ranch dressing
- 1 teaspoon sriracha sauce

**Directions:**

1. Mix flour with garlic powder and salt in a bowl.
2. Dredge the avocado sticks through the flour mixture.
3. Dip them in the eggs and coat them with breadcrumbs.
4. Place the coated fries in the air fryer baskets.
5. Return the air fryer basket 1 to Zone 1, and basket 2 to Zone 2 of the Ninja Foodi 2-Basket Air Fryer.
6. Choose the "Air Fry" mode for Zone 1 at 400 degrees F(205°C) and 6 minutes of cooking time.
7. Select the "MATCH COOK" option to copy the settings for Zone 2.
8. Initiate cooking by pressing the START/PAUSE BUTTON.
9. Flip the fries once cooked halfway through.
10. Mix all the dipping sauce ingredients in a bowl.
11. Serve the fries with dipping sauce.

**Nutrition:**

- (Per serving) Calories 229 | Fat 1.9 |Sodium 567mg | Carbs 1.9g | Fiber 0.4g | Sugar 0.6g | Protein 11.8g

## Pretzels

Servings: 8
Cooking Time: 6 Minutes

**Ingredients:**

- 360ml warm water
- 1 tablespoon dry active yeast
- 1 tablespoon sugar
- 1 tablespoon olive oil
- 500g plain flour
- 1 teaspoon salt
- 1 large egg
- 1 tablespoon water

**Directions:**

1. Combine warm water, yeast, sugar, and olive oil in a large mixing bowl. Stir everything together and leave aside for about 5 minutes.
2. Add 375g flour and a teaspoon of salt to the mixture. Stir well.
3. On a floured surface, roll out the dough. Knead for 3 to 5 minutes, or until the dough is no longer sticky, adding flour 1 tablespoon at a time if necessary.
4. The dough should be divided in half. At a time, work with half of the dough.
5. Each dough half should be divided into eight pieces.
6. Make a 45cm rope out of the dough. Make a U shape out of the dough. Twist the ends two more times.
7. Fold the ends of the dough over the spherical portion.
8. In a small mixing dish, whisk the egg and a tablespoon of water.
9. Brush the egg wash on both sides of the pretzel dough.
10. Press your chosen zone - "Zone 1" or "Zone 2" and then rotate the knob to select "Air Fryer".
11. Set the temperature to 185 degrees C, and then set the time for 5 minutes to preheat.
12. After preheating, arrange pretzels into the basket of each zone.
13. Slide the baskets into Air Fryer and set the time for 6 minutes.
14. After cooking time is completed, place on a wire rack for a few minutes, then transfer onto serving plates and serve.

## Mozzarella Balls

Servings: 6
Cooking Time: 13 Minutes

**Ingredients:**

- 2 cups mozzarella, shredded
- 3 tablespoons cornstarch
- 3 tablespoons water
- 2 eggs, beaten
- 1 cup Italian seasoned breadcrumbs
- 1 tablespoon Italian seasoning
- 1½ teaspoons garlic powder
- 1 teaspoon salt
- 1½ teaspoons Parmesan

**Directions:**

1. Mix mozzarella with parmesan, water and cornstarch in a bowl.
2. Make 1-inch balls out of this mixture.
3. Mix breadcrumbs with seasoning, salt, and garlic powder in a bowl.
4. Dip the balls into the beaten eggs and coat with the breadcrumbs.
5. Place the coated balls in the air fryer baskets.
6. Return the air fryer basket 1 to Zone 1, and basket 2 to Zone 2 of the Ninja Foodi 2-Basket Air Fryer.
7. Choose the "Air Fry" mode for Zone 1 and set the temperature to 360 degrees F(180°C) and 13 minutes of cooking time.
8. Select the "MATCH COOK" option to copy the settings for Zone 2.
9. Initiate cooking by pressing the START/PAUSE BUTTON.
10. Toss the balls once cooked halfway through.
11. Serve.

**Nutrition:**

- (Per serving) Calories 307 | Fat 8.6g |Sodium 510mg | Carbs 22.2g | Fiber 1.4g | Sugar 13g | Protein 33.6g

## Mushroom Rolls

Servings: 10
Cooking Time: 10 Minutes

**Ingredients:**

- 2 tablespoons olive oil
- 200g large portobello mushrooms, finely chopped
- 1 teaspoon dried oregano
- ½ teaspoon crushed red pepper flakes
- ¼ teaspoon salt
- 200g cream cheese, softened
- 100g whole-milk ricotta cheese
- 10 flour tortillas
- Cooking spray

**Directions:**

1. Heat the oil in a frying pan over medium heat. Add the mushrooms and cook for 4 minutes.
2. Sauté until mushrooms are browned, about 4-6 minutes, with oregano, pepper flakes, and salt. Cool.
3. Combine the cheeses in a mixing bowl| fold the mushrooms until thoroughly combined. On the bottom centre of each tortilla, spread 3 tablespoons of the mushroom mixture. Tightly roll up and secure with toothpicks.
4. Press either "Zone 1" or "Zone 2" and then rotate the knob to select "Air Fry".
5. Set the temperature to 200 degrees C, and then set the time for 5 minutes to preheat.
6. After preheating, spray the basket with cooking spray and arrange rolls onto basket.
7. Slide the basket into the Air Fryer and set the time for 10 minutes.
8. After cooking time is completed, transfer them onto serving plates and serve.

## Cheese Stuffed Mushrooms

Servings: 4
Cooking Time: 8 Minutes

**Ingredients:**

- 176g button mushrooms, clean & cut stems
- 46g sour cream
- 17g cream cheese, softened
- ½ tsp garlic powder
- 58g cheddar cheese, shredded
- Pepper
- Salt

**Directions:**

1. In a small bowl, mix cream cheese, garlic powder, sour cream, pepper, and salt.
2. Stuff cream cheese mixture into each mushroom and top each with cheddar cheese.
3. Insert a crisper plate in the Ninja Foodi air fryer baskets.
4. Place the stuffed mushrooms in both baskets.
5. Select zone 1 then select "air fry" mode and set the temperature to 370 degrees F(185°C) for 8 minutes. Press "match" to match zone 2 settings to zone 1. Press "start/stop" to begin.

**Nutrition:**

- (Per serving) Calories 222 | Fat 19.4g |Sodium 220mg | Carbs 5.6g | Fiber 1.2g | Sugar 2.2g | Protein 8.9g

## Roasted Tomato Bruschetta With Toasty Garlic Bread

Servings:4
Cooking Time: 12 Minutes
**Ingredients:**

- FOR THE ROASTED TOMATOES
- 10 ounces cherry tomatoes, cut in half
- 1 tablespoon balsamic vinegar
- 1 tablespoon olive oil
- ¼ teaspoon kosher salt
- ¼ teaspoon freshly ground black pepper
- FOR THE GARLIC BREAD
- 4 slices crusty Italian bread
- 1 tablespoon olive oil
- 3 garlic cloves, minced
- ¼ teaspoon Italian seasoning
- FOR THE BRUSCHETTA
- ¼ cup loosely packed fresh basil, thinly sliced
- ½ cup part-skim ricotta cheese

**Directions:**

1. To prep the tomatoes: In a small bowl, combine the tomatoes, vinegar, oil, salt, and black pepper.
2. To prep the garlic bread: Brush one side of each bread slice with the oil. Sprinkle with the garlic and Italian seasoning.
3. To cook the tomatoes and garlic bread: Install a broil rack in the Zone 1 basket (without the crisper plate installed). Place the tomatoes on the rack in the basket and insert the basket in the unit.
4. Place 2 slices of bread in the Zone 2 basket and insert the basket in the unit.
5. Select Zone 1, select AIR BROIL, set the temperature to 450°F (230°C), and set the time to 12 minutes.
6. Select Zone 2, select AIR FRY, set the temperature to 360°F (180°C), and set the time to 10 minutes. Select SMART FINISH.
7. Press START/PAUSE to begin cooking.
8. When the Zone 2 timer reads 5 minutes, press START/PAUSE. Remove the basket and transfer the garlic bread to a cutting board. Place the remaining 2 slices of garlic bread in the basket. Reinsert the basket in the unit and press START/PAUSE to resume cooking.
9. To assemble the bruschetta: When cooking is complete, add the basil to the tomatoes and stir to combine. Spread 2 tablespoons of ricotta onto each slice of garlic bread and top with the tomatoes. Serve warm or at room temperature.

**Nutrition:**

- (Per serving) Calories: 212; Total fat: 11g; Saturated fat: 2.5g; Carbohydrates: 22g; Fiber: 1.5g; Protein: 6g; Sodium: 286mg

## Cottage Fries

Servings: 2
Cooking Time: 12 Minutes
**Ingredients:**

- 3 medium russet potatoes, sliced
- 1 teaspoon olive oil
- Salt and pepper, to taste

**Directions:**

1. Potatoes should be washed and dried. Cut them into ½ cm slices.
2. Soak the slices in cold water for 3 minutes to remove the starch.
3. Remove the potatoes from the water and pat them dry. Toss them in a bowl with olive oil, pepper and a pinch of salt.
4. Press either "Zone 1" or "Zone 2" and then rotate the knob to select "Air Fryer".
5. Set the temperature to 200 degrees C, and then set the time for 5 minutes to preheat.
6. After preheating, arrange potatoes into the basket.
7. Slide the basket into the Air Fryer and set the time for 12 minutes.
8. While cooking, toss the potato pieces once halfway through.
9. After cooking time is completed, transfer the fries onto serving plates and serve.

## Mexican Jalapeno Poppers

Servings: 8
Cooking Time: 5minutes
**Ingredients:**

- 5 jalapenos, cut in half & remove seeds
- ¼ tsp red pepper flakes, crushed
- 1 tsp onion powder
- 32g salsa
- 113g goat cheese
- 1 tsp garlic powder
- Pepper
- Salt

**Directions:**

1. In a small bowl, mix goat cheese, salsa, red pepper flakes, onion powder, garlic powder, pepper, and salt.
2. Stuff each jalapeno half with goat cheese mixture.
3. Insert a crisper plate in the Ninja Foodi air fryer baskets.
4. Place stuffed peppers in both baskets.
5. Select zone 1 then select "air fry" mode and set the temperature to 360 degrees F(180°C) for 8 minutes—Press "match" to match zone 2 settings to zone 1. Press "start/stop" to begin.

**Nutrition:**

- (Per serving) Calories 112 | Fat 8.2g |Sodium 148mg | Carbs 2.6g | Fiber 0.6g | Sugar 1.5g | Protein 7.4g

## Air Fried Pot Stickers

Servings: 30 Pot Stickers
Cooking Time: 18 To 20 Minutes
**Ingredients:**

- 120 ml finely chopped cabbage
- 60 ml finely chopped red pepper
- 2 spring onions, finely chopped
- 1 egg, beaten
- 2 tablespoons cocktail sauce
- 2 teaspoons low-salt soy sauce
- 30 wonton wrappers
- 1 tablespoon water, for brushing the wrappers

**Directions:**

1. Preheat the air fryer to 180°C.
2. In a small bowl, combine the cabbage, pepper, spring onions, egg, cocktail sauce, and soy sauce, and mix well.
3. Put about 1 teaspoon of the mixture in the centre of each wonton wrapper. Fold the wrapper in half, covering the filling; dampen the edges with water, and seal. You can crimp the edges of the wrapper with your fingers, so they look like the pot stickers you get in restaurants. Brush them with water.
4. Place the pot stickers in the two air fryer baskets and air fry for 9 to 10 minutes, or until the pot stickers are hot and the bottoms are lightly browned.
5. Serve hot.

## Potato Tater Tots

Servings: 4
Cooking Time: 27 Minutes.

**Ingredients:**

- 2 potatoes, peeled
- ½ teaspoon Cajun seasoning
- Olive oil cooking spray
- Sea salt to taste

**Directions:**

1. Boil water in a cooking pot and cook potatoes in it for 15 minutes.
2. Drain and leave the potatoes to cool in a bowl.
3. Grate these potatoes and toss them with Cajun seasoning.
4. Make small tater tots out of this mixture.
5. Divide them into the two crisper plates and spray them with cooking oil.
6. Return the crisper plates to the Ninja Foodi Dual Zone Air Fryer.
7. Choose the Air Fry mode for Zone 1 and set the temperature to 375 degrees F(190°C) and the time to 27 minutes.
8. Select the "MATCH" button to copy the settings for Zone 2.
9. Initiate cooking by pressing the START/STOP button.
10. Flip them once cooked halfway through, and resume cooking.
11. Serve warm

**Nutrition:**

- (Per serving) Calories 185 | Fat 11g |Sodium 355mg | Carbs 21g | Fiber 5.8g | Sugar 3g | Protein 4.7g

## Healthy Spinach Balls

Servings: 4
Cooking Time: 10 Minutes

**Ingredients:**

- 1 egg
- 29g breadcrumbs
- ½ medium onion, chopped
- 225g spinach, blanched & chopped
- 1 carrot, peel & grated
- 1 tbsp cornflour
- 1 tbsp nutritional yeast
- 1 tsp garlic, minced
- ½ tsp garlic powder
- Pepper
- Salt

**Directions:**

1. Add spinach and remaining ingredients into the mixing bowl and mix until well combined.
2. Insert a crisper plate in the Ninja Foodi air fryer baskets.
3. Make small balls from the spinach mixture and place them in both baskets.
4. Select zone 1, then select "air fry" mode and set the temperature to 390 degrees F(200°C) for 10 minutes. Press "match" to match zone 2 settings to zone 1. Press "start/stop" to begin.

**Nutrition:**

- (Per serving) Calories 74 | Fat 1.7g |Sodium 122mg | Carbs 11.1g | Fiber 1.9g | Sugar 2g | Protein 4.2g

## Sausage Balls With Cheese

Servings: 8
Cooking Time: 10 To 11 Minutes

**Ingredients:**

- 340 g mild sausage meat
- 355 ml baking mix
- 240 ml shredded mild Cheddar cheese
- 85 g soft white cheese, at room temperature
- 1 to 2 tablespoons olive oil

**Directions:**

1. Preheat the air fryer to 165°C. Line the two air fryer baskets with parchment paper.
2. Mix together the ground sausage, baking mix, Cheddar cheese, and soft white cheese in a large bowl and stir to incorporate.
3. Divide the sausage mixture into 16 equal portions and roll them into 1-inch balls with your hands.
4. Arrange the sausage balls on the parchment, leaving space between each ball.
5. Brush the sausage balls with the olive oil. Bake in the two baskets for 10 to 11 minutes, shaking the baskets halfway through, or until the balls are firm and lightly browned on both sides.
6. Remove from the baskets to a plate.
7. Serve warm.

## Beef Skewers

Servings: 6
Cooking Time: 5 Minutes

**Ingredients:**

- 1 beef flank steak
- 240ml rice vinegar
- 240ml soy sauce
- 55g packed brown sugar
- 2 tablespoons minced fresh gingerroot
- 6 garlic cloves, minced
- 3 teaspoons sesame oil
- 1 teaspoon hot pepper sauce
- ½ teaspoon cornflour

**Directions:**

1. Cut beef into ½ cm thick strips. Whisk together the following 7 ingredients in a large mixing bowl until well combined.
2. In a shallow dish, pour 1 cup of marinade. Toss in the beef and turn to coat. Refrigerate for 2-8 hours, covered. Cover and keep the remaining marinade refrigerated.
3. Beef should be drained. 12 metal or wet wooden skewers threaded with beef.
4. Press either "Zone 1" or "Zone 2" and then rotate the knob to select "Air Fry".
5. Set the temperature to 200 degrees C, and then set the time for 5 minutes to preheat.
6. After preheating, spray the basket with cooking spray and arrange skewers onto basket.
7. Slide the basket into the Air Fryer and set the time for 5 minutes.
8. After cooking time is completed, transfer them onto serving plates and serve.

## Fried Halloumi Cheese

Servings: 6
Cooking Time: 12 Minutes.

**Ingredients:**

- 1 block of halloumi cheese, sliced
- 2 teaspoons olive oil

**Directions:**

1. Divide the halloumi cheese slices in the crisper plate.
2. Drizzle olive oil over the cheese slices.
3. Return the crisper plate to the Ninja Foodi Dual Zone Air Fryer.
4. Choose the Air Fry mode for Zone 1 and set the temperature to 360 degrees F(180°C) and the time to 12 minutes.
5. Flip the cheese slices once cooked halfway through.
6. Serve.

**Nutrition:**

- (Per serving) Calories 186 | Fat 3g |Sodium 223mg | Carbs 31g | Fiber 8.7g | Sugar 5.5g | Protein 9.7g

## Peppered Asparagus

Servings: 6
Cooking Time: 16 Minutes.

**Ingredients:**

- 1 bunch of asparagus, trimmed
- Avocado or Olive Oil
- Himalayan salt, to taste
- Black pepper, to taste

**Directions:**

1. Divide the asparagus in the two crisper plate.
2. Toss the asparagus with salt, black pepper, and oil.
3. Return the crisper plate to the Ninja Foodi Dual Zone Air Fryer.
4. Choose the Air Fry mode for Zone 1 and set the temperature to 390 degrees F(200°C) and the time to 16 minutes.
5. Select the "MATCH" button to copy the settings for Zone 2.
6. Initiate cooking by pressing the START/STOP button.
7. Serve warm.

**Nutrition:**

- (Per serving) Calories 163 | Fat 11.5g |Sodium 918mg | Carbs 8.3g | Fiber 4.2g | Sugar 0.2g | Protein 7.4g

## Crispy Calamari Rings

Servings: 4
Cooking Time: 10 Minutes

**Ingredients:**

- 455g calamari rings, patted dry
- 3 tablespoons lemon juice
- 60g plain flour
- 1 teaspoon garlic powder
- 2 egg whites
- 60ml milk
- 220g panko breadcrumbs
- 1½ teaspoon salt
- 1½ teaspoon ground black pepper

**Directions:**

1. Allow the squid rings to marinade for at least 30 minutes in a bowl with lemon juice. Drain the water in a colander.
2. In a shallow bowl, combine the flour and garlic powder.
3. In a separate bowl, whisk together the egg whites and milk.
4. In a third bowl, combine the panko breadcrumbs, salt, and pepper.
5. Floured first the calamari rings, then dip in the egg mixture, and finally in the panko breadcrumb mixture.
6. Press either "Zone 1" or "Zone 2" and then rotate the knob to select "Air Fry".
7. Set the temperature to 200 degrees C, and then set the time for 5 minutes to preheat.
8. After preheating, spray the Air-Fryer basket with cooking spray and line with parchment paper. Arrange in a single layer and spritz them with cooking spray.
9. Slide the basket into the Air Fryer and set the time for 10 minutes.
10. After cooking time is completed, transfer them onto serving plates and serve.

## Fried Ravioli

Servings: 6
Cooking Time: 7 Minutes

**Ingredients:**

- 12 frozen raviolis
- 118ml buttermilk
- ½ cup Italian breadcrumbs

**Directions:**

1. Dip the ravioli in the buttermilk then coat with the breadcrumbs.
2. Divide the ravioli into the Ninja Foodi 2 Baskets Air Fryer baskets.
3. Return the air fryer basket 1 to Zone 1, and basket 2 to Zone 2 of the Ninja Foodi 2-Basket Air Fryer.
4. Choose the "Air Fry" mode for Zone 1 and set the temperature to 400 degrees F(205°C) and 7 minutes of cooking time.
5. Select the "MATCH COOK" option to copy the settings for Zone 2.
6. Initiate cooking by pressing the START/PAUSE BUTTON.
7. Flip the ravioli once cooked halfway through.
8. Serve warm.

**Nutrition:**

- (Per serving) Calories 134 | Fat 5.9g |Sodium 343mg | Carbs 9.5g | Fiber 0.5g | Sugar 1.1g | Protein 10.4g

## Onion Rings

Servings: 4
Cooking Time: 7 Minutes

**Ingredients:**

- 170g onion, sliced into rings
- ½ cup breadcrumbs
- 2 eggs, beaten
- ½ cup flour
- Salt and black pepper to taste

**Directions:**

1. Mix flour, black pepper and salt in a bowl.
2. Dredge the onion rings through the flour mixture.
3. Dip them in the eggs and coat with the breadcrumbs.
4. Place the coated onion rings in the air fryer baskets.
5. Return the air fryer basket 1 to Zone 1, and basket 2 to Zone 2 of the Ninja Foodi 2-Basket Air Fryer.
6. Choose the "Air Fry" mode for Zone 1 at 350 degrees F(175°C) and 7 minutes of cooking time.
7. Select the "MATCH COOK" option to copy the settings for Zone 2.
8. Initiate cooking by pressing the START/PAUSE BUTTON.
9. Shake the rings once cooked halfway through.
10. Serve warm.

**Nutrition:**

- (Per serving) Calories 185 | Fat 11g |Sodium 355mg | Carbs 21g | Fiber 5.8g | Sugar 3g | Protein 4.7g

## Five-ingredient Falafel With Garlic-yoghurt Sauce

Servings: 4
Cooking Time: 15 Minutes

**Ingredients:**

- Falafel:
- 1 (425 g) can chickpeas, drained and rinsed
- 120 ml fresh parsley
- 2 garlic cloves, minced
- ½ tablespoon ground cumin
- 1 tablespoon wholemeal flour
- Salt
- Garlic-Yoghurt Sauce:
- 240 ml non-fat plain Greek yoghurt
- 1 garlic clove, minced
- 1 tablespoon chopped fresh dill
- 2 tablespoons lemon juice

**Directions:**

1. Make the Falafel: Preheat the air fryer to 180ºC. 2. Put the chickpeas into a food processor. Pulse until mostly chopped,

then add the parsley, garlic, and cumin and pulse for another 1 to 2 minutes, or until the ingredients are combined and turning into a dough. 3. Add the flour. Pulse a few more times until combined. The dough will have texture, but the chickpeas should be pulsed into small bits. 4. Using clean hands, roll the dough into 8 balls of equal size, then pat the balls down a bit so they are about ½-thick disks. 5. Spray the zone 1 air fryer basket with olive oil cooking spray, then place the falafel patties in the basket in a single layer, making sure they don't touch each other. 6. Fry in the air fryer for 15 minutes. Make the garlic-yoghurt sauce 7. In a small bowl, combine the yoghurt, garlic, dill, and lemon juice. 8. Once the falafel is done cooking and nicely browned on all sides, remove them from the air fryer and season with salt. 9. Serve hot with a side of dipping sauce.

## Mozzarella Arancini

Servings: 16 Arancini
Cooking Time: 8 To 11 Minutes

**Ingredients:**

- 475 ml cooked rice, cooled
- 2 eggs, beaten
- 355 ml panko breadcrumbs, divided
- 120 ml grated Parmesan cheese
- 2 tablespoons minced fresh basil
- 16¾-inch cubes Mozzarella cheese
- 2 tablespoons olive oil

**Directions:**

1. Preheat the air fryer to 205°C.
2. In a medium bowl, combine the rice, eggs, 120 ml of the breadcrumbs, Parmesan cheese, and basil. Form this mixture into 16 1½-inch balls.
3. Poke a hole in each of the balls with your finger and insert a Mozzarella cube. Form the rice mixture firmly around the cheese.
4. On a shallow plate, combine the remaining 240 ml of the breadcrumbs with the olive oil and mix well. Roll the rice balls in the breadcrumbs to coat.
5. Air fry the arancini in two baskets for 8 to 11 minutes or until golden brown.
6. Serve hot.

## Bacon Wrapped Tater Tots

Servings: 8
Cooking Time: 14 Minutes

**Ingredients:**

- 8 bacon slices
- 3 tablespoons honey
- ½ tablespoon chipotle chile powder
- 16 frozen tater tots

**Directions:**

1. Cut the bacon slices in half and wrap each tater tot with a bacon slice.
2. Brush the bacon with honey and drizzle chipotle chile powder over them.
3. Insert a toothpick to seal the bacon.
4. Place the wrapped tots in the air fryer baskets.
5. Return the air fryer basket 1 to Zone 1, and basket 2 to Zone 2 of the Ninja Foodi 2-Basket Air Fryer.
6. Choose the "Air Fry" mode for Zone 1 at 350 degrees F(175°C) and 14 minutes of cooking time.
7. Select the "MATCH COOK" option to copy the settings for Zone 2.
8. Initiate cooking by pressing the START/PAUSE BUTTON.
9. Serve warm.

**Nutrition:**

- (Per serving) Calories 100 | Fat 2g |Sodium 480mg | Carbs 4g | Fiber 2g | Sugar 0g | Protein 18g

## Croquettes

Servings: 6
Cooking Time: 10 Minutes

**Ingredients:**

- 460g mashed potatoes
- 50g grated Parmesan cheese
- 50g shredded Swiss cheese
- 1 shallot, finely chopped
- 2 teaspoons minced fresh rosemary
- ½ teaspoon salt
- ¼ teaspoon pepper
- 420g finely chopped cooked turkey
- 1 large egg
- 2 tablespoons water
- 110g panko bread crumbs
- Cooking spray

**Directions:**

1. Combine mashed potatoes, cheeses, shallot, rosemary, salt, and pepper in a large mixing bowl| stir in turkey.
2. Lightly but completely combine the ingredients. Form into twelve 5cm thick patties.
3. Whisk the egg and water together in a small basin. In a shallow bowl, place the bread crumbs.
4. Dip the croquettes in the egg mixture, then in the bread crumbs, patting them down.
5. Press either "Zone 1" or "Zone 2" and then rotate the knob to select "Air Fry".
6. Set the temperature to 190 degrees C, and then set the time for 5 minutes to preheat.
7. After preheating, spray the Air-Fryer basket with cooking spray and line with parchment paper. Arrange in a single layer and spritz them with cooking spray.
8. Slide the basket into the Air Fryer and set the time for 5 minutes.
9. After that, turn them and again cook for 5 minutes longer.
10. After cooking time is completed, transfer them onto serving plates and serve.

## Bacon-wrapped Dates Bacon-wrapped Scallops

Servings:6
Cooking Time: 12 Minutes

**Ingredients:**

- FOR THE SCALLOPS
- 6 slices bacon, halved crosswise
- 12 large sea scallops, patted dry
- FOR THE DATES
- 4 slices bacon, cut into thirds
- 12 pitted dates

**Directions:**

1. To prep the dates: Wrap each piece of bacon around a date and secure with a toothpick.
2. To cook the dates and the bacon for the scallops: Install a crisper plate in each of the two baskets. Place the bacon for the scallops in the Zone 1 basket in a single layer and insert the basket in the unit. Place the bacon-wrapped dates in the Zone 2 basket in a single layer and insert the basket in the unit.
3. Select Zone 1, select AIR FRY, set the temperature to 400°F (205°C), and set the time to 12 minutes.
4. Select Zone 2, select AIR FRY, set the temperature to 360°F (180°C), and set the time to 10 minutes. Select SMART FINISH.
5. Press START/PAUSE to begin cooking.

6. When the Zone 1 timer reads 9 minutes, press START/PAUSE. Remove the basket from the unit. Wrap each piece of bacon around a scallop and secure with a toothpick. Place the bacon-wrapped scallops in the basket. Reinsert the basket and press START/PAUSE to resume cooking.
7. When the Zone 1 timer reads 4 minutes, press START/PAUSE. Remove the basket and use silicone-tipped tongs to flip the scallops. Reinsert the basket and press START/PAUSE to resume cooking.
8. When cooking is complete, the scallops will be opaque and the bacon around both the scallops and dates will be crisp. Arrange the bacon-wrapped scallops and dates on a serving platter. Serve warm.

**Nutrition:**

- (Per serving) Calories: 191; Total fat: 2.5g; Saturated fat: 1g; Carbohydrates: 39g; Fiber: 4g; Protein: 3g; Sodium: 115mg

## Fried Okra

Servings: 4
Cooking Time: 10 Minutes

**Ingredients:**

- 455g fresh okra
- 240ml buttermilk
- 125g plain flour
- 160g polenta
- 1 teaspoon salt
- 1 teaspoon fresh ground pepper

**Directions:**

1. Wash and trim the ends of the okra before slicing it into 30cm chunks.
2. In a small dish, pour the buttermilk.
3. Combine flour, polenta, salt, and pepper in a separate dish.
4. Coat all sides of okra slices in buttermilk and then in flour mixture.
5. Place a baking sheet on the baskets.
6. Press either "Zone 1" or "Zone 2" and then rotate the knob to select "Air Fryer".
7. Set the temperature to 175 degrees C, and then set the time for 5 minutes to preheat.
8. After preheating, arrange them into the basket.
9. Slide the basket into the Air Fryer and set the time for 8 minutes.
10. After cooking time is completed, place on a wire rack for a few minutes, then transfer onto serving plates and serve.

## Chicken Crescent Wraps

Servings: 6
Cooking Time: 12 Minutes.

**Ingredients:**

- 3 tablespoons chopped onion
- 3 garlic cloves, peeled and minced
- ¾ (8 ounces) package cream cheese
- 6 tablespoons butter
- 2 boneless chicken breasts, cubed, cooked
- 3 (10 ounces) cans refrigerated crescent roll dough

**Directions:**

1. Heat oil in a skillet and add onion and garlic to sauté until soft.
2. Add cooked chicken, sautéed veggies, butter, and cream cheese to a blender.
3. Blend well until smooth. Spread the crescent dough over a flat surface.
4. Slice the dough into 12 rectangles.
5. Spoon the chicken mixture at the center of each rectangle.
6. Roll the dough to wrap the mixture and form a ball.
7. Divide these balls into the two crisper plate.
8. Return the crisper plate to the Ninja Foodi Dual Zone Air Fryer.
9. Choose the Air Fry mode for Zone 1 and set the temperature to 390 degrees F(200°C) and the time to 12 minutes.
10. Select the "MATCH" button to copy the settings for Zone 2.
11. Initiate cooking by pressing the START/STOP button.
12. Serve warm.

**Nutrition:**

- (Per serving) Calories 100 | Fat 2g |Sodium 480mg | Carbs 4g | Fiber 2g | Sugar 0g | Protein 18g

## Potato Tacos

Servings: 6
Cooking Time: 15 Minutes

**Ingredients:**

- 5 small russet potatoes
- 24 mini corn tortillas
- 2 tablespoons rapeseed oil
- ½ teaspoon ground cumin
- ½ teaspoon smoked paprika
- ½ teaspoon granulated garlic
- Salt and pepper, to taste
- 24 long toothpicks

**Directions:**

1. Fill a pot halfway with cold water and add entire potatoes. Bring to a boil over high heat, then reduce to medium-high and simmer until fork-tender, about 15 minutes.
2. It takes about 15-20 minutes. Drain and allow to cool slightly before peeling.
3. In a bowl, combine peeled potatoes and seasonings. Mash until the mixture is relatively smooth. Season to taste.
4. Heat tortillas in a large frying pan until warm and malleable. Cover with a towel while you finish heating the rest of the tortillas.
5. On half of a tortilla, spread roughly one heaping tablespoon of mash. Fold it in half and weave a toothpick through it to seal it.
6. Brush the tacos lightly with oil on both sides.
7. Press your chosen zone - "Zone 1" or "Zone 2" and then rotate the knob to select "Air Fryer".
8. Set the temperature to 200 degrees C, and then set the time for 5 minutes to preheat.
9. After preheating, arrange them into the basket of each zone.
10. Slide the baskets into Air Fryer and set the time for 15 minutes.
11. After cooking time is completed, place on a wire rack for a few minutes, then transfer onto serving plates and serve.

## Crab Rangoon Dip With Crispy Wonton Strips

Servings:6
Cooking Time: 15 Minutes

**Ingredients:**

- FOR THE DIP
- 1 (6-ounce) can pink crab, drained
- 8 ounces (16 tablespoons) cream cheese, at room temperature
- ½ cup sour cream
- 1 tablespoon chopped scallions
- ½ teaspoon garlic powder
- 1 teaspoon Worcestershire sauce
- ¼ teaspoon kosher salt
- 1 cup shredded part-skim mozzarella cheese
- FOR THE WONTON STRIPS
- 12 wonton wrappers

- 1 tablespoon olive oil
- ¼ teaspoon kosher salt

**Directions:**

1. To prep the dip: In a medium bowl, mix the crab, cream cheese, sour cream, scallions, garlic powder, Worcestershire sauce, and salt until smooth.
2. To prep the wonton strips: Brush both sides of the wonton wrappers with the oil and sprinkle with salt. Cut the wonton wrappers into ¾-inch-wide strips.
3. To cook the dip and strips: Pour the dip into the Zone 1 basket, top with the mozzarella cheese, and insert the basket in the unit. Install a crisper plate in the Zone 2 basket, add the wonton strips, and insert the basket in the unit.
4. Select Zone 1, select BAKE, set the temperature to 330°F (165°C), and set the time to 15 minutes.
5. Select Zone 2, select AIR FRY, set the temperature to 350°F (175°C), and set the time to 6 minutes. Select SMART FINISH.
6. Press START/PAUSE to begin cooking.
7. When the Zone 2 timer reads 4 minutes, press START/PAUSE. Remove the basket and shake well to redistribute the wonton strips. Reinsert the basket and press START/PAUSE to resume cooking.
8. When the Zone 2 timer reads 2 minutes, press START/PAUSE. Remove the basket and shake well to redistribute the wonton strips. Reinsert the basket and press START/PAUSE to resume cooking.
9. When cooking is complete, the dip will be bubbling and golden brown on top and the wonton strips will be crunchy. Serve warm.

**Nutrition:**

- (Per serving) Calories: 315; Total fat: 23g; Saturated fat: 12g; Carbohydrates: 14g; Fiber: 0.5g; Protein: 14g; Sodium: 580mg

## Crispy Filo Artichoke Triangles

Servings: 18 Triangles

Cooking Time: 9 To 12 Minutes

**Ingredients:**

- 60 ml Ricotta cheese
- 1 egg white
- 80 ml minced and drained artichoke hearts
- 3 tablespoons grated Mozzarella cheese
- ½ teaspoon dried thyme
- 6 sheets frozen filo pastry, thawed
- 2 tablespoons melted butter

**Directions:**

1. Preheat the air fryer to 205°C.
2. In a small bowl, combine the Ricotta cheese, egg white, artichoke hearts, Mozzarella cheese, and thyme, and mix well.
3. Cover the filo pastry with a damp kitchen towel while you work so it doesn't dry out. Using one sheet at a time, place on the work surface and cut into thirds lengthwise.
4. Put about 1½ teaspoons of the filling on each strip at the base. Fold the bottom right-hand tip of phyllo over the filling to meet the other side in a triangle, then continue folding in a triangle. Brush each triangle with butter to seal the edges. Repeat with the remaining phyllo dough and filling.
5. Place the triangles in the two air fryer baskets. Bake, 6 at a time, in two baskets for about 3 to 4 minutes, or until the filo is golden brown and crisp.
6. Serve hot.

## Crispy Plantain Chips

Servings: 4

Cooking Time: 20 Minutes.

**Ingredients:**

- 1 green plantain
- 1 teaspoon canola oil
- ½ teaspoon sea salt

**Directions:**

1. Peel and cut the plantains into long strips using a mandolin slicer.
2. Grease the crisper plates with ½ teaspoon of canola oil.
3. Toss the plantains with salt and remaining canola oil.
4. Divide these plantains in the two crisper plates.
5. Return the crisper plate to the Ninja Foodi Dual Zone Air Fryer.
6. Choose the Air Fry mode for Zone 1 and set the temperature to 350 degrees F(175°C) and the time to 20 minutes.
7. Select the "MATCH" button to copy the settings for Zone 2.
8. Initiate cooking by pressing the START/STOP button.
9. Toss the plantains after 10 minutes and resume cooking.
10. Serve warm.

**Nutrition:**

- (Per serving) Calories 122 | Fat 1.8g |Sodium 794mg | Carbs 17g | Fiber 8.9g | Sugar 1.6g | Protein 14.9g

# Breakfast Recipes

## Buttermilk Biscuits With Roasted Stone Fruit Compote

Servings:4
Cooking Time: 20 Minutes
**Ingredients:**

- FOR THE BISCUITS
- 1⅓ cups all-purpose flour
- 2 teaspoons sugar
- 2 teaspoons baking powder
- ½ teaspoon baking soda
- ½ teaspoon kosher salt
- 4 tablespoons (½ stick) very cold unsalted butter
- ½ cup plus 1 tablespoon low-fat buttermilk
- FOR THE FRUIT COMPOTE
- 2 peaches, peeled and diced
- 2 plums, peeled and diced
- ¼ cup water
- 2 teaspoons honey
- ⅛ teaspoon ground ginger (optional)

**Directions:**

1. To prep the biscuits: In a small bowl, combine the flour, sugar, baking powder, baking soda, and salt. Using the large holes on a box grater, grate in the butter. Stir in the buttermilk to form a thick dough.
2. Place the dough on a lightly floured surface and gently pat it into a ½-inch-thick disc. Fold the dough in half, then rotate the whole thing 90 degrees, pat into a ½-inch thick disc and fold again. Repeat until you have folded the dough four times.
3. Pat the dough out a final time into a ½-inch-thick disc and use a 3-inch biscuit cutter to cut 4 biscuits from the dough (discard the scraps).
4. To prep the fruit compote: In a large bowl, stir together the peaches, plums, water, honey, and ginger (if using).
5. To cook the biscuits and compote: Install a crisper plate in the Zone 1 basket, place the biscuits in the basket, and insert the basket in the unit. Place the fruit in the Zone 2 basket and insert the basket in the unit.
6. Select Zone 1, select AIR FRY, set the temperature to 400°F (205°C), and set the time to 10 minutes.
7. Select Zone 2, select ROAST, set the temperature to 350°F (175°C), and set the time to 20 minutes. Select SMART FINISH.
8. Press START/PAUSE to begin cooking.
9. When the Zone 2 timer reads 10 minutes, press START/PAUSE. Remove the basket and stir the compote. Reinsert the basket and press START/PAUSE to resume cooking.
10. When cooking is complete, the biscuits will be golden brown and crisp on top and the fruit will be soft. Transfer the biscuits to a plate to cool. Lightly mash the fruit to form a thick, jammy sauce.
11. Split the biscuits in half horizontally and serve topped with fruit compote.

**Nutrition:**

- (Per serving) Calories: 332; Total fat: 12g; Saturated fat: 7.5g; Carbohydrates: 50g; Fiber: 2.5g; Protein: 6g; Sodium: 350mg

## Wholemeal Banana-walnut Bread

Servings: 6
Cooking Time: 23 Minutes
**Ingredients:**

- Olive oil cooking spray
- 2 ripe medium bananas
- 1 large egg
- 60 ml non-fat plain Greek yoghurt
- 60 ml olive oil
- ½ teaspoon vanilla extract
- 2 tablespoons honey
- 235 ml wholemeal flour
- ¼ teaspoon salt
- ¼ teaspoon baking soda
- ½ teaspoon ground cinnamon
- 60 ml chopped walnuts

**Directions:**

1. Lightly coat the inside of two 5 ½-by-3-inch loaf pans with olive oil cooking spray.
2. In a large bowl, mash the bananas with a fork. Add the egg, yoghurt, olive oil, vanilla, and honey. Mix until well combined and mostly smooth. Sift the wholemeal flour, salt, baking soda, and cinnamon into the wet mixture, then stir until just combined. Do not overmix. Gently fold in the walnuts. Pour into the prepared loaf pans and spread to distribute evenly.
3. Place a loaf pan in the zone 1 drawer and another pan into zone 2 drawer. In zone 1, select Bake button and adjust temperature to 180ºC, set time to 20 to 23 minutes. In zone 2, select Match Cook and press Start.
4. Remove until golden brown on top and a toothpick inserted into the center comes out clean. Allow to cool for 5 minutes before serving.

## Red Pepper And Feta Frittata And Bacon Eggs On The Go

Servings: 5
Cooking Time: 20 Minutes
**Ingredients:**

- Red Pepper and Feta Frittàta:
- Olive oil cooking spray
- 8 large eggs
- 1 medium red pepper, diced
- ½ teaspoon salt
- ½ teaspoon black pepper
- 1 garlic clove, minced
- 120 ml feta, divided
- Bacon Eggs on the Go:
- 2 eggs
- 110 g bacon, cooked
- Salt and ground black pepper, to taste

**Directions:**

1. Make the Red Pepper and Feta Frittata :
2. Preheat the air fryer to 180ºC. Lightly coat the inside of a 6-inch round cake pan with olive oil cooking spray.
3. In a large bowl, beat the eggs for 1 to 2 minutes, or until well combined.

4. Add the red pepper, salt, black pepper, and garlic to the eggs, and mix together until the red pepper is distributed throughout.
5. Fold in 60 ml the feta cheese.
6. Pour the egg mixture into the prepared cake pan, and sprinkle the remaining 60 ml feta over the top.
7. Place into the zone 1 air fryer basket and bake for 18 to 20 minutes, or until the eggs are set in the center.
8. Remove from the air fryer and allow to cool for 5 minutes before serving.
9. Make the Bacon Eggs on the Go :
10. Preheat the air fryer to 205ºC. Put liners in a regular cupcake tin.
11. Crack an egg into each of the cups and add the bacon. Season with some pepper and salt.
12. Bake in the preheated zone 2 air fryer basket for 15 minutes, or until the eggs are set. Serve warm.

## French Toasts

Servings: 4
Cooking Time: 6 Minutes
**Ingredients:**

- 4 eggs
- 120g evaporated milk
- 6 tablespoons sugar
- 4 teaspoons olive oil
- ¼ teaspoon ground cinnamon
- ¼ teaspoon vanilla extract
- 8 bread slices

**Directions:**

1. Line each basket of "Zone 1" and "Zone 2" with a greased piece of foil.
2. Then Press your chosen zone - "Zone 1" or "Zone 2" and then rotate the knob to select "Air Fry".
3. Set the temperature to 200 degrees C and then set the time for 5 minutes to preheat.
4. In a large bowl, add all ingredients except for bread slices and beat until well combined.
5. Coat the bread slices with egg mixture evenly.
6. After preheating, arrange 4 bread slices into the basket of each zone.
7. Slide the basket into the Air Fryer and set the time for 6 minutes.
8. While cooking, flip the slices once halfway through.
9. After cooking time is completed, remove the French toasts from Air Fryer and serve warm.

## Cauliflower Avocado Toast And All-in-one Toast

Servings: 3
Cooking Time: 10 Minutes
**Ingredients:**

- Cauliflower Avocado Toast:
- 1 (40 g) steamer bag cauliflower
- 1 large egg
- 120 ml shredded Mozzarella cheese
- 1 ripe medium avocado
- ½ teaspoon garlic powder
- ¼ teaspoon ground black pepper
- All-in-One Toast:
- 1 strip bacon, diced
- 1 slice 1-inch thick bread
- 1 egg
- Salt and freshly ground black pepper, to taste
- 60 ml grated Monterey Jack or Chedday cheese

**Directions:**

1. Make the Cauliflower Avocado Toast :
2. Cook cauliflower according to package instructions. Remove from bag and place into cheesecloth or clean towel to remove excess moisture.
3. Place cauliflower into a large bowl and mix in egg and Mozzarella. Cut a piece of parchment to fit your air fryer drawer. Separate the cauliflower mixture into two, and place it on the parchment in two mounds. Press out the cauliflower mounds into a ¼-inch-thick rectangle. Place the parchment into the zone 1 air fryer drawer.
4. Adjust the temperature to 204ºC and set the timer for 8 minutes.
5. Flip the cauliflower halfway through the cooking time.
6. When the timer beeps, remove the parchment and allow the cauliflower to cool 5 minutes.
7. Cut open the avocado and remove the pit. Scoop out the inside, place it in a medium bowl, and mash it with garlic powder and pepper. Spread onto the cauliflower. Serve immediately.
8. Make the All-in-One Toast :
9. Preheat the zone 2 air fryer drawer to 204ºC.
10. Air fry the bacon for 3 minutes, shaking the zone 2 drawer once or twice while it cooks. Remove the bacon to a paper towel lined plate and set aside.
11. Use a sharp paring knife to score a large circle in the middle of the slice of bread, cutting halfway through, but not all the way through to the cutting board. Press down on the circle in the center of the bread slice to create an indentation.
12. Transfer the slice of bread, hole side up, to the air fryer drawer. Crack the egg into the center of the bread, and season with salt and pepper.
13. Adjust the air fryer temperature to 192ºC and air fry for 5 minutes. Sprinkle the grated cheese around the edges of the bread, leaving the center of the yolk uncovered, and top with the cooked bacon. Press the cheese and bacon into the bread lightly to help anchor it to the bread and prevent it from blowing around in the air fryer.
14. Air fry for one or two more minutes, just to melt the cheese and finish cooking the egg. Serve immediately.

## Bacon-and-eggs Avocado And Simple Scotch Eggs

Servings: 5
Cooking Time: 25 Minutes
**Ingredients:**

- Bacon-and-Eggs Avocado:
- 1 large egg
- 1 avocado, halved, peeled, and pitted
- 2 slices bacon
- Fresh parsley, for serving (optional)
- Sea salt flakes, for garnish (optional)
- Simple Scotch Eggs:
- 4 large hard boiled eggs
- 1 (340 g) package pork sausage meat
- 8 slices thick-cut bacon
- 4 wooden toothpicks, soaked in water for at least 30 minutes

**Directions:**

1. Make the Bacon-and-Eggs Avocado :
2. 1. Spray the zone 1 air fryer basket with avocado oil. Preheat the air fryer to 160ºC. Fill a small bowl with cool water. Soft-boil the egg: Place the egg in the zone 1 air fryer basket. Air fry for 6 minutes for a soft yolk or 7 minutes for a cooked yolk. Transfer the egg to the bowl of cool water and let sit for 2 minutes. Peel and set aside. 3. Use a spoon to carve out extra space in the center of the avocado halves until the cavities are big enough to fit the soft-boiled egg. Place the soft-boiled egg in the center of one half of the avocado and replace the other

half of the avocado on top, so the avocado appears whole on the outside. 4. Starting at one end of the avocado, wrap the bacon around the avocado to completely cover it. Use toothpicks to hold the bacon in place. 5. Place the bacon-wrapped avocado in the zone 1 air fryer basket and air fry for 5 minutes. Flip the avocado over and air fry for another 5 minutes, or until the bacon is cooked to your liking. Serve on a bed of fresh parsley, if desired, and sprinkle with salt flakes, if desired. 6. Best served fresh. Store extras in an airtight container in the fridge for up to 4 days. Reheat in a preheated 160ºC air fryer for 4 minutes, or until heated through.

3. Make the Simple Scotch Eggs :
4. Slice the sausage meat into four parts and place each part into a large circle.
5. Put an egg into each circle and wrap it in the sausage. Put in the refrigerator for 1 hour.
6. Preheat the air fryer to 235ºC.
7. Make a cross with two pieces of thick-cut bacon. Put a wrapped egg in the center, fold the bacon over top of the egg, and secure with a toothpick.
8. Air fry in the preheated zone 2 air fryer basket for 25 minutes.
9. Serve immediately.

## Sausage & Bacon Omelet

Servings: 4
Cooking Time: 10 Minutes
**Ingredients:**

- 8 eggs
- 2 bacon slices, chopped
- 4 sausages, chopped
- 2 yellow onions, chopped

**Directions:**

1. In a bowl, crack the eggs and beat well.
2. Add the remaining ingredients and gently stir to combine.
3. Divide the mixture into 2 small baking pans.
4. Press your chosen zone - "Zone 1" or "Zone 2" and then rotate the knob to select "Air Fry".
5. Set the temperature to 160 degrees C and then set the time for 5 minutes to preheat.
6. After preheating, arrange 1 pan into the basket of each zone.
7. Slide the basket into the Air Fryer and set the time for 10 minutes.
8. After cooking time is completed, remove the both pans from Air Fryer.
9. Cut each omelet in wedges and serve hot.

## Cheesy Scrambled Eggs And Egg And Bacon Muffins

Servings: 3
Cooking Time: 15 Minutes
**Ingredients:**

- Cheesy Scrambled Eggs:
- 1 teaspoon unsalted butter
- 2 large eggs
- 2 tablespoons milk
- 2 tablespoons shredded Cheddar cheese
- Salt and freshly ground black pepper, to taste
- Egg and Bacon Muffins:
- 2 eggs
- Salt and ground black pepper, to taste
- 1 tablespoon green pesto
- 85 g shredded Cheddar cheese
- 140 g cooked bacon
- 1 spring onion, chopped

**Directions:**

1. Make the Cheesy Scrambled Eggs :
2. Preheat the zone 1 air fryer basket to 150ºC. Place the butter in a baking pan and cook for 1 to 2 minutes, until melted.
3. In a small bowl, whisk together the eggs, milk, and cheese. Season with salt and black pepper. Transfer the mixture to the pan.
4. Cook in the zone 1 basket for 3 minutes. Stir the eggs and push them toward the center of the pan.
5. Cook for another 2 minutes, then stir again. Cook for another 2 minutes, until the eggs are just cooked. Serve warm.
6. Make the Egg and Bacon Muffins :
7. Preheat the zone 2 air fryer basket to 175ºC. Line a cupcake tin with parchment paper.
8. Beat the eggs with pepper, salt, and pesto in a bowl. Mix in the cheese.
9. Pour the eggs into the cupcake tin and top with the bacon and spring onion.
10. Bake in the preheated zone 2 air fryer basket for 15 minutes, or until the egg is set.
11. Serve immediately.

## Sausage & Butternut Squash

Servings: 2
Cooking Time: 20 Minutes
**Ingredients:**

- 450g butternut squash, diced
- 70g kielbasa, diced
- ¼ onion, diced
- ¼ tsp garlic powder
- ½ tbsp olive oil
- Pepper
- Salt

**Directions:**

1. In a bowl, toss butternut squash with garlic powder, oil, onion, kielbasa, pepper, and salt.
2. Insert a crisper plate in the Ninja Foodi air fryer baskets.
3. Add sausage and butternut squash mixture in both baskets.
4. Select zone 1, then select "air fry" mode and set the temperature to 375 degrees F(190°C) for 20 minutes. Press "match" to match zone 2 settings to zone 1. Press "start/stop" to begin. Stir halfway through.

**Nutrition:**

- (Per serving) Calories 68 | Fat 3.6g |Sodium 81mg | Carbs 9.7g | Fiber 1.7g | Sugar 2.2g | Protein 0.9g

## Canadian Bacon Muffin Sandwiches And All-in-one Toast

Servings: 5
Cooking Time: 10 Minutes
**Ingredients:**

- Canadian Bacon Muffin Sandwiches:
- 4 English muffins, split
- 8 slices back bacon
- 4 slices cheese
- Cooking spray
- All-in-One Toast:
- 1 strip bacon, diced
- 1 slice 1-inch thick bread
- 1 egg
- Salt and freshly ground black pepper, to taste
- 60 ml grated Monterey Jack or Chedday cheese

**Directions:**

1. Make the Canadian Bacon Muffin Sandwiches :
2. 1. Preheat the air fryer to 190ºC. Make the sandwiches: Top each of 4 muffin halves with 2 slices of bacon, 1 slice of cheese, and finish with the remaining muffin half. 3. Put the

sandwiches in the zone 1 air fryer basket and spritz the tops with cooking spray. 4. Bake for 4 minutes. Flip the sandwiches and bake for another 4 minutes. 5. Divide the sandwiches among four plates and serve warm.

3. Make the All-in-One Toast :
4. Preheat the air fryer to 205ºC.
5. Air fry the bacon in zone 2 basket for 3 minutes, shaking the basket once or twice while it cooks. Remove the bacon to a paper towel lined plate and set aside.
6. Use a sharp paring knife to score a large circle in the middle of the slice of bread, cutting halfway through, but not all the way through to the cutting board. Press down on the circle in the center of the bread slice to create an indentation.
7. Transfer the slice of bread, hole side up, to the zone 2 air fryer basket. Crack the egg into the center of the bread, and season with salt and pepper.
8. Adjust the air fryer temperature to 190ºC and air fry for 5 minutes. Sprinkle the grated cheese around the edges of the bread, leaving the center of the yolk uncovered, and top with the cooked bacon. Press the cheese and bacon into the bread lightly to help anchor it to the bread and prevent it from blowing around in the air fryer.
9. Air fry for one or two more minutes, just to melt the cheese and finish cooking the egg. Serve immediately.

## Breakfast Sammies

Servings: 5
Cooking Time: 20 Minutes
**Ingredients:**

- Biscuits:
- 6 large egg whites
- 475 ml blanched almond flour, plus more if needed
- 1½ teaspoons baking powder
- ½ teaspoon fine sea salt
- 60 ml (½ stick) very cold unsalted butter (or lard for dairy-free), cut into ¼-inch pieces
- Eggs:
- 5 large eggs
- ½ teaspoon fine sea salt
- ¼ teaspoon ground black pepper
- 5 (30 g) slices Cheddar cheese (omit for dairy-free)
- 10 thin slices ham

**Directions:**

1. Spray the two air fryer drawers with avocado oil. Preheat the air fryer to 176ºC. Grease two pie pans or two baking pans that will fit inside your air fryer. 2. Make the biscuits: In a medium-sized bowl, whip the egg whites with a hand mixer until very stiff. Set aside. 3. In a separate medium-sized bowl, stir together the almond flour, baking powder, and salt until well combined. Cut in the butter. Gently fold the flour mixture into the egg whites with a rubber spatula. If the dough is too wet to form into mounds, add a few tablespoons of almond flour until the dough holds together well. 4. Using a large spoon, divide the dough into 5 equal portions and drop them about 1 inch apart on one of the greased pie pans. Place the pan in the two air fryer drawers and bake for 11 to 14 minutes, until the biscuits are golden brown. Remove from the air fryer and set aside to cool. 5. Make the eggs: Set the air fryer to 192ºC. Crack the eggs into the remaining greased pie pan and sprinkle with the salt and pepper. Place the eggs in the air fryer to bake for 5 minutes, or until they are cooked to your liking. 6. Open the air fryer and top each egg yolk with a slice of cheese . Bake for another minute, or until the cheese is melted. 7. Once the biscuits are cool, slice them in half lengthwise. Place 1 cooked egg topped with cheese and 2 slices of ham in each biscuit. 8. Store leftover biscuits, eggs, and ham in separate airtight containers in the fridge for up to 3 days. Reheat the biscuits and eggs on a baking sheet in a preheated 176ºC air fryer for 5 minutes, or until warmed through.

## Spinach And Red Pepper Egg Cups With Coffee-glazed Canadian Bacon

Servings:6
Cooking Time: 13 Minutes
**Ingredients:**

- FOR THE EGG CUPS
- 4 large eggs
- ¼ cup heavy (whipping) cream
- ¼ teaspoon kosher salt
- ¼ teaspoon freshly ground black pepper
- ½ cup roasted red peppers (about 1 whole pepper), drained and chopped
- ½ cup baby spinach, chopped
- FOR THE CANADIAN BACON
- ¼ cup brewed coffee
- 2 tablespoons maple syrup
- 1 tablespoon light brown sugar
- 6 slices Canadian bacon

**Directions:**

1. To prep the egg cups: In a medium bowl, whisk together the eggs and cream until well combined with a uniform, light color. Stir in the salt, black pepper, roasted red peppers, and spinach until combined.
2. Divide the egg mixture among 6 silicone muffin cups.
3. To prep the Canadian bacon: In a small bowl, whisk together the coffee, maple syrup, and brown sugar.
4. Using a basting brush, brush the glaze onto both sides of each slice of bacon.
5. To cook the egg cups and Canadian bacon: Install a crisper plate in each of the two baskets. Place the egg cups in the Zone 1 basket and insert the basket in the unit. Place the glazed bacon in the Zone 2 basket, making sure the slices don't overlap, and insert the basket in the unit. It is okay if the bacon overlaps a little bit.
6. Select Zone 1, select BAKE, set the temperature to 325°F (160°C), and set the time to 13 minutes.
7. Select Zone 2, select AIR FRY, set the temperature to 400°F (205°C), and set the time to 5 minutes. Select SMART FINISH.
8. Press START/PAUSE to begin cooking.
9. When the Zone 2 timer reads 2 minutes, press START/PAUSE. Remove the basket and use silicone-tipped tongs to flip the bacon. Reinsert the basket and press START/PAUSE to resume cooking.
10. When cooking is complete, serve the egg cups with the Canadian bacon.

**Nutrition:**

- (Per serving) Calories: 180; Total fat: 9.5g; Saturated fat: 4.5g; Carbohydrates: 9g; Fiber: 0g; Protein: 14g; Sodium: 688mg

## Savory Soufflé

Servings: 4
Cooking Time: 8 Minutes
**Ingredients:**

- 4 tablespoons light cream
- 4 eggs
- 2 tablespoons fresh parsley, chopped
- 2 fresh red chilies pepper, chopped
- Salt, as required

**Directions:**

1. In a bowl, add all the ingredients and beat until well combined.

2. Divide the mixture into 4 greased soufflé dishes.
3. Press either "Zone 1" and "Zone 2" of Ninja Foodi 2-Basket Air Fryer and then rotate the knob to select "Air Fry".
4. Set the temperature to 200 degrees C, and then set the time for 5 minutes to preheat.
5. After preheating, arrange soufflé dishes into the basket.
6. Slide basket into Air Fryer and set the time for 8 minutes.
7. After cooking time is completed, remove the soufflé dishes from Air Fryer and serve warm.

## Cinnamon Toast

Servings: 6
Cooking Time: 5 Minutes
**Ingredients:**

- 12 slices bread
- 115g butter, at room temperature
- 100g white sugar
- 1½ teaspoons ground cinnamon
- 1½ teaspoons pure vanilla extract
- 1 pinch of salt

**Directions:**

1. Softened butter is mashed with a fork or the back of a spoon, and then sugar, cinnamon, vanilla, and salt are added.
2. Stir everything together thoroughly.
3. Spread one-sixth of the mixture onto each slice of bread, covering the entire surface.
4. Press your chosen zone - "Zone 1" or "Zone 2" and then rotate the knob to select "Air Fryer".
5. Set the temperature to 200 degrees C, and then set the time for 3 minutes to preheat.
6. After preheating, arrange bread into the basket of each zone.
7. Slide the basket into the Air Fryer and set the time for 5 minutes.
8. After cooking time is completed, remove both baskets from Air Fryer.
9. Cut bread slices diagonally and serve.

## Breakfast Casserole

Servings:4
Cooking Time:10
**Ingredients:**

- 1 pound of beef sausage, grounded
- 1/4 cup diced white onion
- 1 diced green bell pepper
- 8 whole eggs, beaten
- ½ cup Colby jack cheese, shredded
- ¼ teaspoon of garlic salt
- Oil spray, for greasing

**Directions:**

1. Take a bowl and add ground sausage to it.
2. Add in the diced onions, bell peppers, eggs and whisk it well.
3. Then season it with garlic salt.
4. Spray both the baskets of the air fryer with oil spray.
5. Divide this mixture among the baskets; remember to remove the crisper plates.
6. Top the mixture with cheese.
7. Now, turn ON the Ninja Foodie 2-Basket Air Fryer zone 1 and select AIR FRY mode and set the time to 10 minutes at 390 degrees F(200°C) .
8. Select the MATCH button for zone 2 baskets, and hit start.
9. Once the cooking cycle completes, take out, and serve.
10. Serve and enjoy.

**Nutrition:**

- (Per serving) Calories 699| Fat 59.1g | Sodium 1217 mg | Carbs 6.8g | Fiber 0.6g| Sugar 2.5g | Protein33.1 g

## Egg And Bacon Muffins

Servings: 1
Cooking Time: 15 Minutes
**Ingredients:**

- 2 eggs
- Salt and ground black pepper, to taste
- 1 tablespoon green pesto
- 85 g shredded Cheddar cheese
- 140 g cooked bacon
- 1 spring onion, chopped

**Directions:**

1. Line a cupcake tin with parchment paper. Beat the eggs with pepper, salt, and pesto in a bowl. Mix in the cheese.
2. Pour the eggs into the cupcake tin and top with the bacon and spring onion.
3. Place the cupcake tin into the zone 1 drawer and bake at 180ºC for 15 minutes, or until the egg is set. Serve immediately.

## Cornbread

Servings: 6
Cooking Time: 15 Minutes
**Ingredients:**

- 1 cup cornmeal
- 1 cup all-purpose flour
- 1 tablespoon sugar
- 2 teaspoons baking powder
- ½ teaspoon baking soda
- ½ teaspoon salt
- 1 stick butter melted
- 1½ cups buttermilk
- 2 eggs
- 113g diced chiles

**Directions:**

1. Mix cornmeal with flour, sugar, baking powder, baking soda, salt, butter, milk, eggs and chiles in a bowl until smooth.
2. Spread this mixture in two greased 4-inch baking pans.
3. Place one pan in each air fryer basket.
4. Return the air fryer basket 1 to Zone 1, and basket 2 to Zone 2 of the Ninja Foodi 2-Basket Air Fryer.
5. Choose the "Air Fry" mode for Zone 1 at 330 degrees F(165°C) and 15 minutes of cooking time.
6. Select the "MATCH COOK" option to copy the settings for Zone 2.
7. Initiate cooking by pressing the START/PAUSE BUTTON.
8. Slice and serve.

**Nutrition:**

- (Per serving) Calories 199 | Fat 11.1g |Sodium 297mg | Carbs 14.9g | Fiber 1g | Sugar 2.5g | Protein 9.9g

## Whole Grain Eggs Avocado Toast And Butternut Squash And Ricotta Frittata

Servings: 7
Cooking Time: 33 Minutes
**Ingredients:**

- Whole Grain Eggs Avocado Toast:
- Olive oil cooking spray
- 4 large eggs
- Salt
- Black pepper
- 4 pieces wholegrain bread
- 1 avocado
- Red pepper flakes (optional)
- Butternut Squash and Ricotta Frittata:
- 235 ml cubed (½-inch) butternut squash (160 g)

- 2 tablespoons olive oil
- Coarse or flaky salt and freshly ground black pepper, to taste
- 4 fresh sage leaves, thinly sliced
- 6 large eggs, lightly beaten
- 120 ml ricotta cheese
- Cayenne pepper

**Directions:**

1. Make the Whole Grain Eggs Avocado Toast :
2. Preheat the air fryer to 160ºC. Lightly coat the inside of four small oven-safe ramekins with olive oil cooking spray.
3. Crack one egg into each ramekin, and season with salt and black pepper.
4. Place the ramekins into the zone 1 air fryer drawer. Close and set the timer to 7 minutes.
5. While the eggs are cooking, toast the bread in a toaster.
6. Slice the avocado in half lengthwise, remove the pit, and scoop the flesh into a small bowl. Season with salt, black pepper, and red pepper flakes, if desired. Using a fork, smash the avocado lightly.
7. Spread a quarter of the smashed avocado evenly over each slice of toast.
8. Remove the eggs from the air fryer, and gently spoon one onto each slice of avocado toast before serving.
9. Make the Butternut Squash and Ricotta Frittata :
10. In a bowl, toss the squash with the olive oil and season with salt and black pepper until evenly coated. Sprinkle the sage on the bottom of a cake pan and place the squash on top. Place the pan in the zone 2 air fryer drawer and bake at 204ºC for 10 minutes. Stir to incorporate the sage, then cook until the squash is tender and lightly caramelized at the edges, about 3 minutes more.
11. Pour the eggs over the squash, dollop the ricotta all over, and sprinkle with cayenne. Bake at 150ºC until the eggs are set and the frittata is golden brown on top, about 20 minutes. Remove the pan from the air fryer and cut the frittata into wedges to serve.

## Eggs In Avocado Cups

Servings: 4
Cooking Time: 12 Minutes

**Ingredients:**

- 2 avocados, halved and pitted
- 4 eggs
- Salt and ground black pepper, as required

**Directions:**

1. Line either basket of "Zone 1" and "Zone 2" of Ninja Foodi 2-Basket Air Fryer with a greased square piece of foil.
2. Press your chosen zone - "Zone 1" and "Zone 2" and then rotate the knob to select "Bake".
3. Set the temperature to 200 degrees C and then set the time for 5 minutes to preheat.
4. Meanwhile, carefully scoop out about 2 teaspoons of flesh from each avocado half.
5. Crack 1 egg in each avocado half and sprinkle with salt and black pepper.
6. After preheating, arrange 2 avocado halves into the basket.
7. Slide the basket into the Air Fryer and set the time for 12 minutes.
8. After cooking time is completed, transfer the avocado halves and onto serving plates and serve hot.

## Bacon And Eggs For Breakfast

Servings:1
Cooking Time:12

**Ingredients:**

- 4 strips of thick-sliced bacon
- 2 small eggs
- Salt and black pepper, to taste
- Oil spray for greasing ramekins

**Directions:**

1. Take 2 ramekins and grease them with oil spray.
2. Crack eggs in a bowl and season it salt and black pepper.
3. Divide the egg mixture between two ramekins.
4. Put the bacon slices into Ninja Foodie 2-Basket Air Fryer zone 1 basket, and ramekins in zone 2 baskets.
5. Now for zone 1 set it to AIR FRY mode at 400 degrees F(205°C) for 12 minutes.
6. And for zone 2 set it 350 degrees F(175°C) for 8 minutes using AIR FRY mode.
7. Press the Smart finish button and press start, it will finish both at the same time.
8. Once done, serve and enjoy.

**Nutrition:**

- (Per serving) Calories131 | Fat 10g| Sodium 187mg | Carbs0.6 g | Fiber 0g | Sugar 0.6g | Protein 10.7

## Breakfast Meatballs

Servings: 18 Meatballs
Cooking Time: 15 Minutes

**Ingredients:**

- 450 g pork sausage meat, removed from casings
- ½ teaspoon salt
- ¼ teaspoon ground black pepper
- 120 ml shredded sharp Cheddar cheese
- 30 g cream cheese, softened
- 1 large egg, whisked

**Directions:**

1. Combine all ingredients in a large bowl. Form mixture into eighteen 1-inch meatballs.
2. Place meatballs into the two ungreased air fryer drawers. Adjust the temperature to 204ºC and air fry for 15 minutes, shaking drawers three times during cooking. Meatballs will be browned on the outside and have an internal temperature of at least 64ºC when completely cooked. Serve warm.

## Quiche Breakfast Peppers

Servings: 4
Cooking Time: 15 Minutes

**Ingredients:**

- 4 eggs
- ½ tsp garlic powder
- 112g mozzarella cheese, shredded
- 125g ricotta cheese
- 2 bell peppers, cut in half & remove seeds
- 7½g baby spinach, chopped
- 22g parmesan cheese, grated
- ¼ tsp dried parsley

**Directions:**

1. In a bowl, whisk eggs, ricotta cheese, garlic powder, parsley, cheese, and spinach.
2. Pour the egg mixture into each bell pepper half and top with mozzarella cheese.
3. Insert a crisper plate in the Ninja Foodi air fryer baskets.
4. Place bell peppers in both the baskets.
5. Select zone 1 then select "air fry" mode and set the temperature to 355 degrees F(180°C) for 15 minutes. Press "match" to match zone 2 settings to zone 1. Press "start/stop" to begin.

**Nutrition:**

- (Per serving) Calories 136 | Fat 7.6g |Sodium 125mg | Carbs 6.9g | Fiber 0.9g | Sugar 3.5g | Protein 10.8g

## Lemon-cream Cheese Danishes Cherry Danishes

Servings:4
Cooking Time: 15 Minutes
**Ingredients:**

- FOR THE CREAM CHEESE DANISHES
- 1 ounce (2 tablespoons) cream cheese, at room temperature
- 1 teaspoon granulated sugar
- ¼ teaspoon freshly squeezed lemon juice
- ⅛ teaspoon vanilla extract
- ½ sheet frozen puff pastry, thawed
- 2 tablespoons lemon curd
- 1 large egg yolk
- 1 tablespoon water
- FOR THE CHERRY DANISHES
- ½ sheet frozen puff pastry, thawed
- 2 tablespoons cherry preserves
- 1 teaspoon coarse sanding sugar

**Directions:**

1. To prep the cream cheese Danishes: In a small bowl, mix the cream cheese, granulated sugar, lemon juice, and vanilla.
2. Cut the puff pastry sheet into 2 squares. Cut a ½-inch-wide strip from each side of the pastry. Brush the edges of the pastry square with water, then layer the strips along the edges, pressing gently to adhere and form a border around the outside of the pastry.
3. Divide the cream cheese mixture between the two pastries, then top each with 1 tablespoon of lemon curd.
4. In a second small bowl, whisk together the egg yolk and water (this will be used for the cherry Danishes, too). Brush the exposed edges of the pastry with half the egg wash.
5. To prep the cherry Danishes: Cut the puff pastry sheet into 2 squares. Cut a ½-inch-wide strip from each side of the pastry. Brush the edges of the pastry square with water, then layer the strips along the edges, pressing gently to adhere and form a border around the outside of the pastry.
6. Spoon 1 tablespoon of cherry preserves into the center of each pastry.
7. Brush the exposed edges of the pastry with the remaining egg wash, then sprinkle with the sanding sugar.
8. To cook both Danishes: Install a crisper plate in each of the two baskets. Place the cream cheese Danishes in the Zone 1 basket and insert the basket in the unit. Place the cherry Danishes in the Zone 2 basket and insert the basket in the unit.
9. Select Zone 1, select AIR FRY, set the temperature to 330°F (165°C), and set the time to 15 minutes. Select MATCH COOK to match Zone 2 settings to Zone 1.
10. Press START/PAUSE to begin cooking.
11. When cooking is complete, transfer the Danishes to a wire rack to cool. Serve warm.

**Nutrition:**

- (Per serving) Calories: 415; Total fat: 24g; Saturated fat: 12g; Carbohydrates: 51g; Fiber: 1.5g; Protein: 7g; Sodium: 274mg

## Yellow Potatoes With Eggs

Servings:2
Cooking Time:35
**Ingredients:**

- 1 pound of Dutch yellow potatoes, quartered
- 1 red bell pepper, chopped
- Salt and black pepper, to taste
- 1 green bell pepper, chopped
- 2 teaspoons of olive oil
- 2 teaspoons of garlic powder
- 1 teaspoon of onion powder
- 1 egg
- ¼ teaspoon of butter

**Directions:**

1. Toss together diced potatoes, green pepper, red pepper, salt, black pepper, and olive oil along with garlic powder and onion powder.
2. Put in the zone 1 basket of the air fryer.
3. Take ramekin and grease it with oil spray.
4. Whisk egg in a bowl and add salt and pepper along with ½ teaspoon of butter.
5. Pour egg into a ramekin and place it in a zone 2 basket.
6. Now start cooking and set a timer for zone 1 basket to 30-35 minutes at 400 degrees at AIR FRY mode.
7. Now for zone 2, set it on AIR FRY mode at 350 degrees F(175°C) for 8-10 minutes.
8. Press the Smart finish button and press start, it will finish both at the same time.
9. Once done, serve and enjoy.

**Nutrition:**

- (Per serving) Calories252 | Fat7.5g | Sodium 37mg | Carbs 40g | Fiber3.9g | Sugar 7g | Protein 6.7g

## Red Pepper And Feta Frittata

Servings: 4
Cooking Time: 20 Minutes
**Ingredients:**

- Olive oil cooking spray
- 8 large eggs
- 1 medium red pepper, diced
- ½ teaspoon salt
- ½ teaspoon black pepper
- 1 garlic clove, minced
- 120 ml feta, divided

**Directions:**

1. Lightly coat the inside of a 6-inch round cake pan with olive oil cooking spray. In a large bowl, beat the eggs for 1 to 2 minutes, or until well combined.
2. Add the red pepper, salt, black pepper, and garlic to the eggs, and mix together until the red pepper is distributed throughout. Fold in 60 ml the feta cheese.
3. Pour the egg mixture into the prepared cake pan, and sprinkle the remaining 60 ml feta over the top. Place into the zone 1 drawer. Select Bake button and adjust temperature to 180ºC, set time to 18 to 20 minutes and press Start.
4. Remove from the air fryer after the end and allow to cool for 5 minutes before serving.

## Cinnamon Toasts

Servings: 4
Cooking Time: 8 Minutes.
**Ingredients:**

- 4 pieces of bread
- 2 tablespoons butter
- 2 eggs, beaten
- 1 pinch salt
- 1 pinch cinnamon ground
- 1 pinch nutmeg ground
- 1 pinch ground clove
- 1 teaspoon icing sugar

**Directions:**

1. Add two eggs to a mixing bowl and stir cinnamon, nutmeg, ground cloves, and salt, then whisk well.
2. Spread butter on both sides of the bread slices and cut them into thick strips.
3. Dip the breadsticks in the egg mixture and place them in the two crisper plates.

4. Return the crisper plates to the Ninja Foodi Dual Zone Air Fryer.
5. Choose the Air Fry mode for Zone 1 and set the temperature to 390 degrees F(200°C) and the time to 8 minutes.
6. Select the "MATCH" button to copy the settings for Zone 2.
7. Initiate cooking by pressing the START/STOP button.
8. Flip the French toast sticks when cooked halfway through.
9. Serve.

**Nutrition:**

- (Per serving) Calories 199 | Fat 11.1g |Sodium 297mg | Carbs 14.9g | Fiber 1g | Sugar 2.5g | Protein 9.9g

## Savory Sweet Potato Hash

Servings: 6
Cooking Time: 18 Minutes

**Ingredients:**

- 2 medium sweet potatoes, peeled and cut into 1-inch cubes
- ½ green pepper, diced
- ½ red onion, diced
- 110 g baby mushrooms, diced
- 2 tablespoons olive oil
- 1 garlic clove, minced
- ½ teaspoon salt
- ½ teaspoon black pepper
- ½ tablespoon chopped fresh rosemary

**Directions:**

1. In a large bowl, toss all ingredients together until the vegetables are well coated and seasonings distributed.
2. Pour half of the vegetables into the zone 1 drawer and the rest into zone 2 drawer. In zone 1, select Roast button and adjust temperature to 190ºC, set time to 18 minutes. In zone 2, select Match Cook and press Start.
3. Pause and toss or flip the vegetables once halfway through. Transfer to a serving bowl or individual plates and enjoy.

## Sweet Potato Hash

Servings: 4
Cooking Time: 15 Minutes

**Ingredients:**

- 3 sweet potatoes, peel & cut into ½-inch pieces
- ½ tsp cinnamon
- 2 tbsp olive oil
- 1 bell pepper, cut into ½-inch pieces
- ½ tsp dried thyme
- ½ tsp nutmeg
- 1 medium onion, cut into ½-inch pieces
- Pepper
- Salt

**Directions:**

1. In a bowl, toss sweet potatoes with the remaining ingredients.
2. Insert a crisper plate in Ninja Foodi air fryer baskets.
3. Add potato mixture in both baskets.
4. Select zone 1 then select "air fry" mode and set the temperature to 355 degrees F(180°C) for 15 minutes. Press "match" to match zone 2 settings to zone 1. Press "start/stop" to begin.

**Nutrition:**

- (Per serving) Calories 167 | Fat 7.3g |Sodium 94mg | Carbs 24.9g | Fiber 4.2g | Sugar 6.8g | Protein 2.2g

## Cinnamon Apple French Toast

Servings: 8
Cooking Time: 10 Minutes

**Ingredients:**

- 1 egg, lightly beaten
- 4 bread slices
- 1 tbsp cinnamon
- 15ml milk
- 23ml maple syrup
- 45 ml applesauce

**Directions:**

1. In a bowl, whisk egg, milk, cinnamon, applesauce, and maple syrup.
2. Insert a crisper plate in the Ninja Foodi air fryer baskets.
3. Dip each slice in egg mixture and place in both baskets.
4. Select zone 1 then select "air fry" mode and set the temperature to 355 degrees F(180°C) for 10 minutes. Press "match" to match zone 2 settings to zone 1. Press "start/stop" to begin.

**Nutrition:**

- (Per serving) Calories 64 | Fat 1.5g |Sodium 79mg | Carbs 10.8g | Fiber 1.3g | Sugar 4.8g | Protein 2.3g

## Breakfast Sausage And Cauliflower

Servings: 4
Cooking Time: 45 Minutes

**Ingredients:**

- 450 g sausage meat, cooked and crumbled
- 475 ml double/whipping cream
- 1 head cauliflower, chopped
- 235 ml grated Cheddar cheese, plus more for topping
- 8 eggs, beaten
- Salt and ground black pepper, to taste

**Directions:**

1. Preheat the air fryer to 176ºC.
2. In a large bowl, mix the sausage, cream, chopped cauliflower, cheese and eggs. Sprinkle with salt and ground black pepper.
3. Pour the mixture into a greased casserole dish. Bake in the preheated air fryer for 45 minutes or until firm.
4. Top with more Cheddar cheese and serve.

## Egg White Muffins

Servings: 8
Cooking Time: 10 Minutes

**Ingredients:**

- 4 slices center-cut bacon, cut into strips
- 4 ounces baby bella mushrooms, roughly chopped
- 2 ounces sun-dried tomatoes
- 2 tablespoon sliced black olives
- 2 tablespoons grated or shredded parmesan
- 2 tablespoons shredded mozzarella
- ¼ teaspoon black pepper
- ¾ cup liquid egg whites
- 2 tablespoons liquid egg whites

**Directions:**

1. Heat a saucepan with a little oil, add the bacon and mushrooms and cook until fully cooked and crispy, about 6–8 minutes.
2. While the bacon and mushrooms cook, mix the ¾ cup liquid egg whites, sun-dried tomato, olives, parmesan, mozzarella, and black pepper together in a large bowl.
3. Add the cooked bacon and mushrooms to the tomato and olive mixture, stirring everything together.
4. Spoon the mixture into muffin molds, followed by 2 tablespoons of egg whites over the top.
5. Place half the muffins mold in zone 1 and half in zone 2, then insert the drawers into the unit.
6. Select zone 1, select AIR FRY, set temperature to 390 degrees F/ 200 degrees C, and set time to 22 minutes.

7. Select MATCH to match zone 2 settings to zone 1. Press the START/STOP button to begin cooking.
8. When cooking is complete, remove the molds and enjoy!

**Nutrition:**

- (Per serving) Calories 104 | Fat 5.6g | Sodium 269mg | Carbs 3.5g | Fiber 0.8g | Sugar 0.3g | Protein 10.3g

## Sausage With Eggs

Servings:2
Cooking Time:13

**Ingredients:**

- 4 sausage links, raw and uncooked
- 4 eggs, uncooked
- 1 tablespoon of green onion
- 2 tablespoons of chopped tomatoes
- Salt and black pepper, to taste
- 2 tablespoons of milk, dairy
- Oil spray, for greasing

**Directions:**

1. Take a bowl and whisk eggs in it.
2. Then pour milk, and add onions and tomatoes.
3. Whisk it all well.
4. Now season it with salt and black pepper.
5. Take one cake pan, that fit inside the air fryer and grease it with oil spray.
6. Pour the omelet in the greased cake pans.
7. Put the cake pan inside zone 1 air fryer basket of Ninja Foodie 2-Basket Air Fryer.
8. Now place the sausage link into the zone 2 basket.
9. Select bake for zone 1 basket and set the timer to 8-10 minutes at 300 degrees F(150°C) .
10. For the zone 2 basket, select the AIR FRY button and set the timer to 12 minutes at 390 degrees.
11. Once the cooking cycle completes, serve by transferring it to plates.
12. Chop the sausage or cut it in round and then mix it with omelet.
13. Enjoy hot as a delicious breakfast.

**Nutrition:**

- (Per serving) Calories 240 | Fat 18.4g| Sodium 396mg | Carbs 2.8g | Fiber0.2g | Sugar 2g | Protein 15.6g

## Egg In Bread Hole

Servings: 1
Cooking Time: 8 Minutes

**Ingredients:**

- 1 tablespoon butter, softened
- 2 eggs
- 2 slices of bread
- Salt and black pepper, to taste

**Directions:**

1. Line either basket of "Zone 1" and "Zone 2" with a greased piece of foil.
2. Press your chosen zone - "Zone 1" or "Zone 2" and then rotate the knob to select "Air Fryer".
3. Set the temperature to 160 degrees C, and then set the time for 3 minutes to preheat.
4. After preheating, place the butter on both sides of the bread. Cut a hole in the centre of the bread and crack the egg.
5. Slide the basket into the Air Fryer and set the time for 6 minutes.
6. After cooking time is completed, transfer the bread to a serving plate and serve.

## Strawberry Baked Oats Chocolate Peanut Butter Baked Oats

Servings:12
Cooking Time: 15 Minutes

**Ingredients:**

- FOR THE STRAWBERRY OATS
- 1 cup whole milk
- 1 cup heavy (whipping) cream
- ½ cup maple syrup
- 2 teaspoons vanilla extract
- 2 large eggs
- 2 cups old-fashioned oats
- 2 teaspoons baking powder
- ½ teaspoon ground cinnamon
- ¼ teaspoon kosher salt
- 1½ cups diced strawberries
- FOR THE CHOCOLATE PEANUT BUTTER OATS
- 2 very ripe bananas
- ½ cup maple syrup
- ¼ cup unsweetened cocoa powder
- 2 teaspoons vanilla extract
- 2 teaspoons baking powder
- 2 large eggs
- ½ teaspoon kosher salt
- 2 cups old-fashioned oats
- 2 tablespoons peanut butter

**Directions:**

1. To prep the strawberry oats: In a large bowl, combine the milk, cream, maple syrup, vanilla, and eggs. Stir in the oats, baking powder, cinnamon, and salt until fully combined. Fold in the strawberries.
2. To prep the chocolate peanut butter oats: In a large bowl, mash the banana with a fork. Stir in the maple syrup, cocoa powder, vanilla, baking powder, and salt until smooth. Beat in the eggs. Stir in the oats until everything is combined.
3. To bake the oats: Place the strawberry oatmeal in the Zone 1 basket and insert the basket in the unit. Place the chocolate peanut butter oatmeal in the Zone 2 basket. Add ½ teaspoon dollops of peanut butter on top and insert the basket in the unit.
4. Select Zone 1, select BAKE, set the temperature to 320°F (160°C), and set the time to 15 minutes. Select MATCH COOK to match Zone 2 settings to Zone 1.
5. Press START/PAUSE to begin cooking.
6. When cooking is complete, serve each oatmeal in a shallow bowl.

**Nutrition:**

- (Per serving) Calories: 367; Total fat: 19g; Saturated fat: 11g; Carbohydrates: 42g; Fiber: 3.5g; Protein: 8g; Sodium: 102mg

## Salmon Quiche

Servings: 4
Cooking Time: 20 Minutes

**Ingredients:**

- 275g salmon fillets, chopped
- Salt and ground black pepper, as required
- 1 tablespoon fresh lemon juice
- 2 egg yolks
- 7 tablespoons chilled butter
- 165g flour
- 2 tablespoons cold water
- 4 eggs
- 6 tablespoons whipping cream
- 2 spring onions, chopped

**Directions:**

1. In a bowl, mix together the salmon, salt, black pepper and lemon juice. Set aside.
2. In another bowl, add egg yolk, butter, flour and water and mix until a dough forms.
3. Divide the dough into 2 portions.
4. Place each dough onto a floured smooth surface and roll into about 17.5cm round.
5. Place each rolled dough into a quiche pan and press firmly in the bottom and along the edges.
6. Then trim the excess edges.
7. In a small bowl, add the eggs, cream, salt and black pepper and beat until well combined.
8. Place the cream mixture over each crust evenly and top with the salmon, followed by the spring onion.
9. Press either "Zone 1" or "Zone 2" of Ninja Foodi 2-Basket Air Fryer and then rotate the knob for each zone to select "Air Fry".
10. Set the temperature to 180 degrees C and then set the time for 5 minutes to preheat.
11. After preheating, arrange 1 quiche pan into the basket of each zone.
12. Slide the basket into the Air Fryer and set the time for 20 minutes.
13. After cooking time is completed, remove the quiche pans from Air Fryer.
14. Cut each quiche in 2 portions and serve hot.

## Lemon-blueberry Muffins

Servings: 6 Muffins
Cooking Time: 20 To 25 Minutes

**Ingredients:**

- 300 ml almond flour
- 3 tablespoons granulated sweetener
- 1 teaspoon baking powder
- 2 large eggs
- 3 tablespoons melted butter
- 1 tablespoon almond milk
- 1 tablespoon fresh lemon juice
- 120 ml fresh blueberries

**Directions:**

1. Preheat the zone 1 air fryer drawer to 176°C. Lightly coat 6 silicone muffin cups with vegetable oil. Set aside.
2. In a large mixing bowl, combine the almond flour, sweetener, and baking soda. Set aside.
3. In a separate small bowl, whisk together the eggs, butter, milk, and lemon juice. Add the egg mixture to the flour mixture and stir until just combined. Fold in the blueberries and let the batter sit for 5 minutes.
4. Spoon the muffin batter into the muffin cups, about two-thirds full. Air fry in the zone 1 drawer for 20 to 25 minutes, or until a toothpick inserted into the center of a muffin comes out clean.
5. Remove the drawer from the air fryer and let the muffins cool for about 5 minutes before transferring them to a wire rack to cool completely.

## Sweet Potatoes Hash

Servings:2
Cooking Time:25

**Ingredients:**

- 450 grams sweet potatoes
- 1/2 white onion, diced
- 3 tablespoons of olive oil
- 1 teaspoon smoked paprika
- 1/4 teaspoon cumin
- 1/3 teaspoon of ground turmeric
- 1/4 teaspoon of garlic salt
- 1 cup guacamole

**Directions:**

1. Peel and cut the potatoes into cubes.
2. Now, transfer the potatoes to a bowl and add oil, white onions, cumin, paprika, turmeric, and garlic salt.
3. Put this mixture between both the baskets of the Ninja Foodie 2-Basket Air Fryer.
4. Set it to AIR FRY mode for 10 minutes at 390 degrees F(200°C) .
5. Then take out the baskets and shake them well.
6. Then again set time to 15 minutes at 390 degrees F(200°C) .
7. Once done, serve it with guacamole.

**Nutrition:**

- (Per serving) Calories691 | Fat 49.7g| Sodium 596mg | Carbs 64g | Fiber15g | Sugar 19g | Protein 8.1g

## Bacon Cheese Egg With Avocado And Potato Nuggets

Servings: 8
Cooking Time: 20 Minutes

**Ingredients:**

- Bacon Cheese Egg with Avocado:
- 6 large eggs
- 60 ml double cream
- 350 ml chopped cauliflower
- 235 ml shredded medium Cheddar cheese
- 1 medium avocado, peeled and pitted
- 8 tablespoons full-fat sour cream
- 2 spring onions, sliced on the bias
- 12 slices bacon, cooked and crumbled
- Potato Nuggets:
- 1 teaspoon extra virgin olive oil
- 1 clove garlic, minced
- 1 L kale, rinsed and chopped
- 475 ml potatoes, boiled and mashed
- 30 ml milk
- Salt and ground black pepper, to taste
- Cooking spray

**Directions:**

1. Make the Bacon Cheese Egg with Avocado :
2. In a medium bowl, whisk eggs and cream together. Pour into a round baking dish.
3. Add cauliflower and mix, then top with Cheddar. Place dish into the zone 1 air fryer drawer.
4. Adjust the temperature to 160°C and set the timer for 20 minutes.
5. When completely cooked, eggs will be firm and cheese will be browned. Slice into four pieces.
6. Slice avocado and divide evenly among pieces. Top each piece with 2 tablespoons sour cream, sliced spring onions, and crumbled bacon.
7. Make the Potato Nuggets :
8. Preheat the zone 2 air fryer drawer to 200°C.
9. In a skillet over medium heat, sauté the garlic in the olive oil, until it turns golden brown. Sauté with the kale for an additional 3 minutes and remove from the heat.
10. Mix the mashed potatoes, kale and garlic in a bowl. Pour in the milk and sprinkle with salt and pepper.
11. Shape the mixture into nuggets and spritz with cooking spray.
12. Put in the zone 2 air fryer drawer and air fry for 15 minutes, flip the nuggets halfway through cooking to make sure the nuggets fry evenly.
13. Serve immediately.

## Baked Mushroom And Mozzarella Frittata With Breakfast Potatoes

Servings:4
Cooking Time: 35 Minutes
**Ingredients:**

- FOR THE FRITTATA
- 8 large eggs
- ⅓ cup whole milk
- 1 teaspoon kosher salt
- ½ teaspoon freshly ground black pepper
- 1 cup sliced cremini mushrooms (about 2 ounces)
- 1 teaspoon olive oil
- 2 ounces part-skim mozzarella cheese, cut into ½-inch cubes
- FOR THE POTATOES
- 2 russet potatoes, cut into ½-inch cubes
- 1 tablespoon olive oil
- ½ teaspoon garlic powder
- ¼ teaspoon kosher salt
- ¼ teaspoon freshly ground black pepper

**Directions:**

1. To prep the frittata: In a large bowl, whisk together the eggs, milk, salt, and pepper. Stir in the mushrooms.
2. To prep the potatoes: In a large bowl, combine the potatoes, olive oil, garlic powder, salt, and black pepper.
3. To cook the frittata and potatoes: Brush the bottom of the Zone 1 basket with 1 teaspoon of olive oil. Add the egg mixture to the basket, top with the mozzarella cubes, and insert the basket in the unit. Install a crisper plate in the Zone 2 basket. Place the potatoes in the basket and insert the basket in the unit.
4. Select Zone 1, select BAKE, set the temperature to 350°F (175°C), and set the time to 30 minutes.
5. Select Zone 2, select AIR FRY, set the temperature to 400°F (205°C), and set the time to 35 minutes. Select SMART FINISH.
6. Press START/PAUSE to begin cooking.
7. When the Zone 2 timer reads 15 minutes, press START/PAUSE. Remove the basket and shake the potatoes for 10 seconds. Reinsert the basket and press START/PAUSE to resume cooking.
8. When cooking is complete, the frittata will pull away from the edges of the basket and the potatoes will be golden brown. Transfer the frittata to a cutting board and cut into 4 portions. Serve with the potatoes.

**Nutrition:**

- (Per serving) Calories: 307; Total fat: 17g; Saturated fat: 5.5g; Carbohydrates: 18g; Fiber: 1g; Protein: 19g; Sodium: 600mg

## Jalapeño Popper Egg Cups And Cheddar Soufflés

Servings: 6
Cooking Time: 12 Minutes
**Ingredients:**

- Jalapeño Popper Egg Cups:
- 4 large eggs
- 60 ml chopped pickled jalapeños
- 60 g full-fat cream cheese
- 120 ml shredded sharp Cheddar cheese
- Cheddar Soufflés:
- 3 large eggs, whites and yolks separated
- ¼ teaspoon cream of tartar
- 120 ml shredded sharp Cheddar cheese
- 85 g cream cheese, softened

**Directions:**

1. Make the Jalapeño Popper Egg Cups :
2. In a medium bowl, beat the eggs, then pour into four silicone muffin cups.
3. In a large microwave-safe bowl, place jalapeños, cream cheese, and Cheddar. Microwave for 30 seconds and stir. Take a spoonful, approximately ¼ of the mixture, and place it in the center of one of the egg cups. Repeat with remaining mixture.
4. Place egg cups into the zone 1 air fryer drawer.
5. Adjust the temperature to 160°C and bake for 10 minutes.
6. Serve warm.
7. Make the Cheddar Soufflés :
8. In a large bowl, beat egg whites together with cream of tartar until soft peaks form, about 2 minutes.
9. In a separate medium bowl, beat egg yolks, Cheddar, and cream cheese together until frothy, about 1 minute. Add egg yolk mixture to whites, gently folding until combined.
10. Pour mixture evenly into four ramekins greased with cooking spray. Place ramekins into the zone 2 air fryer drawer. Adjust the temperature to 176°C and bake for 12 minutes. Eggs will be browned on the top and firm in the center when done. Serve warm.

## Gyro Breakfast Patties With Tzatziki

Servings: 16
Cooking Time: 20 Minutes
**Ingredients:**

- patties
- Patties:
- 900 g lamb or beef mince
- 120 ml diced red onions
- 60 ml sliced black olives
- 2 tablespoons tomato sauce
- 1 teaspoon dried oregano leaves
- 2 cloves garlic, minced
- 1 teaspoon fine sea salt
- Tzatziki:
- 235 ml full-fat sour cream
- 1 small cucumber, chopped
- ½ teaspoon fine sea salt
- ½ teaspoon garlic powder, or 1 clove garlic, minced
- ¼ teaspoon dried dill, or 1 teaspoon finely chopped fresh dill
- For Garnish/Serving:
- 120 ml crumbled feta cheese (about 60 g)
- Diced red onions
- Sliced black olives
- Sliced cucumbers

**Directions:**

1. Preheat the air fryer to 176°C. 2. Place the lamb, onions, olives, tomato sauce, oregano, garlic, and salt in a large bowl. Mix well to combine the ingredients. 3. Using your hands, form the mixture into sixteen 3-inch patties. Place the patties in the two air fryer drawers and air fry for 20 minutes, flipping halfway through. Remove the patties and place them on a serving platter. 4. While the patties cook, make the tzatziki: Place all the ingredients in a small bowl and stir well. Cover and store in the fridge until ready to serve. Garnish with ground black pepper before serving. 5. Serve the patties with a dollop of tzatziki, a sprinkle of crumbled feta cheese, diced red onions, sliced black olives, and sliced cucumbers. 6. Store leftovers in an airtight container in the refrigerator for up to 5 days or in the freezer for up to a month. Reheat the patties in a preheated 200°C air fryer for a few minutes, until warmed through.

## Breakfast Pitta

Servings: 2
Cooking Time: 6 Minutes
**Ingredients:**

- 1 wholemeal pitta
- 2 teaspoons olive oil
- ½ shallot, diced
- ¼ teaspoon garlic, minced
- 1 large egg
- ¼ teaspoon dried oregano
- ¼ teaspoon dried thyme
- ⅛ teaspoon salt
- 2 tablespoons shredded Parmesan cheese

**Directions:**

1. Brush the top of the pitta with olive oil, then spread the diced shallot and minced garlic over the pitta. Crack the egg into a small bowl or ramekin, and season it with oregano, thyme, and salt.
2. Place the pitta into the zone 1 drawer, and gently pour the egg onto the top of the pitta. Sprinkle with cheese over the top.
3. Select Bake button and adjust temperature to 190ºC, set time to 6 minutes and press Start. After the end, allow to cool for 5 minutes before cutting into pieces for serving.

## Breakfast Stuffed Peppers

Servings: 4
Cooking Time: 13 Minutes
**Ingredients:**

- 2 capsicums, halved, seeds removed
- 4 eggs
- 1 teaspoon olive oil
- 1 pinch salt and pepper
- 1 pinch sriracha flakes

**Directions:**

1. Cut each capsicum in half and place two halves in each air fryer basket.
2. Crack one egg into each capsicum and top it with black pepper, salt, sriracha flakes and olive oil.
3. Return the air fryer basket 1 to Zone 1, and basket 2 to Zone 2 of the Ninja Foodi 2-Basket Air Fryer.
4. Choose the "Air Fry" mode for Zone 1 at 390 degrees F(200°C) and 13 minutes of cooking time.
5. Select the "MATCH COOK" option to copy the settings for Zone 2.
6. Initiate cooking by pressing the START/PAUSE BUTTON.
7. Serve warm.

**Nutrition:**

- (Per serving) Calories 237 | Fat 19g |Sodium 518mg | Carbs 7g | Fiber 1.5g | Sugar 3.4g | Protein 12g

## Quick And Easy Blueberry Muffins

Servings: 8 Muffins
Cooking Time: 12 Minutes
**Ingredients:**

- 315 ml flour
- 120 ml sugar
- 2 teaspoons baking powder
- ¼ teaspoon salt
- 80 ml rapeseed oil
- 1 egg
- 120 ml milk
- 160 ml blueberries, fresh or frozen and thawed

**Directions:**

1. Preheat the air fryer to 165ºC.
2. In a medium bowl, stir together flour, sugar, baking powder, and salt.
3. In a separate bowl, combine oil, egg, and milk and mix well.
4. Add egg mixture to dry ingredients and stir just until moistened.
5. Gently stir in the blueberries.
6. Spoon batter evenly into parchment paper-lined muffin cups.
7. Put the muffin cups in the two air fryer baskets and bake for 12 minutes or until tops spring back when touched lightly.
8. Serve immediately.

## Air Fried Sausage

Servings: 4
Cooking Time: 13 Minutes.
**Ingredients:**

- 4 sausage links, raw and uncooked

**Directions:**

1. Divide the sausages in the two crisper plates.
2. Return the crisper plate to the Ninja Foodi Dual Zone Air Fryer.
3. Choose the Air Fry mode for Zone 1 and set the temperature to 390 degrees F(200°C) and set the time to 13 minutes.
4. Select the "MATCH" button to copy the settings for Zone 2.
5. Initiate cooking by pressing the START/STOP button.
6. Serve warm and fresh.

**Nutrition:**

- (Per serving) Calories 267 | Fat 12g |Sodium 165mg | Carbs 39g | Fiber 1.4g | Sugar 22g | Protein 3.3g

## Crispy Hash Browns

Servings: 4
Cooking Time: 13 Minutes.
**Ingredients:**

- 3 russet potatoes
- ¼ cup chopped green peppers
- ¼ cup chopped red peppers
- ¼ cup chopped onions
- 2 garlic cloves chopped
- 1 teaspoon paprika
- Salt and black pepper, to taste
- 2 teaspoons olive oil

**Directions:**

1. Peel and grate all the potatoes with the help of a cheese grater.
2. Add potato shreds to a bowl filled with cold water and leave it soaked for 25 minutes.
3. Drain the water and place the potato shreds on a plate lined with a paper towel.
4. Transfer the shreds to a dry bowl and add olive oil, paprika, garlic, and black pepper.
5. Make four flat patties out of the potato mixture and place two into each of the crisper plate.
6. Return the crisper plate to the Ninja Foodi Dual Zone Air Fryer.
7. Choose the Air Fry mode for Zone 1 and set the temperature to 390 degrees F(200°C) and set the time to 13 minutes.
8. Select the "MATCH" button to copy the settings for Zone 2.
9. Initiate cooking by pressing the START/STOP button.
10. Flip the potato hash browns once cooked halfway through, then resume cooking.
11. Once done, serve warm.

**Nutrition:**

- (Per serving) Calories 190 | Fat 18g |Sodium 150mg | Carbs 0.6g | Fiber 0.4g | Sugar 0.4g | Protein 7.2g

## Glazed Apple Fritters Glazed Peach Fritters

Servings:4
Cooking Time: 12 Minutes
**Ingredients:**

- FOR THE FRITTERS
- ¾ cup all-purpose flour
- 2 tablespoons granulated sugar
- 1 teaspoon baking powder
- ½ teaspoon kosher salt
- ½ teaspoon ground cinnamon
- ⅓ cup whole milk
- 2 tablespoons cold unsalted butter, grated
- 1 large egg
- 1 teaspoon fresh lemon juice
- 1 apple, peeled and diced
- 1 peach, peeled and diced
- FOR THE GLAZE
- ½ cup powdered sugar
- 1 tablespoon whole milk
- ½ teaspoon vanilla extract
- ½ teaspoon ground cinnamon
- Pinch salt

**Directions:**

1. To prep the fritters: In a large bowl, combine the flour, granulated sugar, baking powder, salt, and cinnamon. Stir in the milk, butter, egg, and lemon juice to form a thick batter.
2. Transfer half of the batter to a second bowl. Fold the apples into one bowl and the peaches into the other.
3. To prep the glaze: In a small bowl, whisk together the powdered sugar, milk, vanilla, cinnamon, and salt until smooth. Set aside.
4. To cook the fritters: Install a crisper plate in each of the two baskets. Drop two ¼-cup scoops of the apple fritter batter into the Zone 1 basket and insert the basket in the unit. Drop two ¼-cup scoops of the peach fritter batter into the Zone 2 basket and insert the basket in the unit.
5. Select Zone 1, select AIR FRY, set the temperature to 345°F (175°C), and set the time to 10 minutes.
6. Select Zone 2, select AIR FRY, set the temperature to 345°F (175°C), and set the time to 12 minutes. Select SMART FINISH.
7. Press START/PAUSE to begin cooking.
8. When cooking is complete, transfer the fritters to a wire rack and drizzle the glaze over them. Serve warm or at room temperature.

**Nutrition:**

- (Per serving) Calories: 298; Total fat: 8g; Saturated fat: 4.5g; Carbohydrates: 53g; Fiber: 3g; Protein: 5g; Sodium: 170mg

## Broccoli-mushroom Frittata And Chimichanga Breakfast Burrito

Servings: 4
Cooking Time: 20 Minutes
**Ingredients:**

- Broccoli-Mushroom Frittata:
- 1 tablespoon olive oil
- 350 ml broccoli florets, finely chopped
- 120 ml sliced brown mushrooms
- 60 ml finely chopped onion
- ½ teaspoon salt
- ¼ teaspoon freshly ground black pepper
- 6 eggs
- 60 ml Parmesan cheese
- Chimichanga Breakfast Burrito:
- 2 large (10- to 12-inch) flour tortillas
- 120 ml canned refried beans (pinto or black work equally well)
- 4 large eggs, cooked scrambled
- 4 corn tortilla chips, crushed
- 120 ml grated chili cheese
- 12 pickled jalapeño slices
- 1 tablespoon vegetable oil
- Guacamole, salsa, and sour cream, for serving (optional)

**Directions:**

1. Make the Broccoli-Mushroom Frittata :
2. In a nonstick cake pan, combine the olive oil, broccoli, mushrooms, onion, salt, and pepper. Stir until the vegetables are thoroughly coated with oil. Place the cake pan in the zone 1 air fryer basket and set the air fryer to 205ºC. Air fry for 5 minutes until the vegetables soften.
3. Meanwhile, in a medium bowl, whisk the eggs and Parmesan until thoroughly combined. Pour the egg mixture into the pan and shake gently to distribute the vegetables. Air fry for another 15 minutes until the eggs are set.
4. Remove from the air fryer and let sit for 5 minutes to cool slightly. Use a silicone spatula to gently lift the frittata onto a plate before serving.
5. Make the Chimichanga Breakfast Burrito :
6. Place the tortillas on a work surface and divide the refried beans between them, spreading them in a rough rectangle in the center of the tortillas. Top the beans with the scrambled eggs, crushed chips, cheese, and jalapeños. Fold one side over the fillings, then fold in each short side and roll up the rest of the way like a burrito.
7. Brush the outside of the burritos with the oil, then transfer to the zone 2 air fryer basket, seam-side down. Air fry at 175ºC until the tortillas are browned and crisp and the filling is warm throughout, about 10 minutes.
8. Transfer the chimichangas to plates and serve warm with guacamole, salsa, and sour cream, if you like.

## Honey-apricot Granola With Greek Yoghurt

Servings: 6
Cooking Time: 30 Minutes
**Ingredients:**

- 235 ml rolled oats
- 60 ml dried apricots, diced
- 60 ml almond slivers
- 60 ml walnuts, chopped
- 60 ml pumpkin seeds
- 60 to 80 ml honey, plus more for drizzling
- 1 tablespoon olive oil
- 1 teaspoon ground cinnamon
- ¼ teaspoon ground nutmeg
- ¼ teaspoon salt
- 2 tablespoons sugar-free dark chocolate chips (optional)
- 700 ml fat-free plain Greek yoghurt

**Directions:**

1. Line the zone 1 and zone 2 drawer with two parchment papers. In a large bowl, combine the oats, apricots, almonds, walnuts, pumpkin seeds, honey, olive oil, cinnamon, nutmeg, and salt, mixing so that the honey, oil, and spices are well distributed. Pour the mixture onto the parchment papers and spread it into an even layer.
2. Bake at 130ºC for 10 minutes, then shake or stir and spread back out into an even layer. Continue baking for 10 minutes more, then repeat the process of shaking or stirring the mixture.

3. Bake for an additional 10 minutes before removing from the air fryer. Allow the granola to cool completely before stirring in the chocolate chips and pouring into an airtight container for storage. For each serving, top 120 ml Greek yoghurt with 80 ml granola and a drizzle of honey, if needed.

## Perfect Cinnamon Toast

Servings: 6
Cooking Time: 10 Minutes
**Ingredients:**

- 12 slices whole-wheat bread
- 1 stick butter, room temperature
- ½ cup white sugar
- 1½ teaspoons ground cinnamon
- 1½ teaspoons pure vanilla extract
- 1 pinch kosher salt
- 2 pinches freshly ground black pepper (optional)

**Directions:**

1. Mash the softened butter with a fork or the back of a spoon in a bowl. Add the sugar, cinnamon, vanilla, and salt. Stir until everything is well combined.
2. Spread one-sixth of the mixture onto each slice of bread, making sure to cover the entire surface.
3. Install a crisper plate in both drawers. Place half the bread sliced in the zone 1 drawer and half in the zone 2 drawer, then insert the drawers into the unit.
4. Select zone 1, select AIR FRY, set temperature to 400 degrees F/ 205 degrees C, and set time to 5 minutes. Select MATCH to match zone 2 settings to zone 1. Press theSTART/STOP button to begin cooking
5. When cooking is complete, remove the slices and cut them diagonally.
6. Serve immediately.

**Nutrition:**

- (Per serving) Calories 322 | Fat 16.5g | Sodium 249mg | Carbs 39.3g | Fiber 4.2g | Sugar 18.2g | Protein 8.2g

## Bacon And Egg Omelet

Servings:2
Cooking Time:10
**Ingredients:**

- 2 eggs, whisked
- ½ teaspoon of chopped tomatoes
- Sea Salt and black pepper, to taste
- 2 teaspoons of almond milk
- 1 teaspoon of cilantro, chopped
- 1 small green chili, chopped
- 4 slices of bacon

**Directions:**

1. Take a bowl and whisk eggs in it.
2. Then add green chili salt, black pepper, cilantro, almond milk, and chopped tomatoes.
3. Oil greases the ramekins.
4. Pour this into ramekins.
5. Put the bacon in the zone 1 basket and ramekins in zone 2 basket of the Ninja Foodie 2-Basket Air Fryer.
6. Now for zone 1, set it to AIR FRY mode at 400 degrees F(205°C) for 10 minutes
7. And for zone 2, set it 350 degrees F(175°C) for 10 minutes in AIR FRY mode.
8. Press the Smart finish button and press start, it will finish both at the same time.
9. Once done, serve and enjoy.

**Nutrition:**

- (Per serving) Calories 285| Fat 21.5g| Sodium1000 mg | Carbs 2.2g | Fiber 0.1g| Sugar1 g | Protein 19.7g

## French Toast Sticks

Servings: 5
Cooking Time: 12 Minutes
**Ingredients:**

- 10 teaspoons sugar, divided
- 3¼ teaspoons cinnamon, divided
- 3 slices toast
- 1 egg
- 1 egg yolks
- 80ml milk
- 1 teaspoon sugar
- 1 teaspoon brown sugar
- 1 teaspoon vanilla
- ¼ teaspoon cinnamon

**Directions:**

1. Line either basket "Zone 1" and "Zone 2" with a greased piece of foil.
2. Press your chosen zone - "Zone 1" and "Zone 2" and then rotate the knob to select "Air Fryer".
3. Set the temperature to 175 degrees C, and then set the time for 3 minutes to preheat.
4. Three teaspoons of sugar and 3 teaspoons of cinnamon are whisked together in a shallow bowl. Set aside.
5. Cut each slice of bread in thirds.
6. Combine the eggs, egg yolks, milk, brown sugar, remaining sugar, vanilla, and remaining cinnamon in a shallow pan.
7. Blend everything until it's smooth.
8. Allow the bread to soak in the egg mixture for a few seconds. Flip over and dip the other side.
9. Coat both sides of the bread in the cinnamon-sugar mixture. Place in the basket.
10. Slide the basket into the Air Fryer and set the time for 8 minutes.
11. After cooking time is completed, transfer the bread to a serving plate and serve.

## Pumpkin French Toast Casserole With Sweet And Spicy Twisted Bacon

Servings:4
Cooking Time: 35 Minutes
**Ingredients:**

- FOR THE FRENCH TOAST CASSEROLE
- 3 large eggs
- 1 cup unsweetened almond milk
- 1 cup canned unsweetened pumpkin puree
- 2 teaspoons pumpkin pie spice
- ¼ cup packed light brown sugar
- 1 teaspoon vanilla extract
- 6 cups French bread cubes
- 1 teaspoon vegetable oil
- ¼ cup maple syrup
- FOR THE BACON
- 2 tablespoons light brown sugar
- ⅛ teaspoon cayenne pepper
- 8 slices bacon

**Directions:**

1. To prep the French toast casserole: In a shallow bowl, whisk together the eggs, almond milk, pumpkin puree, pumpkin pie spice, brown sugar, and vanilla.
2. Add the bread cubes to the egg mixture, making sure the bread is fully coated in the custard. Let sit for at least 10 minutes to allow the bread to soak up the custard.
3. To prep the bacon: In a small bowl, combine the brown sugar and cayenne.

4. Arrange the bacon on a cutting board in a single layer. Evenly sprinkle the strips with the brown sugar mixture. Fold the bacon strip in half lengthwise. Hold one end of the bacon steady and twist the other end so the bacon resembles a straw.
5. To cook the casserole and bacon: Brush the Zone 1 basket with the oil. Pour the French toast casserole into the Zone 1 basket, drizzle with maple syrup, and insert the basket in the unit. Install a crisper plate in the Zone 2 basket, add the bacon twists in a single layer, and insert the basket in the unit. For the best fit, arrange the bacon twists across the unit, front to back.
6. Select Zone 1, select BAKE, set the temperature to 330°F (165°C), and set the time to 35 minutes.
7. Select Zone 2, select AIR FRY, set the temperature to 400°F (205°C), and set the time to 12 minutes. Select SMART FINISH.
8. Press START/PAUSE to begin cooking.
9. When cooking is complete, transfer the bacon to a plate lined with paper towels. Let cool for 2 to 3 minutes before serving with the French toast casserole.

**Nutrition:**

- (Per serving) Calories: 601; Total fat: 28g; Saturated fat: 9g; Carbohydrates: 67g; Fiber: 2.5g; Protein: 17g; Sodium: 814mg

## Egg With Baby Spinach

Servings:4
Cooking Time:12

**Ingredients:**

- Nonstick spray, for greasing ramekins
- 2 tablespoons olive oil
- 6 ounces baby spinach
- 2 garlic cloves, minced
- 1/3 teaspoon kosher salt
- 6-8 large eggs
- ½ cup half and half
- Salt and black pepper, to taste
- 8 Sourdough bread slices, toasted

**Directions:**

1. Grease 4 ramekins with oil spray and set aside for further use.
2. Take a skillet and heat oil in it.
3. Then cook spinach for 2 minutes and add garlic and salt black pepper.
4. Let it simmer for2more minutes.
5. Once the spinach is wilted, transfer it to a plate.
6. Whisk an egg into a small bowl.
7. Add in the spinach.
8. Whisk it well and then pour half and half.
9. Divide this mixture between 4 ramekins and remember not to overfill it to the top, leave a little space on top.
10. Put the ramekins in zone 1 and zone 2 baskets of the Ninja Foodie 2-Basket Air Fryer.
11. Press start and set zone 1 to AIR fry it at 350 degrees F(175°C) for 8-12 minutes.
12. Press the MATCH button for zone 2.
13. Once it's cooked and eggs are done, serve with sourdough bread slices.

**Nutrition:**

- (Per serving) Calories 404| Fat 19.6g| Sodium 761mg | Carbs 40.1g | Fiber 2.5g| Sugar 2.5g | Protein 19.2g

## Baked Eggs

Servings: 10
Cooking Time: 12 Minutes

**Ingredients:**

- 450g marinara sauce, divided
- 2 tablespoons capers, drained and divided
- 16 eggs
- 120g whipping cream, divided
- 50g Parmesan cheese, shredded and divided
- Salt and ground black pepper, as required

**Directions:**

1. Press "Zone 1" and "Zone 2" and then rotate the knob to select "Bake".
2. Set the temperature to 200 degrees C and then set the time for 5 minutes to preheat.
3. Divide the marinara sauce in the bottom of 8 greased ramekins evenly and top with capers.
4. Carefully crack 2 eggs over marinara sauce into each ramekin and top with cream, followed by the Parmesan cheese.
5. Sprinkle each ramekin with salt and black pepper.
6. After preheating, arrange the ramekins into the basket of each zone.
7. Slide the basket into the Air Fryer and set the time for 12 minutes.
8. After cooking time is completed, remove the ramekins from Air Fryer.
9. Serve hot.

## Breakfast Potatoes

Servings: 6
Cooking Time: 20 Minutes

**Ingredients:**

- 3 potatoes, peeled and diced
- 1 onion yellow, diced
- 1 green pepper diced
- 2 teaspoons salt
- ½ teaspoon pepper
- 2 tablespoons olive oil
- 1 cup cheese shredded

**Directions:**

1. Toss potatoes with onion, green peppers, black pepper, salt and cheese in a bowl.
2. Divide the potato mixture into the Ninja Foodi 2 Baskets Air Fryer baskets.
3. Return the air fryer basket 1 to Zone 1, and basket 2 to Zone 2 of the Ninja Foodi 2-Basket Air Fryer.
4. Choose the "Air Fry" mode for Zone 1 at 400 degrees F(205°C) temperature and 20 minutes of cooking time.
5. Select the "MATCH COOK" option to copy the settings for Zone 2.
6. Initiate cooking by pressing the START/PAUSE BUTTON.
7. Toss the veggies once cooked halfway through.
8. Serve warm.

**Nutrition:**

- (Per serving) Calories 209 | Fat 7.5g |Sodium 321mg | Carbs 34.1g | Fiber 4g | Sugar 3.8g | Protein 4.3g

## Parmesan Ranch Risotto And Oat And Chia Porridge

Servings: 6
Cooking Time: 30 Minutes

**Ingredients:**

- Parmesan Ranch Risotto:
- 1 tablespoon olive oil
- 1 clove garlic, minced
- 1 tablespoon unsalted butter
- 1 onion, diced
- 180 ml Arborio rice
- 475 ml chicken stock, boiling
- 120 ml Parmesan cheese, grated
- Oat and Chia Porridge:
- 2 tablespoons peanut butter

- 4 tablespoons honey
- 1 tablespoon butter, melted
- 1 L milk
- 475 ml oats
- 235 ml chia seeds

**Directions:**

1. Make the Parmesan Ranch Risotto :
2. Preheat the air fryer to 200ºC.
3. Grease a round baking tin with olive oil and stir in the garlic, butter, and onion.
4. Transfer the tin to the zone 1 air fryer basket and bake for 4 minutes. Add the rice and bake for 4 more minutes.
5. Turn the air fryer to 160ºC and pour in the chicken stock. Cover and bake for 22 minutes.
6. Scatter with cheese and serve.
7. Make the Oat and Chia Porridge :
8. Preheat the air fryer to 200ºC.
9. Put the peanut butter, honey, butter, and milk in a bowl and stir to mix. Add the oats and chia seeds and stir.
10. Transfer the mixture to a bowl and bake in the zone 2 air fryer basket for 5 minutes. Give another stir before serving.

## Buffalo Chicken Breakfast Muffins

Servings: 10

Cooking Time: 13 To 16 Minutes

**Ingredients:**

- 170 g shredded cooked chicken
- 85 g blue cheese, crumbled
- 2 tablespoons unsalted butter, melted
- 80 ml Buffalo hot sauce, such as Frank's RedHot
- 1 teaspoon minced garlic
- 6 large eggs
- Sea salt and freshly ground black pepper, to taste
- Avocado oil spray

**Directions:**

1. In a large bowl, stir together the chicken, blue cheese, melted butter, hot sauce, and garlic.
2. In a medium bowl or large liquid measuring cup, beat the eggs. Season with salt and pepper.
3. Spray 10 silicone muffin cups with oil. Divide the chicken mixture among the cups, and pour the egg mixture over top.
4. Place the cups in the two air fryer baskets and set to 150ºC. Bake for 13 to 16 minutes, until the muffins are set and cooked through.

## Banana Bread

Servings: 8

Cooking Time: 35 Minutes

**Ingredients:**

- 95g flour
- 1 teaspoon ground cinnamon
- ¼ teaspoon ground nutmeg
- ½ teaspoon salt
- ¼ teaspoon baking soda
- 2 medium-sized ripe bananas mashed
- 2 large eggs lightly beaten
- 100g granulated sugar
- 2 tablespoons whole milk
- 1 tablespoon plain nonfat yoghurt
- 2 tablespoons vegetable oil
- 1 teaspoon vanilla
- 2 tablespoons walnuts roughly chopped

**Directions:**

1. Combine flour, cinnamon, nutmeg, baking soda, and salt in a large mixing basin.
2. Mash the banana in a separate dish before adding the eggs, sugar, milk, yoghurt, oil, and vanilla extract.
3. Combine the wet and dry ingredients in a mixing bowl and stir until just incorporated.
4. Pour the batter into the loaf pan and top with chopped walnuts.
5. Press either "Zone 1" and "Zone 2" and then rotate the knob select "Air Fryer".
6. Set the temperature to 155 degrees C, and then set the time for 3 minutes to preheat.
7. After preheating, arrange 1 loaf pan into the basket.
8. Slide basket into Air Fryer and set the time for 35 minutes.
9. After cooking time is completed, remove pan from Air Fryer.
10. Place the loaf pan onto a wire rack to cool for about 10 minutes.
11. Carefully invert the bread onto a wire rack to cool completely before slicing
12. Cut the bread into desired-sized slices and serve.

## Hard Boiled Eggs

Servings: 6

Cooking Time: 18 Minutes

**Ingredients:**

- 6 eggs
- Cold water

**Directions:**

1. Press your chosen zone - "Zone 1" or "Zone 2" and then rotate the knob to select "Air Fryer".
2. Set the temperature to 120 degrees C, and then set the time for 5 minutes to preheat.
3. After preheating, arrange eggs into the basket of each zone.
4. Slide the baskets into Air Fryer and set the time for 18 minutes.
5. After cooking time is completed, transfer the eggs into cold water and serve.

# Beef, Pork, And Lamb Recipes

## Paprika Pork Chops

Servings: 4
Cooking Time: 12 Minutes
**Ingredients:**

- 4 bone-in pork chops (6–8 ounces each)
- 1½ tablespoons brown sugar
- 1¼ teaspoons kosher salt
- 1 teaspoon dried Italian seasoning
- 1 teaspoon smoked paprika
- ¼ teaspoon garlic powder
- ¼ teaspoon onion powder
- ¼ teaspoon black pepper
- 1 teaspoon sweet paprika
- 3 tablespoons butter, melted
- 2 tablespoons chopped fresh parsley
- Cooking spray

**Directions:**

1. In a small mixing bowl, combine the brown sugar, salt, Italian seasoning, smoked paprika, garlic powder, onion powder, black pepper, and sweet paprika. Mix thoroughly.
2. Brush the pork chops on both sides with the melted butter.
3. Rub the spice mixture all over the meat on both sides.
4. Install a crisper plate in both drawers. Place half the chops in the zone 1 drawer and half in zone 2's, then insert the drawers into the unit.
5. Select zone 1, select AIR FRY, set temperature to 390 degrees F/ 200 degrees C, and set time to 12 minutes. Select MATCH to match zone 2 settings to zone 1. Press the START/STOP button to begin cooking.
6. When the time reaches 10 minutes, press START/STOP to pause the unit. Remove the drawers and flip the chops. Re-insert the drawers into the unit and press START/STOP to resume cooking.
7. Serve and enjoy!

**Nutrition:**

- (Per serving) Calories 338 | Fat 21.2g | Sodium 1503mg | Carbs 5.1g | Fiber 0.3g | Sugar 4.6g | Protein 29.3g

## Bacon Wrapped Pork Tenderloin

Servings: 2
Cooking Time: 20 Minutes
**Ingredients:**

- ½ teaspoon salt
- ¼ teaspoon black pepper
- 1 pork tenderloin
- 6 center cut strips bacon
- cooking string

**Directions:**

1. Cut two bacon strips in half and place them on the working surface.
2. Place the other bacon strips on top and lay the tenderloin over the bacon strip.
3. Wrap the bacon around the tenderloin and tie the roast with a kitchen string.
4. Place the roast in the first air fryer basket.
5. Return the air fryer basket 1 to Zone 1, and basket 2 to Zone 2 of the Ninja Foodi 2-Basket Air Fryer.
6. Choose the "Air Fry" mode for Zone 1 and set the temperature to 400 degrees F(205°C) and 20 minutes of cooking time.
7. Initiate cooking by pressing the START/PAUSE BUTTON.
8. Slice and serve warm.

**Nutrition:**

- (Per serving) Calories 459 | Fat 17.7g |Sodium 1516mg | Carbs 1.7g | Fiber 0.5g | Sugar 0.4g | Protein 69.2g

## Sumptuous Pizza Tortilla Rolls

Servings: 4
Cooking Time: 6 Minutes
**Ingredients:**

- 1 teaspoon butter
- ½ medium onion, slivered
- ½ red or green pepper, julienned
- 110 g fresh white mushrooms, chopped
- 120 ml pizza sauce
- 8 flour tortillas
- 8 thin slices wafer-thinham
- 24 pepperoni slices
- 235 ml shredded Mozzarella cheese
- Cooking spray

**Directions:**

1. Preheat the air fryer to 200ºC.
2. Put butter, onions, pepper, and mushrooms in a baking pan. Bake in the preheated air fryer for 3 minutes. Stir and cook 3 to 4 minutes longer until just crisp and tender. Remove pan and set aside.
3. To assemble rolls, spread about 2 teaspoons of pizza sauce on one half of each tortilla. Top with a slice of ham and 3 slices of pepperoni. Divide sautéed vegetables among tortillas and top with cheese.
4. Roll up tortillas, secure with toothpicks if needed, and spray with oil.
5. Put the rolls in the two air fryer drawers and air fry for 4 minutes. Turn and air fry 4 minutes, until heated through and lightly browned.
6. Serve immediately.

## Jerk-rubbed Pork Loin With Carrots And Sage

Servings: 4
Cooking Time: 35 Minutes
**Ingredients:**

- 1½ pounds pork loin
- 3 teaspoons canola oil, divided
- 2 tablespoons jerk seasoning
- 1-pound carrots, peeled, cut into 1-inch pieces
- 1 tablespoon honey
- ½ teaspoon kosher salt
- ½ teaspoon chopped fresh sage

**Directions:**

1. Place the pork loin in a pan or a dish with a high wall. Using a paper towel, pat the meat dry.

2. Rub 2 teaspoons of canola oil evenly over the pork with your hands. Then spread the jerk seasoning evenly over it with your hands.
3. Allow the pork loin to marinate for at least 10 minutes or up to 8 hours in the refrigerator after wrapping it in plastic wrap or sealing it in a plastic bag.
4. Toss the carrots with the remaining canola oil and ½ teaspoon of salt in a medium mixing bowl.
5. Place a crisper plate in each of the drawers. Put the marinated pork loin in the zone 1 drawer and place it in the unit. Place the carrots in the zone 2 drawer and place the drawer in the unit.
6. Select zone 1 and select AIR FRY. Set the temperature to 390 degrees F/ 200 degrees C and the time setting to 25 minutes. Select zone 2 and select AIR FRY. Set the temperature to 390 degrees F/ 200 degrees C and the time setting to 16 minutes. Select SYNC. Press START/STOP to begin cooking.
7. Check the pork loin for doneness after the zones have finished cooking. When the internal temperature of the loin hits 145°F(60°C) on an instant-read thermometer, the pork is ready.
8. Allow the pork loin to rest for at least 5 minutes on a plate or cutting board.
9. Combine the carrots and sage in a mixing bowl.
10. When the pork loin has rested, slice it into the desired thickness of slices and serve with the carrots.

**Nutrition:**

- (Per serving) Calories 500 | Fat 19.8g | Sodium 680mg | Carbs 50.1g | Fiber 4.1g | Sugar 0g | Protein 27.9g

## Barbecue Ribs With Roasted Green Beans And Shallots

Servings:4
Cooking Time: 40 Minutes

**Ingredients:**

- FOR THE RIBS
- 1 tablespoon light brown sugar
- 1 tablespoon smoked paprika
- 1 tablespoon chili powder
- 2 teaspoons kosher salt
- 1 teaspoon freshly ground black pepper
- 1 teaspoon garlic powder
- ¼ teaspoon cayenne pepper (optional)
- 2 pounds pork ribs
- 1 cup barbecue sauce (your favorite), for serving
- FOR THE GREEN BEANS AND SHALLOTS
- 1 pound green beans, trimmed
- 2 shallots, sliced
- 1 tablespoon olive oil
- ¼ teaspoon kosher salt

**Directions:**

1. To prep the ribs: In a small bowl, combine the brown sugar, paprika, chili powder, salt, black pepper, garlic powder, and cayenne (if using).
2. Rub the spice blend all over both sides of the ribs.
3. To prep the green beans and shallots: In a large bowl, combine the green beans, shallots, and oil. Toss to coat. Season with the salt.
4. To cook the ribs and vegetables: Install a crisper plate in each of the two baskets. Place the ribs in the Zone 1 basket and insert the basket in the unit. Place the green beans in the Zone 2 basket and insert the basket in the unit.
5. Select Zone 1, select AIR FRY, set the temperature to 375°F (190°C), and set the time to 40 minutes.
6. Select Zone 2, select ROAST, set the temperature to 400°F (205°C), and set the time to 20 minutes. Select SMART FINISH.
7. Press START/PAUSE to begin cooking.
8. When the Zone 1 timer reads 10 minutes, press START/PAUSE. Increase the temperature of Zone 1 to 400°F (205°C). Press START/PAUSE to resume cooking.
9. When cooking is complete, an instant-read thermometer inserted into the ribs should read 170°F (75°C) and the green beans should be tender-crisp. Serve topped with your favorite barbecue sauce.

**Nutrition:**

- (Per serving) Calories: 541; Total fat: 27g; Saturated fat: 9g; Carbohydrates: 48g; Fiber: 4.5g; Protein: 28g; Sodium: 1,291mg

## Pork Chops

Servings:2
Cooking Time:17

**Ingredients:**

- 1 tablespoon of rosemary, chopped
- Salt and black pepper, to taste
- 2 garlic cloves
- 1-inch ginger
- 2 tablespoons of olive oil
- 8 pork chops

**Directions:**

1. Take a blender and pulse together rosemary, salt, pepper, garlic cloves, ginger, and olive oil.
2. Rub this marinade over pork chops and let it rest for 1 hour.
3. Then divide it amongst air fryer baskets and set it to AIR FRY mode for 17 minutes at 375 degrees F(190°C) .
4. Once the cooking cycle is done, take out and serve hot.

**Nutrition:**

- (Per serving) Calories 1154| Fat 93.8g| Sodium 225mg | Carbs 2.1g | Fiber0.8 g| Sugar 0g | Protein 72.2g

## Pork Katsu With Seasoned Rice

Servings:4
Cooking Time: 15 Minutes

**Ingredients:**

- FOR THE PORK KATSU
- 4 thin-sliced boneless pork chops (4 ounces each)
- 2 tablespoons all-purpose flour
- 2 large eggs
- 1 cup panko bread crumbs
- ¼ teaspoon kosher salt
- ¼ teaspoon freshly ground black pepper
- 1 teaspoon vegetable oil
- 3 tablespoons ketchup
- 3 tablespoons Worcestershire sauce
- 1 tablespoon oyster sauce
- ⅛ teaspoon granulated sugar
- FOR THE RICE
- 2 cups dried instant rice (not microwavable)
- 2½ cups water
- 1 tablespoon sesame oil
- 1 teaspoon soy sauce
- 1 tablespoon toasted sesame seeds
- 3 scallions, sliced

**Directions:**

1. To prep the pork katsu: Place the pork chops between two slices of plastic wrap. Using a meat mallet or rolling pin, pound the pork into ½-inch-thick cutlets.
2. Set up a breading station with three small shallow bowls. Place the flour in the first bowl. In the second bowl, whisk the eggs. Combine the panko, salt, and black pepper in the third bowl.

3. Bread the cutlets in this order: First, dip them in the flour, coating both sides. Then, dip them into the beaten egg. Finally, coat them in panko, gently pressing the bread crumbs to adhere to the pork. Drizzle both sides of the cutlets with the oil.
4. To prep the rice: In the Zone 2 basket, combine the rice, water, sesame oil, and soy sauce. Stir well to ensure all of the rice is submerged in the liquid.
5. To cook the pork and rice: Install a crisper plate in the Zone 1 basket. Place the pork in the basket and insert the basket in the unit. Insert the Zone 2 basket in the unit.
6. Select Zone 1, select AIR FRY, set the temperature to 390°F (200°C), and set the time to 15 minutes.
7. Select Zone 2, select BAKE, set the temperature to 350°F (175°C), and set the time to 10 minutes. Select SMART FINISH.
8. Press START/PAUSE to begin cooking.
9. When the Zone 1 timer reads 10 minutes, press START/PAUSE. Remove the basket and use silicone-tipped tongs to flip the pork. Reinsert the basket and press START/PAUSE to resume cooking.
10. When cooking is complete, the pork should be crisp and cooked through and the rice tender.
11. Stir the sesame seeds and scallions into the rice. For the sauce to go with the pork, in a small bowl, whisk together the ketchup, Worcestershire sauce, oyster sauce, and sugar. Drizzle the sauce over the pork and serve with the hot rice.

**Nutrition:**

- (Per serving) Calories: 563; Total fat: 20g; Saturated fat: 5.5g; Carbohydrates: 62g; Fiber: 1g; Protein: 34g; Sodium: 665mg

## Spice-rubbed Pork Loin

Servings: 6
Cooking Time: 20 Minutes

**Ingredients:**

- 1 teaspoon paprika
- ½ teaspoon ground cumin
- ½ teaspoon chili powder
- ½ teaspoon garlic powder
- 2 tablespoons coconut oil
- 1 (680 g) boneless pork loin
- ½ teaspoon salt
- ¼ teaspoon ground black pepper

**Directions:**

1. In a small bowl, mix paprika, cumin, chili powder, and garlic powder.
2. Drizzle coconut oil over pork. Sprinkle pork loin with salt and pepper, then rub spice mixture evenly on all sides.
3. Place pork loin into the two ungreased air fryer drawer. Adjust the temperature to 204°C and air fry for 20 minutes, turning pork halfway through cooking. Pork loin will be browned and have an internal temperature of at least 64°C when done. Serve warm.

## Beef And Bean Taquitos With Mexican Rice

Servings:4
Cooking Time: 15 Minutes

**Ingredients:**

- FOR THE TAQUITOS
- ½ pound ground beef (85 percent lean)
- 1 tablespoon taco seasoning
- 8 (6-inch) soft white corn tortillas
- Nonstick cooking spray
- ¾ cup canned refried beans
- ½ cup shredded Mexican blend cheese (optional)
- FOR THE MEXICAN RICE
- 1 cup dried instant white rice (not microwavable)
- 1½ cups chicken broth
- ¼ cup jarred salsa
- 2 tablespoons canned tomato sauce
- 1 tablespoon vegetable oil
- ½ teaspoon kosher salt

**Directions:**

1. To prep the taquitos: In a large bowl, mix the ground beef and taco seasoning until well combined.
2. Mist both sides of each tortilla lightly with cooking spray.
3. To prep the Mexican rice: In the Zone 2 basket, combine the rice, broth, salsa, tomato sauce, oil, and salt. Stir well to ensure all of the rice is submerged in the liquid.
4. To cook the taquitos and rice: Install a crisper plate in the Zone 1 basket. Place the seasoned beef in the basket and insert the basket in the unit. Insert the Zone 2 basket in the unit.
5. Select Zone 1, select AIR FRY, set the temperature to 390°F (200°C), and set the time to 15 minutes.
6. Select Zone 2, select BAKE, set the temperature to 350°F (175°C), and set the time to 10 minutes. Select SMART FINISH.
7. Press START/PAUSE to begin cooking.
8. When the Zone 1 timer reads 10 minutes, press START/PAUSE. Remove the basket and transfer the beef to a medium bowl. Add the refried beans and cheese (if using) and combine well. Spoon 2 tablespoons of the filling onto each tortilla and roll tightly. Place the taquitos in the Zone 1 basket seam-side down. Reinsert the basket in the unit and press START/PAUSE to resume cooking.
9. When cooking is complete, the taquitos should be crisp and golden brown and the rice cooked through. Serve hot.

**Nutrition:**

- (Per serving) Calories: 431; Total fat: 18g; Saturated fat: 4g; Carbohydrates: 52g; Fiber: 5.5g; Protein: 18g; Sodium: 923mg

## Bacon-wrapped Cheese Pork

Servings: 4
Cooking Time: 20 Minutes

**Ingredients:**

- 4 (1-inch-thick) boneless pork chops
- 2 (150 g) packages Boursin cheese
- 8 slices thin-cut bacon

**Directions:**

1. Spray the air fryer drawer with avocado oil. Preheat the air fryer to 204°C.
2. Place one of the chops on a cutting board. With a sharp knife held parallel to the cutting board, make a 1-inch-wide incision on the top edge of the chop. Carefully cut into the chop to form a large pocket, leaving a ½-inch border along the sides and bottom. Repeat with the other 3 chops.
3. Snip the corner of a large resealable plastic bag to form a ¾-inch hole. Place the Boursin cheese in the bag and pipe the cheese into the pockets in the chops, dividing the cheese evenly among them.
4. Wrap 2 slices of bacon around each chop and secure the ends with toothpicks. Place the bacon-wrapped chops in the two air fryer drawers and cook for 10 minutes, then flip the chops and cook for another 8 to 10 minutes, until the bacon is crisp, the chops are cooked through, and the internal temperature reaches 64°C.
5. Store leftovers in an airtight container in the refrigerator for up to 3 days. Reheat in a preheated 204°C air fryer for 5 minutes, or until warmed through.

## Cheeseburgers With Barbecue Potato Chips

Servings:4
Cooking Time: 15 Minutes
**Ingredients:**

- FOR THE CHEESEBURGERS
- 1 pound ground beef (85 percent lean)
- ¼ teaspoon kosher salt
- ¼ teaspoon freshly ground black pepper
- ½ teaspoon olive oil
- 4 slices American cheese
- 4 hamburger rolls
- FOR THE POTATO CHIPS
- 2 large russet potatoes
- 2 teaspoons vegetable oil
- 1½ teaspoons smoked paprika
- 1 teaspoon light brown sugar
- ½ teaspoon garlic powder
- ½ teaspoon kosher salt
- ¼ teaspoon chili powder

**Directions:**

1. To prep the cheeseburgers: Season the beef with the salt and black pepper. Form the beef into 4 patties about 1 inch thick. Brush both sides of the beef patties with the oil.
2. To prep the potato chips: Fill a large bowl with ice water. Using a mandoline or sharp knife, cut the potatoes into very thin (⅛- to 1/16-inch) slices. Soak the potatoes in the ice water for 30 minutes.
3. Drain the potatoes and pat dry with a paper towel. Place in a large bowl and toss with the oil, smoked paprika, brown sugar, garlic powder, salt, and chili powder.
4. To cook the cheeseburgers and potato chips: Install a crisper plate in each of the two baskets. Place the burgers in the Zone 1 basket and insert the basket in the unit. Place the potato slices in the Zone 2 basket and insert the basket in the unit.
5. Select Zone 1, select AIR FRY, set the temperature to 390°F (200°C), and set the time to 12 minutes.
6. Select Zone 2, select AIR FRY, set the temperature to 390°F (200°C), and set the time to 15 minutes. Select SMART FINISH.
7. Press START/PAUSE to begin cooking.
8. At 5-minute intervals, press START/PAUSE. Remove the Zone 2 basket and shake the potato chips to keep them from sticking to each other. Reinsert the basket and press START/PAUSE to resume cooking.
9. When cooking is complete, the burgers should be cooked to your preferred doneness and the potato chips should be crisp and golden brown.
10. Top each burger patty in the basket with a slice of cheese. Turn the air fryer off and let the cheese melt inside the unit, or cover the basket with aluminum foil and let stand for 1 to 2 minutes, until the cheese is melted. Serve the cheeseburgers on buns with the chips on the side.

**Nutrition:**

- (Per serving) Calories: 475; Total fat: 22g; Saturated fat: 8g; Carbohydrates: 38g; Fiber: 2g; Protein: 32g; Sodium: 733mg

## Chorizo And Beef Burger

Servings: 4
Cooking Time: 15 Minutes
**Ingredients:**

- 340 g 80/20 beef mince
- 110 g Mexican-style chorizo crumb
- 60 ml chopped onion
- 5 slices pickled jalapeños, chopped
- 2 teaspoons chili powder
- 1 teaspoon minced garlic
- ¼ teaspoon cumin

**Directions:**

1. In a large bowl, mix all ingredients. Divide the mixture into four sections and form them into burger patties.
2. Place burger patties into the two air fryer drawers.
3. Adjust the temperature to 192ºC and air fry for 15 minutes.
4. Flip the patties halfway through the cooking time. Serve warm.

## Honey-baked Pork Loin

Servings: 6
Cooking Time: 22 To 25 Minutes
**Ingredients:**

- 60 ml honey
- 60 ml freshly squeezed lemon juice
- 2 tablespoons soy sauce
- 1 teaspoon garlic powder
- 1 (900 g) pork loin
- 2 tablespoons vegetable oil

**Directions:**

1. In a medium bowl, whisk together the honey, lemon juice, soy sauce, and garlic powder. Reserve half of the mixture for basting during cooking.
2. Cut 5 slits in the pork loin and transfer it to a resealable bag. Add the remaining honey mixture. Seal the bag and refrigerate to marinate for at least 2 hours.
3. Preheat the air fryer to 204ºC. Line the two air fryer drawers with parchment paper.
4. Remove the pork from the marinade, and place it on the parchment. Spritz with oil, then baste with the reserved marinade.
5. Cook for 15 minutes. Flip the pork, baste with more marinade and spritz with oil again. Cook for 7 to 10 minutes more until the internal temperature reaches 64ºC. Let rest for 5 minutes before serving.

## Spicy Lamb Chops

Servings:4
Cooking Time:15
**Ingredients:**

- 12 lamb chops, bone-in
- Salt and black pepper, to taste
- ½ teaspoon of lemon zest
- 1 tablespoon of lemon juice
- 1 teaspoon of paprika
- 1 teaspoon of garlic powder
- ½ teaspoon of Italian seasoning
- ¼ teaspoon of onion powder

**Directions:**

1. Add the lamb chops to the bowl and sprinkle salt, garlic powder, Italian seasoning, onion powder, black pepper, lemon zest, lemon juice, and paprika.
2. Rub the chops well, and divide it between both the baskets of the air fryer.
3. Set zone 1 basket to 400 degrees F(205°C) , for 15 minutes at AIR FRY mode.
4. Select MATCH for zone2 basket.
5. After 10 minutes, take out the baskets and flip the chops cook for the remaining minutes, and then serve.

**Nutrition:**

- (Per serving) Calories 787| Fat 45.3g| Sodium1 mg | Carbs 16.1g | Fiber0.3g | Sugar 0.4g | Protein 75.3g

## Gochujang Brisket

Servings: 6
Cooking Time: 55 Minutes.
**Ingredients:**

- ½ tablespoons sweet paprika
- ½ teaspoon toasted sesame oil
- 2 lbs. beef brisket, cut into 4 pieces
- Salt, to taste
- ⅛ cup Gochujang, Korean chili paste
- Black pepper, to taste
- 1 small onion, diced
- 2 garlic cloves, minced
- 1 teaspoon Asian fish sauce
- 1 ½ tablespoons peanut oil, as needed
- ½ tablespoon fresh ginger, grated
- ¼ teaspoon red chili flakes
- ½ cup of water
- 1 tablespoon ketchup
- 1 tablespoon soy sauce

**Directions:**

1. Thoroughly rub the beef brisket with olive oil, paprika, chili flakes, black pepper, and salt.
2. Cut the brisket in half, then divide the beef in the two crisper plate.
3. Return the crisper plate to the Ninja Foodi Dual Zone Air Fryer.
4. Choose the Air Fry mode for Zone 1 and set the temperature to 390 degrees F(200°C) and the time to 35 minutes.
5. Select the "MATCH" button to copy the settings for Zone 2.
6. Initiate cooking by pressing the START/STOP button.
7. Flip the brisket halfway through, and resume cooking.
8. Meanwhile, heat oil in a skillet and add ginger, onion, and garlic.
9. Sauté for 5 minutes, then add all the remaining ingredients.
10. Cook the mixture for 15 minutes approximately until well thoroughly mixed.
11. Serve the brisket with this sauce on top.

**Nutrition:**

- (Per serving) Calories 374 | Fat 25g |Sodium 275mg | Carbs 7.3g | Fiber 0g | Sugar 6g | Protein 12.3g

## Kheema Burgers

Servings: 4
Cooking Time: 12 Minutes
**Ingredients:**

- Burgers:
- 450 g 85% lean beef mince or lamb mince
- 2 large eggs, lightly beaten
- 1 medium brown onion, diced
- 60 ml chopped fresh coriander
- 1 tablespoon minced fresh ginger
- 3 cloves garlic, minced
- 2 teaspoons garam masala
- 1 teaspoon ground turmeric
- ½ teaspoon ground cinnamon
- ⅛ teaspoon ground cardamom
- 1 teaspoon coarse or flaky salt
- 1 teaspoon cayenne pepper
- Raita Sauce:
- 235 ml grated cucumber
- 120 ml sour cream
- ¼ teaspoon coarse or flaky salt
- ¼ teaspoon black pepper
- For Serving:
- 4 lettuce leaves, hamburger buns, or naan breads

**Directions:**

1. For the burgers: In a large bowl, combine the beef mince, eggs, onion, coriander, ginger, garlic, garam masala, turmeric, cinnamon, cardamom, salt, and cayenne. Gently mix until ingredients are thoroughly combined. 2. Divide the meat into four portions and form into round patties. Make a slight depression in the middle of each patty with your thumb to prevent them from puffing up into a dome shape while cooking. 3. Place the patties in the zone 1 air fryer drawer. Set the temperature to 176ºC for 12 minutes. Use a meat thermometer to ensure the burgers have reached an internal temperature of 72ºC . 4. Meanwhile, for the sauce: In a small bowl, combine the cucumber, sour cream, salt, and pepper. 5. To serve: Place the burgers on the lettuce, buns, or naan and top with the sauce.

## Juicy Pork Chops

Servings: 4
Cooking Time: 15 Minutes
**Ingredients:**

- 450g pork chops
- ¼ tsp garlic powder
- 15ml olive oil
- ¼ tsp smoked paprika
- Pepper
- Salt

**Directions:**

1. In a small bowl, mix the garlic powder, paprika, pepper, and salt.
2. Brush the pork chops with oil and rub with spice mixture.
3. Insert a crisper plate in the Ninja Foodi air fryer baskets.
4. Place the pork chops in both baskets.
5. Select zone 1, then select "bake" mode and set the temperature to 410 degrees F(210°C) for 15 minutes. Press "match" to match zone 2 settings to zone 1. Press "start/stop" to begin. Turn halfway through.

**Nutrition:**

- (Per serving) Calories 394 | Fat 31.7g |Sodium 118mg | Carbs 0.2g | Fiber 0.1g | Sugar 0.1g | Protein 25.5g

## Bacon-wrapped Filet Mignon

Servings: 4
Cooking Time: 15 Minutes
**Ingredients:**

- 4 bacon slices
- 4 (4-ounce) filet mignon
- Salt and ground black pepper, as required
- Olive oil cooking spray

**Directions:**

1. Wrap 1 bacon slice around each filet mignon and secure with toothpicks.
2. Spray the filet mignon with cooking spray evenly. Season the filets with salt and black pepper lightly.
3. Grease each basket of "Zone 1" and "Zone 2" of Ninja Foodi 2-Basket Air Fryer.
4. Press "Zone 1" and "Zone 2" and then rotate the knob for each zone to select "Air Fry".
5. Set the temperature to 400 degrees F/ 205 degrees C for both zones and then set the time for 5 minutes to preheat.
6. After preheating, arrange 2 filets into the basket of each zone.
7. Slide each basket into Air Fryer and set the time for 15 minutes.
8. While cooking, flip the filets once halfway through.
9. After cooking time is completed, remove the filets from Air Fryer and serve hot.

## Pork With Green Beans And Potatoes

Servings: 4
Cooking Time: 15 Minutes.
**Ingredients:**

- ¼ cup Dijon mustard
- 2 tablespoons brown sugar
- 1 teaspoon dried parsley flake
- ½ teaspoon dried thyme
- ¼ teaspoons salt
- ¼ teaspoons black pepper
- 1 ¼ lbs. pork tenderloin
- ¾ lb. small potatoes halved
- 1 (12-oz) package green beans, trimmed
- 1 tablespoon olive oil
- Salt and black pepper ground to taste

**Directions:**

1. Preheat your Air Fryer Machine to 400 degrees F(205°C) .
2. Add mustard, parsley, brown sugar, salt, black pepper, and thyme in a large bowl, then mix well.
3. Add tenderloin to the spice mixture and coat well.
4. Toss potatoes with olive oil, salt, black pepper, and green beans in another bowl.
5. Place the prepared tenderloin in the crisper plate.
6. Return this crisper plate to the Zone 1 of the Ninja Foodi Dual Zone Air Fryer.
7. Choose the Air Fry mode for Zone 1 and set the temperature to 390 degrees F(200°C) and the time to 15 minutes.
8. Add potatoes and green beans to the Zone 2.
9. Choose the Air Fry mode for Zone 2 with 350 degrees F(175°C) and the time to 10 minutes.
10. Press the SYNC button to sync the finish time for both Zones.
11. Initiate cooking by pressing the START/STOP button.
12. Serve the tenderloin with Air Fried potatoes

**Nutrition:**

- (Per serving) Calories 400 | Fat 32g |Sodium 721mg | Carbs 2.6g | Fiber 0g | Sugar 0g | Protein 27.4g

## Beef Cheeseburgers

Servings: 4
Cooking Time: 13 Minutes.
**Ingredients:**

- 1 lb. ground beef
- Salt, to taste
- 2 garlic cloves, minced
- 1 tablespoon soy sauce
- Black pepper, to taste
- 4 American cheese slices
- 4 hamburger buns
- Mayonnaise, to serve
- Lettuce, to serve
- Sliced tomatoes, to serve
- Sliced red onion, to serve

**Directions:**

1. Mix beef with soy sauce and garlic in a large bowl.
2. Make 4 patties of 4 inches in diameter.
3. Rub them with salt and black pepper on both sides.
4. Place the 2 patties in each of the crisper plate.
5. Return the crisper plate to the Ninja Foodi Dual Zone Air Fryer.
6. Choose the Air Fry mode for Zone 1 and set the temperature to 390 degrees F(200°C) and the time to 13 minutes.
7. Select the "MATCH" button to copy the settings for Zone 2.
8. Initiate cooking by pressing the START/STOP button.
9. Flip each patty once cooked halfway through, and resume cooking.
10. Add each patty to the hamburger buns along with mayo, tomatoes, onions, and lettuce.
11. Serve.

**Nutrition:**

- (Per serving) Calories 437 | Fat 28g |Sodium 1221mg | Carbs 22.3g | Fiber 0.9g | Sugar 8g | Protein 30.3g

## Stuffed Beef Fillet With Feta Cheese

Servings: 4
Cooking Time: 10 Minutes
**Ingredients:**

- 680 g beef fillet, pounded to ¼ inch thick
- 3 teaspoons sea salt
- 1 teaspoon ground black pepper
- 60 g creamy goat cheese
- 120 ml crumbled feta cheese
- 60 ml finely chopped onions
- 2 cloves garlic, minced
- Cooking spray

**Directions:**

1. Preheat the air fryer to 204ºC. Spritz the two air fryer drawers with cooking spray. 2. Unfold the beef on a clean work surface. Rub the salt and pepper all over the beef to season. 3. Make the filling for the stuffed beef fillet: Combine the goat cheese, feta, onions, and garlic in a medium bowl. Stir until well blended. 4. Spoon the mixture in the center of the fillet. Roll the fillet up tightly like rolling a burrito and use some kitchen twine to tie the fillet. 5. Arrange the fillet in the two air fryer drawers and air fry for 10 minutes, flipping the fillet halfway through to ensure even cooking, or until an instant-read thermometer inserted in the center of the fillet registers 57ºC for medium-rare. 6. Transfer to a platter and serve immediately.

## Curry-crusted Lamb Chops With Baked Brown Sugar Acorn Squash

Servings:4
Cooking Time: 20 Minutes
**Ingredients:**

- FOR THE LAMB CHOPS
- 4 lamb loin chops (4 ounces each)
- 1 tablespoon olive oil
- 2 teaspoons curry powder
- ¼ teaspoon kosher salt
- FOR THE ACORN SQUASH
- 2 small acorn squash
- 4 teaspoons dark brown sugar
- 2 teaspoons salted butter
- ⅛ teaspoon kosher salt

**Directions:**

1. To prep the lamb chops: Brush both sides of the lamb chops with the oil and season with the curry powder and salt.
2. To prep the acorn squash: Cut the squash in half through the stem end and remove the seeds. Place 1 teaspoon of brown sugar and ½ teaspoon of butter into the well of each squash half.
3. To cook the lamb and squash: Install a crisper plate in each of the two baskets. Place the lamb chops in the Zone 1 basket and insert the basket in the unit. Place the squash cut-side up in the Zone 2 basket and insert the basket in the unit.

4. Select Zone 1, select AIR FRY, set the temperature to 400°F (205°C), and set the timer to 15 minutes.
5. Select Zone 2, select BAKE, set the temperature to 400°F (205°C), and set the time to 20 minutes. Select SMART FINISH.
6. Press START/PAUSE to begin cooking.
7. When both timers read 5 minutes, press START/PAUSE. Remove the Zone 1 basket and use a pair of silicone-tipped tongs to flip the lamb chops. Reinsert the basket in the unit. Remove the Zone 2 basket and spoon the melted butter and sugar over the top edges of the squash. Reinsert the basket and press START/PAUSE to resume cooking.
8. When cooking is complete, the lamb should be cooked to your liking and the squash soft when pierced with a fork.
9. Remove the lamb chops from the basket and let rest for 5 minutes. Season the acorn squash with salt before serving.

**Nutrition:**

- (Per serving) Calories: 328; Total fat: 19g; Saturated fat: 7.5g; Carbohydrates: 23g; Fiber: 3g; Protein: 16g; Sodium: 172mg

## Bacon-wrapped Hot Dogs With Mayo-ketchup Sauce

Servings: 5
Cooking Time: 10 To 12 Minutes

**Ingredients:**

- 10 thin slices of bacon
- 5 pork hot dogs, halved
- 1 teaspoon cayenne pepper
- Sauce:
- 60 ml mayonnaise
- 4 tablespoons ketchup
- 1 teaspoon rice vinegar
- 1 teaspoon chili powder

**Directions:**

1. Preheat the air fryer to 200ºC. 2. Arrange the slices of bacon on a clean work surface. One by one, place the halved hot dog on one end of each slice, season with cayenne pepper and wrap the hot dog with the bacon slices and secure with toothpicks as needed. 3. Place half the wrapped hot dogs in the two air fryer drawers and air fry for 10 to 12 minutes or until the bacon becomes browned and crispy. 4. Make the sauce: Stir all the ingredients for the sauce in a small bowl. Wrap the bowl in plastic and set in the refrigerator until ready to serve. 5. Transfer the hot dogs to a platter and serve hot with the sauce.

## Meat And Rice Stuffed Peppers

Servings: 4
Cooking Time: 18 Minutes

**Ingredients:**

- 340 g lean beef mince
- 110 g lean pork mince
- 60 ml onion, minced
- 1 (425 g) can finely-chopped tomatoes
- 1 teaspoon Worcestershire sauce
- 1 teaspoon barbecue seasoning
- 1 teaspoon honey
- ½ teaspoon dried basil
- 120 ml cooked brown rice
- ½ teaspoon garlic powder
- ½ teaspoon oregano
- ½ teaspoon salt
- 2 small peppers, cut in half, stems removed, deseeded
- Cooking spray

**Directions:**

1. Preheat the zone 1 air fryer drawer to 182ºC and spritz a baking pan with cooking spray.
2. Arrange the beef, pork, and onion in the baking pan and bake in the preheated air fryer drawer for 8 minutes. Break the ground meat into chunks halfway through the cooking.
3. Meanwhile, combine the tomatoes, Worcestershire sauce, barbecue seasoning, honey, and basil in a saucepan. Stir to mix well.
4. Transfer the cooked meat mixture to a large bowl and add the cooked rice, garlic powder, oregano, salt, and 60 ml of the tomato mixture. Stir to mix well.
5. Stuff the pepper halves with the mixture, then arrange the pepper halves in the zone 1 air fryer drawer and air fry for 10 minutes or until the peppers are lightly charred.
6. Serve the stuffed peppers with the remaining tomato sauce on top.

## Italian Sausage And Cheese Meatballs

Servings: 4
Cooking Time: 20 Minutes

**Ingredients:**

- 230 g sausage meat with Italian seasoning added to taste
- 230 g 85% lean beef mince
- 120 ml shredded sharp Cheddar cheese
- ½ teaspoon onion granules
- ½ teaspoon garlic powder
- ½ teaspoon black pepper

**Directions:**

1. In a large bowl, gently mix the sausage meat, beef mince, cheese, onion granules, garlic powder, and pepper until well combined.
2. Form the mixture into 16 meatballs. Place the meatballs in a single layer in the two air fryer drawers. Set the air fryer to 176ºC for 20 minutes, turning the meatballs halfway through the cooking time. Use a meat thermometer to ensure the meatballs have reached an internal temperature of 72ºC .

## Blue Cheese Steak Salad

Servings: 4
Cooking Time: 22 Minutes

**Ingredients:**

- 2 tablespoons balsamic vinegar
- 2 tablespoons red wine vinegar
- 1 tablespoon Dijon mustard
- 1 tablespoon granulated sweetener
- 1 teaspoon minced garlic
- Sea salt and freshly ground black pepper, to taste
- 180 ml extra-virgin olive oil
- 450 g boneless rump steak
- Avocado oil spray
- 1 small red onion, cut into ¼-inch-thick rounds
- 170 g baby spinach
- 120 ml cherry tomatoes, halved
- 85 g blue cheese, crumbled

**Directions:**

1. In a blender, combine the balsamic vinegar, red wine vinegar, Dijon mustard, sweetener, and garlic. Season with salt and pepper and process until smooth. With the blender running, drizzle in the olive oil. Process until well combined. Transfer to a jar with a tight-fitting lid, and refrigerate until ready to serve .
2. Season the steak with salt and pepper and let sit at room temperature for at least 45 minutes, time permitting.
3. Set the zone 1 air fryer drawer to 204ºC. Spray the steak with oil and place it in the zone 1 air fryer drawer. Spray the onion slices with oil and place them in the zone 2 air fryer drawer.

4. In zone 1, air fry for 6 minutes. Flip the steak and spray it with more oil. Air fry for 6 minutes more for medium-rare or until the steak is done to your liking.
5. In zone 2, cook at 204ºC for 5 minutes. Flip the onion slices and spray them with more oil. Air fry for 5 minutes more.
6. Transfer the steak to a plate, tent with a piece of aluminum foil, and allow it to rest. Slice the steak diagonally into thin strips. Place the spinach, cherry tomatoes, onion slices, and steak in a large bowl. Toss with the desired amount of dressing. Sprinkle with crumbled blue cheese and serve.

## Panko Crusted Calf' s Liver Strips

Servings: 4
Cooking Time: 23 To 25 Minutes
**Ingredients:**

- 450 g sliced calf's liver, cut into ½-inch wide strips
- 2 eggs
- 2 tablespoons milk
- 120 ml whole wheat flour
- 475 ml panko breadcrumbs
- Salt and ground black pepper, to taste
- Cooking spray

**Directions:**

1. Preheat the air fryer to 200ºC and spritz with cooking spray.
2. Rub the calf's liver strips with salt and ground black pepper on a clean work surface.
3. Whisk the eggs with milk in a large bowl. Pour the flour in a shallow dish. Pour the panko on a separate shallow dish.
4. Dunk the liver strips in the flour, then in the egg mixture. Shake the excess off and roll the strips over the panko to coat well.
5. Arrange the liver strips in a single layer in the two preheated air fryer drawers and spritz with cooking spray.
6. Air fry for 5 minutes or until browned. Flip the strips halfway through.
7. Serve immediately.

## Steak Fajitas With Onions And Peppers

Servings: 6
Cooking Time: 15 Minutes
**Ingredients:**

- 1 pound steak
- 1 green bell pepper, sliced
- 1 yellow bell pepper, sliced
- 1 red bell pepper, sliced
- ½ cup sliced white onions
- 1 packet gluten-free fajita seasoning
- Olive oil spray

**Directions:**

1. Thinly slice the steak against the grain. These should be about ¼-inch slices.
2. Mix the steak with the peppers and onions.
3. Evenly coat with the fajita seasoning.
4. Install a crisper plate in both drawers. Place half the steak mixture in the zone 1 drawer and half in zone 2's, then insert the drawers into the unit.
5. Select zone 1, select AIR FRY, set temperature to 390 degrees F/ 200 degrees C, and set time to 15 minutes. Select MATCH to match zone 2 settings to zone 1. Press the START/STOP button to begin cooking.
6. When the time reaches 10 minutes, press START/STOP to pause the unit. Remove the drawers and flip the steak strips. Re-insert the drawers into the unit and press START/STOP to resume cooking.
7. Serve in warm tortillas.

**Nutrition:**

- (Per serving) Calories 305 | Fat 17g | Sodium 418mg | Carbs 15g | Fiber 2g | Sugar 4g | Protein 22g

## Roast Souvlaki-style Pork With Lemon-feta Baby Potatoes

Servings:4
Cooking Time: 40 Minutes
**Ingredients:**

- FOR THE PORK
- 1½ pounds pork tenderloin, cut into bite-size cubes
- ¼ cup olive oil
- ¼ cup fresh lemon juice
- 2 teaspoons minced garlic
- 2 teaspoons honey
- 1½ teaspoons dried oregano
- ¼ teaspoon kosher salt
- ¼ teaspoon freshly ground black pepper
- FOR THE POTATOES
- 1 pound baby red or yellow potatoes, halved
- 1 tablespoon olive oil
- Grated zest and juice of 1 lemon
- ½ teaspoon kosher salt
- ¼ teaspoon freshly ground black pepper
- ⅓ cup crumbled feta cheese
- 2 tablespoons chopped fresh parsley

**Directions:**

1. To prep the pork: In a large bowl, combine the pork, oil, lemon juice, garlic, honey, oregano, salt, and black pepper. If desired, cover and refrigerate up to 24 hours.
2. To prep the potatoes: In a large bowl, combine the potatoes, oil, lemon zest, lemon juice, salt, and black pepper. Mix to coat the potatoes.
3. To cook the pork and potatoes: Install a crisper plate in each of the two baskets. Place the pork in the Zone 1 basket and insert the basket in the unit. Place the potatoes in the Zone 2 basket and insert the basket in the unit.
4. Select Zone 1, select ROAST, set the temperature to 390°F (200°C), and set the time to 20 minutes.
5. Select Zone 2, select AIR FRY, set the temperature to 400°F (205°C), and set the time to 40 minutes. Select SMART FINISH.
6. Press START/PAUSE to begin cooking.
7. When cooking is complete, the pork will be cooked through (an instant-read thermometer should read 145°F (60°C)) and the potatoes will be tender and beginning to brown around the edges.
8. Stir the feta and parsley into the potatoes. Serve the pork and potatoes while hot.

**Nutrition:**

- (Per serving) Calories: 395; Total fat: 17g; Saturated fat: 4.5g; Carbohydrates: 24g; Fiber: 2g; Protein: 37g; Sodium: 399mg

## Seasoned Flank Steak

Servings: 12
Cooking Time: 30 Minutes
**Ingredients:**

- 2 (2-pound) flank steaks
- 3 tablespoons taco seasoning rub

**Directions:**

1. Grease each basket of "Zone 1" and "Zone 2" of Ninja Foodi 2-Basket Air Fryer.
2. Press "Zone 1" and "Zone 2" and then rotate the knob for each zone to select "Bake".
3. Set the temperature to 420 degrees F/ 215 degrees C for both zones and then set the time for 5 minutes to preheat.
4. Rub the steaks with taco seasoning evenly.
5. After preheating, arrange 1 steak into the basket of each zone.

6. Slide each basket into Air Fryer and set the time for 30 minutes.
7. After cooking time is completed, remove the steaks from Air Fryer and place onto a cutting board for about 10-15 minutes before slicing.
8. With a sharp knife, cut each steak into desired size slices and serve.

## Bacon And Cheese Stuffed Pork Chops

Servings: 4
Cooking Time: 12 Minutes
**Ingredients:**

- 15 g plain pork scratchings, finely crushed
- 120 ml shredded sharp Cheddar cheese
- 4 slices cooked bacon, crumbled
- 4 (110 g) boneless pork chops
- ½ teaspoon salt
- ¼ teaspoon ground black pepper

**Directions:**

1. In a small bowl, mix pork scratchings, Cheddar, and bacon.
2. Make a 3-inch slit in the side of each pork chop and stuff with ¼ pork rind mixture. Sprinkle each side of pork chops with salt and pepper.
3. Place pork chops into the two ungreased air fryer drawers, stuffed side up. Adjust the temperature to 204ºC and air fry for 12 minutes. Pork chops will be browned and have an internal temperature of at least 64ºC when done. Serve warm.

## Turkey And Beef Meatballs

Servings: 6
Cooking Time: 24 Minutes.
**Ingredients:**

- 1 medium shallot, minced
- 2 tablespoons olive oil
- 3 garlic cloves, minced
- ¼ cup panko crumbs
- 2 tablespoons whole milk
- ⅔ lb. lean ground beef
- ⅓ lb. bulk turkey sausage
- 1 large egg, lightly beaten
- ¼ cup parsley, chopped
- 1 tablespoon fresh thyme, chopped
- 1 tablespoon fresh rosemary, chopped
- 1 tablespoon Dijon mustard
- ½ teaspoon salt

**Directions:**

1. Preheat your oven to 400 degrees F(205°C) . Place a medium non-stick pan over medium-high heat.
2. Add oil and shallot, then sauté for 2 minutes.
3. Toss in the garlic and cook for 1 minute.
4. Remove this pan from the heat.
5. Whisk panko with milk in a large bowl and leave it for 5 minutes.
6. Add cooked shallot mixture and mix well.
7. Stir in egg, parsley, turkey sausage, beef, thyme, rosemary, salt, and mustard.
8. Mix well, then divide the mixture into 1 ½-inch balls.
9. Divide these balls into the two crisper plates and spray them with cooking oil.
10. Return the crisper plates to the Ninja Foodi Dual Zone Air Fryer.
11. Choose the Air Fry mode for Zone 1 and set the temperature to 400 degrees F(205°C) and the time to 21 minutes.
12. Select the "MATCH" button to copy the settings for Zone 2.
13. Initiate cooking by pressing the START/STOP button.
14. Serve warm.

**Nutrition:**

- (Per serving) Calories 551 | Fat 31g |Sodium 1329mg | Carbs 1.5g | Fiber 0.8g | Sugar 0.4g | Protein 64g

## Air Fryer Meatloaves

Servings: 4
Cooking Time: 22 Minutes.
**Ingredients:**

- ⅓ cup milk
- 2 tablespoons basil pesto
- 1 egg, beaten
- 1 garlic clove, minced
- ¼ teaspoons black pepper
- 1 lb. ground beef
- ⅓ cup panko bread crumbs
- 8 pepperoni slices
- ½ cup marinara sauce, warmed
- 1 tablespoon fresh basil, chopped

**Directions:**

1. Mix pesto, milk, egg, garlic, and black pepper in a medium-sized bowl.
2. Stir in ground beef and bread crumbs, then mix.
3. Make the 4 small-sized loaves with this mixture and top them with 2 pepperoni slices.
4. Press the slices into the meatloaves.
5. Place the meatloaves in the two crisper plates.
6. Return the crisper plate to the Ninja Foodi Dual Zone Air Fryer.
7. Choose the Air Fry mode for Zone 1 and set the temperature to 390 degrees F(200°C) and the time to 22 minutes.
8. Select the "MATCH" button to copy the settings for Zone 2.
9. Initiate cooking by pressing the START/STOP button.
10. Top them with marinara sauce and basil to serve.
11. Serve warm.

**Nutrition:**

- (Per serving) Calories 316 | Fat 12.2g |Sodium 587mg | Carbs 12.2g | Fiber 1g | Sugar 1.8g | Protein 25.8g

## Marinated Pork Chops

Servings: 2
Cooking Time: 12 Minutes
**Ingredients:**

- 2 pork chops, boneless
- 18g sugar
- 1 tbsp water
- 15ml rice wine
- 15ml dark soy sauce
- 15ml light soy sauce
- ½ tsp cinnamon
- ½ tsp five-spice powder
- 1 tsp black pepper

**Directions:**

1. Add pork chops and remaining ingredients into a zip-lock bag. Seal the bag and place in the refrigerator for 4 hours.
2. Insert a crisper plate in the Ninja Foodi air fryer baskets.
3. Place the marinated pork chops in both baskets.
4. Select zone 1, then select air fry mode and set the temperature to 380 degrees F(195°C) for 12 minutes. Press "match" to match zone 2 settings to zone 1. Press "start/stop" to begin.

**Nutrition:**

- (Per serving) Calories 306 | Fat 19.9g |Sodium 122mg | Carbs 13.7g | Fiber 0.6g | Sugar 11g | Protein 18.1g

## Steaks With Walnut-blue Cheese Butter

Servings: 6
Cooking Time: 10 Minutes
**Ingredients:**
- 120 ml unsalted butter, at room temperature
- 120 ml crumbled blue cheese
- 2 tablespoons finely chopped walnuts
- 1 tablespoon minced fresh rosemary
- 1 teaspoon minced garlic
- ¼ teaspoon cayenne pepper
- Sea salt and freshly ground black pepper, to taste
- 680 g sirloin steaks, at room temperature

**Directions:**
1. In a medium bowl, combine the butter, blue cheese, walnuts, rosemary, garlic, and cayenne pepper and salt and black pepper to taste. Use clean hands to ensure that everything is well combined. Place the mixture on a sheet of parchment paper and form it into a log. Wrap it tightly in plastic wrap. Refrigerate for at least 2 hours or freeze for 30 minutes.
2. Season the steaks generously with salt and pepper.
3. Set the air fryer to 204°C and let it preheat for 5 minutes.
4. Place the steaks in the two drawers in a single layer and air fry for 5 minutes. Flip the steaks, and cook for 5 minutes more, until an instant-read thermometer reads 49°C for medium-rare .
5. Transfer the steaks to a plate. Cut the butter into pieces and place the desired amount on top of the steaks. Tent a piece of aluminum foil over the steaks and allow to sit for 10 minutes before serving.
6. Store any remaining butter in a sealed container in the refrigerator for up to 2 weeks.

## Roasted Beef

Servings: 8
Cooking Time: 50 Minutes
**Ingredients:**
- 1 (1-pound) beef roast
- Salt and ground black pepper, as required

**Directions:**
1. Grease each basket of "Zone 1" and "Zone 2" of Ninja Foodi 2-Basket Air Fryer.
2. Press "Zone 1" and "Zone 2" and then rotate the knob for each zone to select "Roast".
3. Set the temperature to 350 degrees F/ 175 degrees C for both zones and then set the time for 5 minutes to preheat.
4. Rub ach roast with salt and black pepper generously.
5. After preheating, arrange the roast into the basket of each zone.
6. Slide each basket into Air Fryer and set the time for 50 minutes.
7. After cooking time is completed, remove each roast from Air Fryer and place onto a platter for about 10 minutes before slicing.
8. With a sharp knife, cut each roast into desired-sized slices and serve.

## Minute Steak Roll-ups

Servings: 4
Cooking Time: 8 To 10 Minutes
**Ingredients:**
- 4 minute steaks (170 g each)
- 1 (450 g) bottle Italian dressing
- 1 teaspoon salt
- ½ teaspoon freshly ground black pepper
- 120 ml finely chopped brown onion
- 120 ml finely chopped green pepper
- 120 ml finely chopped mushrooms
- 1 to 2 tablespoons oil

**Directions:**
1. In a large resealable bag or airtight storage container, combine the steaks and Italian dressing. Seal the bag and refrigerate to marinate for 2 hours.
2. Remove the steaks from the marinade and place them on a cutting board. Discard the marinade. Evenly season the steaks with salt and pepper.
3. In a small bowl, stir together the onion, pepper, and mushrooms. Sprinkle the onion mixture evenly over the steaks. Roll up the steaks, jelly roll-style, and secure with toothpicks.
4. Preheat the air fryer to 204°C.
5. Place the steaks in the two air fryer drawers.
6. Cook for 4 minutes. Flip the steaks and spritz them with oil. Cook for 4 to 6 minutes more until the internal temperature reaches 64°C. Let rest for 5 minutes before serving.

## Sausage And Pork Meatballs

Servings: 8
Cooking Time: 8 To 12 Minutes
**Ingredients:**
- 1 large egg
- 1 teaspoon gelatin
- 450 g pork mince
- 230 g Italian-seasoned sausage, casings removed, crumbled
- 80 ml Parmesan cheese
- 60 ml finely diced onion
- 1 tablespoon tomato paste
- 1 teaspoon minced garlic
- 1 teaspoon dried oregano
- ¼ teaspoon red pepper flakes
- Sea salt and freshly ground black pepper, to taste
- Keto-friendly marinara sauce, for serving

**Directions:**
1. Beat the egg in a small bowl and sprinkle with the gelatin. Allow to sit for 5 minutes.
2. In a large bowl, combine the pork mince, sausage, Parmesan, onion, tomato paste, garlic, oregano, and red pepper flakes. Season with salt and black pepper.
3. Stir the gelatin mixture, then add it to the other ingredients and, using clean hands, mix to ensure that everything is well combined. Form into 1½-inch round meatballs.
4. Set the air fryer to 204°C. Place the meatballs in the two air fryer drawers in a single layer. Air fry for 5 minutes. Flip and cook for 3 to 7 minutes more, or until an instant-read thermometer reads 72°C.

## Steak And Mashed Creamy Potatoes

Servings:1
Cooking Time:45
**Ingredients:**
- 2 Russet potatoes, peeled and cubed
- ¼ cup butter, divided
- 1/3 cup heavy cream
- ½ cup shredded cheddar cheese
- Salt and black pepper, to taste
- 1 New York strip steak, about a pound
- 1 teaspoon of olive oil
- Oil spray, for greasing

**Directions:**
1. Rub the potatoes with salt and a little amount of olive oil about a teaspoon.
2. Next, season the steak with salt and black pepper.
3. Place the russet potatoes in a zone 1 basket.

4. Oil spray the steak from both sides and then place it in the zone 2 basket.
5. Set zone 1 to AIR fry mode for 45 minutes at 390 degrees F(200°C) .
6. Set the zone 2 basket, at 12 minutes at 375 degrees F(190°C) .
7. Hot start and Lethe ninja foodie do its magic.
8. One the cooking cycle completes, take out the steak and potatoes.
9. Mash the potatoes and then add butter, heavy cream, and cheese along with salt and black pepper.
10. Serve the mashed potatoes with steak.
11. Enjoy.

**Nutrition:**

- (Per serving) Calories1932 | Fat 85.2g| Sodium 3069mg | Carbs 82g | Fiber10.3 g| Sugar 5.3g | Protein 22.5g

## Pork Chops And Potatoes

Servings: 3
Cooking Time: 12 Minutes

**Ingredients:**

- 455g red potatoes
- Olive oil
- Salt and pepper
- 1 teaspoon garlic powder
- 1 teaspoon fresh rosemary, chopped
- 2 tablespoons brown sugar
- 1 tablespoon soy sauce
- 1 tablespoon Worcestershire sauce
- 1 teaspoon lemon juice
- 3 small pork chops

**Directions:**

1. Mix potatoes and pork chops with remaining ingredients in a bowl.
2. Divide the ingredients in the air fryer baskets.
3. Return the air fryer basket 1 to Zone 1, and basket 2 to Zone 2 of the Ninja Foodi 2-Basket Air Fryer.
4. Choose the "Air Fry" mode for Zone 1 at 400 degrees F(205°C) and 12 minutes of cooking time.
5. Select the "MATCH COOK" option to copy the settings for Zone 2.
6. Initiate cooking by pressing the START/PAUSE BUTTON.
7. Flip the chops and toss potatoes once cooked halfway through.
8. Serve warm.

**Nutrition:**

- (Per serving) Calories 352 | Fat 9.1g |Sodium 1294mg | Carbs 3.9g | Fiber 1g | Sugar 1g | Protein 61g

## Steak In Air Fry

Servings:1
Cooking Time:20

**Ingredients:**

- 2 teaspoons of canola oil
- 1 tablespoon of Montreal steaks seasoning
- 1 pound of beef steak

**Directions:**

1. The first step is to season the steak on both sides with canola oil and then rub a generous amount of steak seasoning all over.
2. We are using the AIR BROIL feature of the ninja air fryer and it works with one basket.
3. Put the steak in the basket and set it to AIR BROIL at 450 degrees F(230°C) for 20 -22 minutes.
4. After 7 minutes, hit pause and take out the basket to flip the steak, and cover it with foil on top, for the remaining 14 minutes.
5. Once done, serve the medium-rare steak and enjoy it by resting for 10 minutes.
6. Serve by cutting in slices.
7. Enjoy.

**Nutrition:**

- (Per serving) Calories 935| Fat 37.2g| Sodium 1419mg | Carbs 0g | Fiber 0g| Sugar 0g | Protein137.5 g

## Simple Strip Steak

Servings: 4
Cooking Time: 10 Minutes

**Ingredients:**

- 2 (9½-ounce) New York strip steaks
- Salt and ground black pepper, as required
- 3 teaspoons olive oil

**Directions:**

1. Grease each basket of "Zone 1" and "Zone 2" of Ninja Foodi 2-Basket Air Fryer.
2. Press "Zone 1" and "Zone 2" and then rotate the knob for each zone to select "Air Fry".
3. Set the temperature to 400 degrees F/ 205 degrees C for both zones and then set the time for 5 minutes to preheat.
4. Coat the steaks with oil and then sprinkle with salt and black pepper evenly.
5. After preheating, arrange 1 steak into the basket of each zone.
6. Slide each basket into Air Fryer and set the time for 10 minutes.
7. While cooking, flip the steak once halfway through.
8. After cooking time is completed, remove the steaks from Air Fryer and place onto a platter for about 10 minutes.
9. Cut each steak into desired size slices and serve immediately.

## Garlic-rosemary Pork Loin With Scalloped Potatoes And Cauliflower

Servings:6
Cooking Time: 50 Minutes

**Ingredients:**

- FOR THE PORK LOIN
- 2 pounds pork loin roast
- 2 tablespoons vegetable oil
- 2 teaspoons dried thyme
- 2 teaspoons dried crushed rosemary
- 1 teaspoon minced garlic
- ¾ teaspoon kosher salt
- FOR THE SCALLOPED POTATOES AND CAULIFLOWER
- 1 teaspoon vegetable oil
- ¾ pound Yukon Gold potatoes, peeled and very thinly sliced
- 1½ cups cauliflower florets
- ¼ teaspoon kosher salt
- ¼ teaspoon freshly ground black pepper
- 1 tablespoon very cold unsalted butter, grated
- 3 tablespoons all-purpose flour
- 1 cup whole milk
- 1 cup shredded Gruyère cheese

**Directions:**

1. To prep the pork loin: Coat the pork with the oil. Season with thyme, rosemary, garlic, and salt.

2. To prep the potatoes and cauliflower: Brush the bottom and sides of the Zone 2 basket with the oil. Add one-third of the potatoes to the bottom of the basket and arrange in a single layer. Top with ½ cup of cauliflower florets. Sprinkle a third of the salt and black pepper on top. Scatter one-third of the butter on top and sprinkle on 1 tablespoon of flour. Repeat this step twice more for a total of three layers.
3. Pour the milk over the layered potatoes and cauliflower; it should just cover the top layer. Top with the Gruyère.
4. To cook the pork and scalloped vegetables: Install a crisper plate in the Zone 1 basket. Place the pork loin in the basket and insert the basket in the unit. Insert the Zone 2 basket in the unit.
5. Select Zone 1, select AIR FRY, set the temperature to 390°F (200°C), and set the time to 50 minutes.
6. Select Zone 2, select BAKE, set the temperature to 350°F (175°C), and set the time to 45 minutes. Select SMART FINISH.
7. Press START/PAUSE to begin cooking.
8. When cooking is complete, the pork will be cooked through (an instant-read thermometer should read 145°F (60°C)) and the potatoes and cauliflower will be tender.
9. Let the pork rest for at least 15 minutes before slicing and serving with the scalloped vegetables.

**Nutrition:**

- (Per serving) Calories: 439; Total fat: 25g; Saturated fat: 10g; Carbohydrates: 17g; Fiber: 1.5g; Protein: 37g; Sodium: 431mg

## Bbq Pork Chops

Servings: 4
Cooking Time: 12 Minutes

**Ingredients:**

- 4 pork chops
- Salt and black pepper to taste
- 1 package BBQ Shake & Bake
- Olive oil

**Directions:**

1. Season pork chops with black pepper, salt, BBQ shake and olive oil.
2. Place these chops in the air fryer baskets.
3. Return the air fryer basket 1 to Zone 1, and basket 2 to Zone 2 of the Ninja Foodi 2-Basket Air Fryer.
4. Choose the "Air Fry" mode for Zone 1 at 375 degrees F(190°C) and 12 minutes of cooking time.
5. Select the "MATCH COOK" option to copy the settings for Zone 2.
6. Initiate cooking by pressing the START/PAUSE BUTTON.
7. Flip the pork chops once cooked halfway through.
8. Serve warm.

**Nutrition:**

- (Per serving) Calories 437 | Fat 28g |Sodium 1221mg | Carbs 22.3g | Fiber 0.9g | Sugar 8g | Protein 30.3g

## Mozzarella Stuffed Beef And Pork Meatballs

Servings: 4 To 6
Cooking Time: 12 Minutes

**Ingredients:**

- 1 tablespoon olive oil
- 1 small onion, finely chopped
- 1 to 2 cloves garlic, minced
- 340 g beef mince
- 340 g pork mince
- 180 ml bread crumbs
- 60 ml grated Parmesan cheese
- 60 ml finely chopped fresh parsley
- ½ teaspoon dried oregano
- 1½ teaspoons salt
- Freshly ground black pepper, to taste
- 2 eggs, lightly beaten
- 140 g low-moisture Mozzarella or other melting cheese, cut into 1-inch cubes

**Directions:**

1. Preheat a skillet over medium-high heat. Add the oil and cook the onion and garlic until tender, but not browned. 2. Transfer the onion and garlic to a large bowl and add the beef, pork, bread crumbs, Parmesan cheese, parsley, oregano, salt, pepper and eggs. Mix well until all the ingredients are combined. Divide the mixture into 12 evenly sized balls. Make one meatball at a time, by pressing a hole in the meatball mixture with the finger and pushing a piece of Mozzarella cheese into the hole. Mold the meat back into a ball, enclosing the cheese. 3. Preheat the air fryer to 192ºC. 4. Transfer meatballs to the two air fryer drawers and air fry for 12 minutes, shaking the drawers and turning the meatballs twice during the cooking process. Serve warm.

## Short Ribs & Root Vegetables

Servings:2
Cooking Time:45

**Ingredients:**

- 1 pound of beef short ribs, bone-in and trimmed
- Salt and black pepper, to taste
- 2 tablespoons canola oil, divided
- 1/4 cup red wine
- 3 tablespoons brown sugar
- 2 cloves garlic, peeled, minced
- 4 carrots, peeled, cut into 1-inch pieces
- 2 parsnips, peeled, cut into 1-inch pieces
- ½ cup pearl onions

**Directions:**

1. Season the ribs with salt and black pepper and rub a little amount of canola oil on both sides.
2. Place it in zone 1 basket of the air fryer.
3. Next, take a bowl and add pearl onions, parsnip, carrots, garlic, brown sugar, red wine, salt, and black pepper.
4. Add the vegetable mixture to the zone 2 basket.
5. Set the zone 1 basket time to 12 minutes at 375 degrees F(190°C) at AIR FRY mode.
6. Set the zone 2 basket at AIR FRY mode at 390 degrees F(200°C) for 18 minutes.
7. Hit start so the cooking cycle being.
8. Once the cooking complete, take out the ingredient and serve short ribs with the mixed vegetables and liquid collect at the bottom of zone 2 basket
9. Enjoy it hot.

**Nutrition:**

- (Per serving) Calories1262 | Fat 98.6g| Sodium 595mg | Carbs 57g | Fiber 10.1g| Sugar 28.2g | Protein 35.8g

## Kielbasa And Cabbage

Servings: 4
Cooking Time: 20 To 25 Minutes

**Ingredients:**

- 450 g smoked kielbasa sausage, sliced into ½-inch pieces
- 1 head cabbage, very coarsely chopped
- ½ brown onion, chopped
- 2 cloves garlic, chopped
- 2 tablespoons olive oil
- ½ teaspoon salt
- ½ teaspoon freshly ground black pepper
- 60 ml water

**Directions:**

1. Preheat the zone 1 air fryer drawer to 204ºC.
2. In a large bowl, combine the sausage, cabbage, onion, garlic, olive oil, salt, and black pepper. Toss until thoroughly combined.
3. Transfer the mixture to the zone 1 drawer of the air fryer and pour the water over the top. Pausing two or three times during the cooking time to shake the drawer, air fry for 20 to 25 minutes, until the sausage is browned and the vegetables are tender.

## Hot Dogs Wrapped In Bacon

Servings: 2
Cooking Time: 20 Minutes
**Ingredients:**

- 2 bacon strips
- 2 hot dogs
- Salt and black pepper, to taste

**Directions:**

1. Wrap each hot dog with bacon strip and season with salt and black pepper.
2. Grease each basket of "Zone 1" and "Zone 2" of Ninja Foodi 2-Basket Air Fryer.
3. Press "Zone 1" and "Zone 2" and then rotate the knob for each zone to select "Air Fry".
4. Set the temperature to 400 degrees F/ 205 degrees C for both zones and then set the time for 5 minutes to preheat.
5. After preheating, arrange bacon wrapped hot dogs into the basket of each zone.
6. Slide each basket into Air Fryer and set the time for 15 minutes.
7. While cooking, flip the hot dogs once halfway through.
8. After cooking time is completed, remove the filets from Air Fryer and serve hot.

## Pork Chops With Brussels Sprouts

Servings: 4
Cooking Time: 15 Minutes.
**Ingredients:**

- 4 bone-in center-cut pork chop
- Cooking spray
- Salt, to taste
- Black pepper, to taste
- 2 teaspoons olive oil
- 2 teaspoons pure maple syrup
- 2 teaspoons Dijon mustard
- 6 ounces Brussels sprouts, quartered

**Directions:**

1. Rub pork chop with salt, ¼ teaspoons black pepper, and cooking spray.
2. Toss Brussels sprouts with mustard, syrup, oil, ¼ teaspoon of black pepper in a medium bowl.
3. Add pork chop to the crisper plate of Zone 1 of the Ninja Foodi Dual Zone Air Fryer.
4. Return the crisper plate to the Ninja Foodi Dual Zone Air Fryer.
5. Choose the Air Fry mode for Zone 1 and set the temperature to 400 degrees F(205°C) and the time to 15 minutes.
6. Add the Brussels sprouts to the crisper plate of Zone 2 and return it to the unit.
7. Choose the Air Fry mode for Zone 2 with 350 degrees F(175°C) and the time to 13 minutes.
8. Press the SYNC button to sync the finish time for both Zones.
9. Initiate cooking by pressing the START/STOP button.
10. Serve warm and fresh

**Nutrition:**

- (Per serving) Calories 336 | Fat 27.1g |Sodium 66mg | Carbs 1.1g | Fiber 0.4g | Sugar 0.2g | Protein 19.7g

## Rosemary Ribeye Steaks And Mongolian-style Beef

Servings: 6
Cooking Time: 15 Minutes
**Ingredients:**

- Rosemary Ribeye Steaks:
- 60 ml butter
- 1 clove garlic, minced
- Salt and ground black pepper, to taste
- 1½ tablespoons balsamic vinegar
- 60 ml rosemary, chopped
- 2 ribeye steaks
- Mongolian-Style Beef:
- Oil, for spraying
- 60 ml cornflour
- 450 g bavette or skirt steak, thinly sliced
- 180 ml packed light brown sugar
- 120 ml soy sauce
- 2 teaspoons toasted sesame oil
- 1 tablespoon minced garlic
- ½ teaspoon ground ginger
- 120 ml water
- Cooked white rice or ramen noodles, for serving

**Directions:**

1. Make the Rosemary Ribeye Steaks :
2. Melt the butter in a skillet over medium heat. Add the garlic and fry until fragrant.
3. Remove the skillet from the heat and add the salt, pepper, and vinegar. Allow it to cool.
4. Add the rosemary, then pour the mixture into a Ziploc bag.
5. Put the ribeye steaks in the bag and shake well, coating the meat well. Refrigerate for an hour, then allow to sit for a further twenty minutes.
6. Preheat the zone 1 air fryer drawer to 204ºC.
7. Air fry the ribeye steaks for 15 minutes.
8. Take care when removing the steaks from the air fryer and plate up.
9. Serve immediately.
10. Make the Mongolian-Style Beef :
11. Line the zone 2 air fryer drawer with parchment and spray lightly with oil.
12. Place the cornflour in a bowl and dredge the steak until evenly coated. Shake off any excess cornflour.
13. Place the steak in the prepared drawer and spray lightly with oil.
14. Roast at 200ºC for 5 minutes, flip, and cook for another 5 minutes.
15. In a small saucepan, combine the brown sugar, soy sauce, sesame oil, garlic, ginger, and water and bring to a boil over medium-high heat, stirring frequently. Remove from the heat.
16. Transfer the meat to the sauce and toss until evenly coated. Let sit for about 5 minutes so the steak absorbs the flavors. Serve with white rice or ramen noodles.

## Tasty Pork Skewers

Servings: 3
Cooking Time: 10 Minutes
**Ingredients:**

- 450g pork shoulder, cut into ¼-inch pieces
- 66ml soy sauce
- ½ tbsp garlic, crushed
- 1 tbsp ginger paste
- 1 ½ tsp sesame oil
- 22ml rice vinegar

- 21ml honey
- Pepper
- Salt

**Directions:**

1. In a bowl, mix meat with the remaining ingredients. Cover and place in the refrigerator for 30 minutes.
2. Thread the marinated meat onto the soaked skewers.
3. Insert a crisper plate in the Ninja Foodi air fryer baskets.
4. Place the pork skewers in both baskets.
5. Select zone 1, then select "air fry" mode and set the temperature to 360 degrees F(180°C) for 10 minutes. Press "match" and then press "start/stop" to begin. Turn halfway through.

**Nutrition:**

- (Per serving) Calories 520 | Fat 34.7g |Sodium 1507mg | Carbs 12.2g | Fiber 0.5g | Sugar 9.1g | Protein 37g

## Kielbasa Sausage With Pineapple And Kheema Meatloaf

Servings: 6 To 8
Cooking Time: 15 Minutes

**Ingredients:**

- Kielbasa Sausage with Pineapple:
- 340 g kielbasa sausage, cut into ½-inch slices
- 1 (230 g) can pineapple chunks in juice, drained
- 235 ml pepper chunks
- 1 tablespoon barbecue seasoning
- 1 tablespoon soy sauce
- Cooking spray
- Kheema Meatloaf:
- 450 g 85% lean beef mince
- 2 large eggs, lightly beaten
- 235 ml diced brown onion
- 60 ml chopped fresh coriander
- 1 tablespoon minced fresh ginger
- 1 tablespoon minced garlic
- 2 teaspoons garam masala
- 1 teaspoon coarse or flaky salt
- 1 teaspoon ground turmeric
- 1 teaspoon cayenne pepper
- ½ teaspoon ground cinnamon
- ⅛ teaspoon ground cardamom

**Directions:**

1. Make the Kielbasa Sausage with Pineapple :
2. Preheat the air fryer to 200ºC. Spritz the zone 1 air fryer drawer with cooking spray.
3. Combine all the ingredients in a large bowl. Toss to mix well.
4. Pour the sausage mixture in the preheated zone 1 air fryer drawer.
5. Air fry for 10 minutes or until the sausage is lightly browned and the pepper and pineapple are soft. Shake the drawer halfway through. Serve immediately.
6. Make the Kheema Meatloaf :
7. In a large bowl, gently mix the beef mince, eggs, onion, coriander, ginger, garlic, garam masala, salt, turmeric, cayenne, cinnamon, and cardamom until thoroughly combined.
8. Place the seasoned meat in a baking pan. Place the pan in the zone 2 air fryer drawer. Set the temperature to 176ºC for 15 minutes. Use a meat thermometer to ensure the meat loaf has reached an internal temperature of 72ºC .
9. Drain the fat and liquid from the pan and let stand for 5 minutes before slicing.
10. Slice and serve hot.

## Roast Beef

Servings: 4
Cooking Time: 35 Minutes

**Ingredients:**

- 2 pounds beef roast
- 1 tablespoon olive oil
- 1 medium onion (optional)
- 1 teaspoon salt
- 2 teaspoons rosemary and thyme, chopped (fresh or dried)

**Directions:**

1. Combine the sea salt, rosemary, and oil in a large, shallow dish.
2. Using paper towels, pat the meat dry. Place it on a dish and turn it to coat the outside with the oil-herb mixture.
3. Peel the onion and split it in half (if using).
4. Install a crisper plate in both drawers. Place half the beef roast and half an onion in the zone 1 drawer and half the beef and half the onion in zone 2's, then insert the drawers into the unit.
5. Select zone 1, select AIR FRY, set temperature to 360 degrees F/ 180 degrees C, and set time to 22 minutes. Select MATCH to match zone 2 settings to zone 1. Press the START/STOP button to begin cooking.
6. When the time reaches 11 minutes, press START/STOP to pause the unit. Remove the drawers and flip the roast. Re-insert the drawers into the unit and press START/STOP to resume cooking.

**Nutrition:**

- (Per serving) Calories 463 | Fat 17.8g | Sodium 732mg | Carbs 2.8g | Fiber 0.7g | Sugar 1.2g | Protein 69g

## Chinese Bbq Pork

Servings:35
Cooking Time:25

**Ingredients:**

- 4 tablespoons of soy sauce
- ¼ cup red wine
- 2 tablespoons of oyster sauce
- ¼ tablespoons of hoisin sauce
- ¼ cup honey
- ¼ cup brown sugar
- Pinch of salt
- Pinch of black pepper
- 1 teaspoon of ginger garlic, paste
- 1 teaspoon of five-spice powder
- 1.5 pounds of pork shoulder, sliced

**Directions:**

1. Take a bowl and mix all the ingredients listed under sauce ingredients.
2. Transfer half of it to a sauce pan and let it cook for 10 minutes.
3. Set it aside.
4. Let the pork marinate in the remaining sauce for 2 hours.
5. Afterward, put the pork slices in the basket and set it to AIRBORIL mode 450 degrees F(230°C) for 25 minutes.
6. Make sure the internal temperature is above 160 degrees F(70°C) once cooked.
7. If not add a few more minutes to the overall cooking time.
8. Once done, take it out and baste it with prepared sauce.
9. Serve and Enjoy.

**Nutrition:**

- (Per serving) Calories 1239| Fat 73 g| Sodium 2185 mg | Carbs 57.3 g | Fiber 0.4g| Sugar53.7 g | Protein 81.5 g

## Easy Breaded Pork Chops

Servings: 8
Cooking Time: 12 Minutes

**Ingredients:**

- 1 egg
- 118ml milk
- 8 pork chops
- 1 packet ranch seasoning
- 238g breadcrumbs
- Pepper
- Salt

**Directions:**

1. In a small bowl, whisk the egg and milk.
2. In a separate shallow dish, mix breadcrumbs, ranch seasoning, pepper, and salt.
3. Dip each pork chop in the egg mixture, then coat with breadcrumbs.
4. Insert a crisper plate in the Ninja Foodi air fryer baskets.
5. Place the coated pork chops in both baskets.
6. Select zone 1, then select air fry mode and set the temperature to 360 degrees F(180°C) for 12 minutes. Press "match" to match zone 2 settings to zone 1. Press "start/stop" to begin. Turn halfway through.

**Nutrition:**

- (Per serving) Calories 378 | Fat 22.2g |Sodium 298mg | Carbs 20.2g | Fiber 1.2g | Sugar 2.4g | Protein 22.8g

## Pigs In A Blanket With Spinach-artichoke Stuffed Mushrooms

Servings:4
Cooking Time: 15 Minutes

**Ingredients:**

- FOR THE PIGS IN A BLANKET
- Half an 8-ounce tube refrigerated crescent roll dough
- 4 hot dogs
- ½ teaspoon everything bagel seasoning (optional)
- FOR THE STUFFED MUSHROOMS
- 1 cup frozen chopped spinach, thawed and drained
- 1 (14-ounce) can artichoke hearts, drained and chopped
- 2 ounces (¼ cup) cream cheese, at room temperature
- ¼ cup grated Parmesan cheese
- ½ teaspoon garlic powder
- 1 (8-ounce) package whole cremini mushrooms, stems removed

**Directions:**

1. To prep the pigs in a blanket: Unroll the crescent roll dough. It will be scored into 4 triangular pieces, but leave them in place and pinch together at the seams to form 1 large square of dough. Cut the dough into 4 strips.
2. Wrap one strip of dough around each hot dog, starting with a short end of the strips and wrapping in a spiral motion around the hot dog. If desired, sprinkle each pig in a blanket with everything bagel seasoning.
3. To prep the stuffed mushrooms: In a medium bowl, combine the spinach, artichoke hearts, cream cheese, Parmesan, and garlic powder. Stuff about 1 tablespoon of filling into each mushroom cap.
4. To cook the pigs in a blanket and mushrooms: Install a crisper plate in each of the two baskets. Place the pigs in a blanket in the Zone 1 basket and insert the basket in the unit. Place the mushrooms in the Zone 2 basket and insert the basket in the unit.
5. Select Zone 1, select AIR FRY, set the temperature to 370°F (185°C), and set the time to 8 minutes.
6. Select Zone 2, select BAKE, set the temperature to 370°F (185°C), and set the time to 15 minutes. Select SMART FINISH.
7. Press START/PAUSE to begin cooking.
8. When cooking is complete, the crescent roll dough should be cooked through and golden brown, and the mushrooms should be tender.

**Nutrition:**

- (Per serving) Calories: 371; Total fat: 25g; Saturated fat: 11g; Carbohydrates: 22g; Fiber: 2.5g; Protein: 14g; Sodium: 1,059mg

## Rosemary And Garlic Lamb Chops

Servings: 4
Cooking Time: 15 Minutes

**Ingredients:**

- 8 lamb chops
- 3 tablespoons olive oil
- 2 tablespoons chopped fresh rosemary
- 1 teaspoon garlic powder or 3 cloves garlic, minced
- 1 teaspoon salt, or to taste
- ½ teaspoon black pepper, or to taste

**Directions:**

1. Dry the lamb chops with a paper towel.
2. Combine the olive oil, rosemary, garlic, salt, and pepper in a large mixing bowl. Toss the lamb in the marinade gently to coat it. Cover and set aside to marinate for 1 hour or up to overnight.
3. Install a crisper plate in both drawers. Place half the lamb chops in the zone 1 drawer and half in zone 2's, then insert the drawers into the unit.
4. Select zone 1, select AIR FRY, set temperature to 390 degrees F/ 200 degrees C, and set time to 15 minutes. Select MATCH to match zone 2 settings to zone 1. Press the START/STOP button to begin cooking.
5. When the time reaches 10 minutes, press START/STOP to pause the unit. Remove the drawers and flip the chops. Re-insert the drawers into the unit and press START/STOP to resume cooking.
6. Serve and enjoy!

**Nutrition:**

- (Per serving) Calories 427 | Fat 34g | Sodium 668mg | Carbs 1g | Fiber 1g | Sugar 1g | Protein 31g

## Cilantro Lime Steak

Servings: 4
Cooking Time: 10 Minutes

**Ingredients:**

- 450g flank steak, sliced
- 1 tsp cumin
- 1 tsp olive oil
- 4 tsp soy sauce
- 12g cilantro, chopped
- ¼ tsp cayenne
- 45ml lime juice
- 2 tsp chilli powder
- ¼ tsp salt

**Directions:**

1. Add the sliced steak pieces and the remaining ingredients into a zip-lock bag. Seal the bag and place in the refrigerator for 2 hours.
2. Insert a crisper plate in the Ninja Foodi air fryer baskets.
3. Place the marinated steak pieces in both baskets.
4. Select zone 1, then select "air fry" mode and set the temperature to 380 degrees F(195°C) for 10 minutes. Press "match" to match zone 2 settings to zone 1. Press "start/stop" to begin.

**Nutrition:**

- (Per serving) Calories 240 | Fat 11g |Sodium 524mg | Carbs 1.5g | Fiber 0.6g | Sugar 0.2g | Protein 32.2g

## Sweet And Spicy Country-style Ribs

Servings: 4
Cooking Time: 25 Minutes
**Ingredients:**

- 2 tablespoons brown sugar
- 2 tablespoons smoked paprika
- 1 teaspoon garlic powder
- 1 teaspoon onion granules
- 1 teaspoon mustard powder
- 1 teaspoon ground cumin
- 1 teaspoon coarse or flaky salt
- 1 teaspoon black pepper
- ¼ to ½ teaspoon cayenne pepper
- 680 g boneless pork steaks
- 235 ml barbecue sauce

**Directions:**

1. In a small bowl, stir together the brown sugar, paprika, garlic powder, onion granules, mustard powder, cumin, salt, black pepper, and cayenne. Mix until well combined.
2. Pat the ribs dry with a paper towel. Generously sprinkle the rub evenly over both sides of the ribs and rub in with your fingers.
3. Place the ribs in the two air fryer drawers. Set the air fryer to 176ºC for 15 minutes. Turn the ribs and brush with 120 ml of the barbecue sauce. Cook for an additional 10 minutes. Use a meat thermometer to ensure the pork has reached an internal temperature of 64ºC.
4. Serve with remaining barbecue sauce.

## Garlic Butter Steak Bites

Servings: 3
Cooking Time: 16 Minutes
**Ingredients:**

- Oil, for spraying
- 450 g boneless steak, cut into 1-inch pieces
- 2 tablespoons olive oil
- 1 teaspoon Worcestershire sauce
- ½ teaspoon granulated garlic
- ½ teaspoon salt
- ¼ teaspoon freshly ground black pepper

**Directions:**

1. Preheat the air fryer to 204ºC. Line the two air fryer drawers with parchment and spray lightly with oil.
2. In a medium bowl, combine the steak, olive oil, Worcestershire sauce, garlic, salt, and black pepper and toss until evenly coated.
3. Place the steak in a single layer in the two prepared drawers.
4. Cook for 10 to 16 minutes, flipping every 3 to 4 minutes. The total cooking time will depend on the thickness of the meat and your preferred doneness. If you want it well done, it may take up to 5 additional minutes.

# Poultry Recipes

## Ranch Turkey Tenders With Roasted Vegetable Salad

Servings:4
Cooking Time: 20 Minutes
**Ingredients:**

- FOR THE TURKEY TENDERS
- 1 pound turkey tenderloin
- ¼ cup ranch dressing
- ½ cup panko bread crumbs
- Nonstick cooking spray
- FOR THE VEGETABLE SALAD
- 1 large sweet potato, peeled and diced
- 1 zucchini, diced
- 1 red bell pepper, diced
- 1 small red onion, sliced
- 1 tablespoon vegetable oil
- ¼ teaspoon kosher salt
- ½ teaspoon freshly ground black pepper
- 2 cups baby spinach
- ½ cup store-bought balsamic vinaigrette
- ¼ cup chopped walnuts

**Directions:**

1. To prep the turkey tenders: Slice the turkey crosswise into 16 strips. Brush both sides of each strip with ranch dressing, then coat with the panko. Press the bread crumbs into the turkey to help them adhere. Mist both sides of the strips with cooking spray.
2. To prep the vegetables: In a large bowl, combine the sweet potato, zucchini, bell pepper, onion, and vegetable oil. Stir well to coat the vegetables. Season with the salt and black pepper.
3. To cook the turkey and vegetables: Install a crisper plate in the Zone 1 basket. Place the turkey tenders in the basket in a single layer and insert the basket in the unit. Place the vegetables in the Zone 2 basket and insert the basket in the unit.
4. Select Zone 1, select AIR FRY, set the temperature to 375°F (190°C), and set the time to 20 minutes.
5. Select Zone 2, select ROAST, set the temperature to 400°F (205°C), and set the time to 20 minutes. Select SMART FINISH.
6. Press START/PAUSE to begin cooking.
7. When both timers read 10 minutes, press START/PAUSE. Remove the Zone 1 basket and use silicone-tipped tongs to flip the turkey tenders. Reinsert the basket in the unit. Remove the Zone 2 basket and shake to redistribute the vegetables. Reinsert the basket and press START/PAUSE to resume cooking.
8. When cooking is complete, the turkey will be golden brown and cooked through (an instant-read thermometer should read 165°F (75°C)) and the vegetables will be fork-tender.
9. Place the spinach in a large serving bowl. Mix in the roasted vegetables and balsamic vinaigrette. Sprinkle with walnuts. Serve warm with the turkey tenders.

**Nutrition:**

- (Per serving) Calories: 470; Total fat: 28g; Saturated fat: 2.5g; Carbohydrates: 28g; Fiber: 4g; Protein: 31g; Sodium: 718mg

## African Piri-piri Chicken Drumsticks

Servings: 2
Cooking Time: 20 Minutes
**Ingredients:**

- Chicken:
- 1 tablespoon chopped fresh thyme leaves
- 1 tablespoon minced fresh ginger
- 1 small shallot, finely chopped
- 2 garlic cloves, minced
- 80 ml piri-piri sauce or hot sauce
- 3 tablespoons extra-virgin olive oil
- Zest and juice of 1 lemon
- 1 teaspoon smoked paprika
- ½ teaspoon kosher salt
- ½ teaspoon black pepper
- 4 chicken drumsticks
- Glaze:
- 2 tablespoons butter or ghee
- 1 teaspoon chopped fresh thyme leaves
- 1 garlic clove, minced
- 1 tablespoon piri-piri sauce
- 1 tablespoon fresh lemon juice

**Directions:**

1. For the chicken: In a small bowl, stir together all the ingredients except the chicken. Place the chicken and the marinade in a gallon-size resealable plastic bag. Seal the bag and massage to coat. Refrigerate for at least 2 hours or up to 24 hours, turning the bag occasionally. 2. Place the chicken legs in the zone 1 air fryer basket. Set the air fryer to 200ºC for 20 minutes, turning the chicken halfway through the cooking time. 3. Meanwhile, for the glaze: Melt the butter in a small saucepan over medium-high heat. Add the thyme and garlic. Cook, stirring, until the garlic just begins to brown, 1 to 2 minutes. Add the piri-piri sauce and lemon juice. Reduce the heat to medium-low and simmer for 1 to 2 minutes. 4. Transfer the chicken to a serving platter. Pour the glaze over the chicken. Serve immediately.

## Glazed Thighs With French Fries

Servings:3
Cooking Time:35
**Ingredients:**

- 2 tablespoons of Soy Sauce
- Salt, to taste
- 1 teaspoon of Worcestershire Sauce
- 2 teaspoons Brown Sugar
- 1 teaspoon of Ginger, paste
- 1 teaspoon of Garlic, paste
- 6 Boneless Chicken Thighs
- 1 pound of hand-cut potato fries
- 2 tablespoons of canola oil

**Directions:**

1. Coat the French fries well with canola oil.
2. Season it with salt.

3. In a small bowl, combine the soy sauce, Worcestershire sauce, brown sugar, ginger, and garlic.
4. Place the chicken in this marinade and let it sit for 40 minutes.
5. Put the chicken thighs into the zone 1 basket and fries into the zone 2 basket.
6. Press button 1 for the first basket, and set it to ROAST mode at 350 degrees F(175°C) for 35 minutes.
7. For the second basket hit 2 and set time to 30 minutes at 360 degrees F(180°C) , by selecting AIR FRY mode.
8. Once the cooking cycle completely take out the fries and chicken and serve it hot.

**Nutrition:**

- (Per serving) Calories 858| Fat39g | Sodium 1509mg | Carbs 45.6g | Fiber 4.4g | Sugar3 g | Protein 90g

## Curried Orange Honey Chicken

Servings: 4
Cooking Time: 16 To 19 Minutes

**Ingredients:**

- 340 g boneless, skinless chicken thighs, cut into 1-inch pieces
- 1 yellow bell pepper, cut into 1½-inch pieces
- 1 small red onion, sliced
- Olive oil for misting
- 60 ml chicken stock
- 2 tablespoons honey
- 60 ml orange juice
- 1 tablespoon cornflour
- 2 to 3 teaspoons curry powder

**Directions:**

1. Preheat the air fryer to 190ºC.
2. Put the chicken thighs, pepper, and red onion in the zone 1 air fryer drawer and mist with olive oil.
3. Roast for 12 to 14 minutes or until the chicken is cooked to 76ºC, shaking the drawer halfway through cooking time.
4. Remove the chicken and vegetables from the air fryer drawer and set aside.
5. In a metal bowl, combine the stock, honey, orange juice, cornflour, and curry powder, and mix well. Add the chicken and vegetables, stir, and put the bowl in the drawer.
6. Return the drawer to the air fryer and roast for 2 minutes. Remove and stir, then roast for 2 to 3 minutes or until the sauce is thickened and bubbly.
7. Serve warm.

## Crispy Fried Quail

Servings: 8
Cooking Time: 6 Minutes

**Ingredients:**

- 8 boneless quail breasts
- 2 tablespoons Sichuan pepper dry rub mix
- ¾ cup rice flour
- ¼ cup all-purpose flour
- 2-3 cups peanut oil
- Garnish
- Sliced jalapenos
- Fresh lime wedges
- Fresh coriander

**Directions:**

1. Split the quail breasts in half.
2. Mix Sichuan mix with flours in a bowl.
3. Coat the quail breasts with flour mixture and place in the air fryer baskets.
4. Return the air fryer basket 1 to Zone 1, and basket 2 to Zone 2 of the Ninja Foodi 2-Basket Air Fryer.
5. Choose the "Air Fry" mode for Zone 1 at 300 degrees F(150°C) and 6 minutes of cooking time.
6. Select the "MATCH COOK" option to copy the settings for Zone 2.
7. Initiate cooking by pressing the START/PAUSE BUTTON.
8. Flip the quail breasts once cooked halfway through.
9. Serve warm.

**Nutrition:**

- (Per serving) Calories 351 | Fat 11g |Sodium 150mg | Carbs 3.3g | Fiber 0.2g | Sugar 1g | Protein 33.2g

## Chicken Ranch Wraps

Servings: 4
Cooking Time: 22 Minutes

**Ingredients:**

- 1½ ounces breaded chicken breast tenders
- 4 (12-inch) whole-wheat tortilla wraps
- 2 heads romaine lettuce, chopped
- ½ cup shredded mozzarella cheese
- 4 tablespoons ranch dressing

**Directions:**

1. Place a crisper plate in each drawer. Place half of the chicken tenders in one drawer and half in the other. Insert the drawers into the unit.
2. Select zone 1, then AIR FRY, and set the temperature to 390 degrees F/ 200 degrees C with a 22-minute timer. To match zone 2 settings to zone 1, choose MATCH. To begin cooking, press the START/STOP button.
3. To pause the unit, press START/STOP when the timer reaches 11 minutes. Remove the drawers from the unit and flip the tenders over. To resume cooking, re-insert the drawers into the device and press START/STOP.
4. Remove the chicken from the drawers when they're done cooking and chop them up.
5. Divide the chopped chicken between warmed-up wraps. Top with some lettuce, cheese, and ranch dressing. Wrap and serve.

**Nutrition:**

- (Per serving) Calories 212 | Fat 7.8g | Sodium 567mg | Carbs 9.1g | Fiber 34.4g | Sugar 9.7g | Protein 10.6g

## Thai Chicken With Cucumber And Chili Salad

Servings: 6
Cooking Time: 25 Minutes

**Ingredients:**

- 2 (570 g) small chickens, giblets discarded
- 1 tablespoon fish sauce
- 6 tablespoons chopped fresh coriander
- 2 teaspoons lime zest
- 1 teaspoon ground coriander
- 2 garlic cloves, minced
- 2 tablespoons packed light brown sugar
- 2 teaspoons vegetable oil
- Salt and ground black pepper, to taste
- 1 English cucumber, halved lengthwise and sliced thin
- 1 Thai chili, stemmed, deseeded, and minced
- 2 tablespoons chopped dry-roasted peanuts
- 1 small shallot, sliced thinly
- 1 tablespoon lime juice
- Lime wedges, for serving
- Cooking spray

**Directions:**

1. Arrange a chicken on a clean work surface, remove the backbone with kitchen shears, then pound the chicken breast to flat. Cut the breast in half. Repeat with the remaining chicken.
2. Loose the breast and thigh skin with your fingers, then pat the chickens dry and pierce about 10 holes into the fat deposits of the chickens. Tuck the wings under the chickens.
3. Combine 2 teaspoons of fish sauce, coriander, lime zest, coriander, garlic, 4 teaspoons of sugar, 1 teaspoon of vegetable oil, ½ teaspoon of salt, and ⅛ teaspoon of ground black pepper in a small bowl. Stir to mix well.
4. Rub the fish sauce mixture under the breast and thigh skin of the game chickens, then let sit for 10 minutes to marinate.
5. Preheat the air fryer to 200ºC. Spritz the two air fryer baskets with cooking spray.
6. Arrange the marinated chickens in the preheated air fryer, skin side down.
7. Air fry for 15 minutes, then gently turn the game hens over and air fry for 10 more minutes or until the skin is golden brown and the internal temperature of the chickens reads at least 75ºC.
8. Meanwhile, combine all the remaining ingredients, except for the lime wedges, in a large bowl and sprinkle with salt and black pepper. Toss to mix well.
9. Transfer the fried chickens on a large plate, then sit the salad aside and squeeze the lime wedges over before serving.

## Thai Curry Meatballs

Servings: 4
Cooking Time: 10 Minutes
**Ingredients:**
- 450 g chicken mince
- 15 g chopped fresh coriander
- 1 teaspoon chopped fresh mint
- 1 tablespoon fresh lime juice
- 1 tablespoon Thai red, green, or yellow curry paste
- 1 tablespoon fish sauce
- 2 garlic cloves, minced
- 2 teaspoons minced fresh ginger
- ½ teaspoon kosher salt
- ½ teaspoon black pepper
- ¼ teaspoon red pepper flakes

**Directions:**
1. Preheat the zone 1 air fryer drawer to 200ºC.
2. In a large bowl, gently mix the chicken mince, coriander, mint, lime juice, curry paste, fish sauce, garlic, ginger, salt, black pepper, and red pepper flakes until thoroughly combined.
3. Form the mixture into 16 meatballs. Place the meatballs in a single layer in the zone 1 air fryer drawer. Air fry for 10 minutes, turning the meatballs halfway through the cooking time. Use a meat thermometer to ensure the meatballs have reached an internal temperature of 76ºC. Serve immediately.

## Barbecue Chicken Drumsticks With Crispy Kale Chips

Servings:4
Cooking Time: 20 Minutes
**Ingredients:**
- FOR THE DRUMSTICKS
- 1 tablespoon chili powder
- 2 teaspoons smoked paprika
- ¼ teaspoon kosher salt
- ¼ teaspoon garlic powder
- ¼ teaspoon freshly ground black pepper
- 2 teaspoons dark brown sugar
- 4 chicken drumsticks
- 1 cup barbecue sauce (your favorite)
- FOR THE KALE CHIPS
- 5 cups kale, stems and midribs removed, if needed
- ½ teaspoon garlic powder
- ½ teaspoon kosher salt
- ¼ teaspoon freshly ground black pepper

**Directions:**
1. To prep the drumsticks: In a small bowl, combine the chili powder, smoked paprika, salt, garlic powder, black pepper, and brown sugar. Rub the spice mixture all over the chicken.
2. To cook the chicken and kale chips: Install a crisper plate in each of the two baskets. Add the chicken drumsticks to the Zone 1 basket and insert the basket in the unit. Add the kale to the Zone 2 basket, sprinkle the kale with the garlic powder, salt, and black pepper and insert the basket in the unit.
3. Select Zone 1, select BAKE, set the temperature to 390°F (200°C), and set the time to 20 minutes.
4. Select Zone 2, select AIR FRY, set the temperature to 300°F (150°C), and set the time to 15 minutes. Select SMART FINISH.
5. Press START/PAUSE to begin cooking.
6. When the Zone 1 timer reads 5 minutes, press START/PAUSE. Remove the basket and brush the drumsticks with the barbecue sauce. Reinsert the basket and press START/PAUSE to resume cooking.
7. When cooking is complete, the chicken should be cooked through (an instant-read thermometer should read 165°F (75°C)) and the kale chips will be crispy. Serve hot.

**Nutrition:**
- (Per serving) Calories: 335; Total fat: 11g; Saturated fat: 3g; Carbohydrates: 31g; Fiber: 1.5g; Protein: 26g; Sodium: 1,045mg

## Bacon Wrapped Stuffed Chicken

Servings: 4
Cooking Time: 25 Minutes
**Ingredients:**
- 3 boneless chicken breasts
- 6 jalapenos, sliced
- ¾ cup (170g) cream cheese
- ½ cup Monterey Jack cheese, shredded
- 1 teaspoon ground cumin
- 12 strips thick bacon

**Directions:**
1. Cut the chicken breasts in half crosswise and pound them with a mallet.
2. Mix cream cheese with cumin and Monterey jacket cheese in a bowl.
3. Spread the cream cheese mixture over the chicken breast slices.
4. Add jalapeno slices on top and wrap the chicken slices.
5. Wrap each chicken rolls with a bacon slice.
6. Place the wrapped rolls into the Ninja Foodi 2 Baskets Air Fryer baskets.
7. Return the air fryer basket 1 to Zone 1, and basket 2 to Zone 2 of the Ninja Foodi 2-Basket Air Fryer.
8. Choose the "Air Fry" mode for Zone 1 at 340 degrees F(170°C) and 25 minutes of cooking time.
9. Select the "MATCH COOK" option to copy the settings for Zone 2.
10. Initiate cooking by pressing the START/PAUSE BUTTON.
11. Serve warm.

**Nutrition:**
- (Per serving) Calories 220 | Fat 1.7g |Sodium 178mg | Carbs 1.7g | Fiber 0.2g | Sugar 0.2g | Protein 32.9g

## Chicken Drumettes

Servings: 5
Cooking Time: 52 Minutes.

**Ingredients:**

- 10 large chicken drumettes
- Cooking spray
- ¼ cup of rice vinegar
- 3 tablespoons honey
- 2 tablespoons unsalted chicken stock
- 1 tablespoon soy sauce
- 1 tablespoon toasted sesame oil
- ⅜ teaspoons crushed red pepper
- 1 garlic clove, chopped
- 2 tablespoons chopped unsalted roasted peanuts
- 1 tablespoon chopped fresh chives

**Directions:**

1. Spread the chicken in the two crisper plates in an even layer and spray cooking spray on top.
2. Return the crisper plate to the Ninja Foodi Dual Zone Air Fryer.
3. Choose the Air Fry mode for Zone 1 and set the temperature to 390 degrees F(200°C) and the time to 47 minutes.
4. Select the "MATCH" button to copy the settings for Zone 2.
5. Initiate cooking by pressing the START/STOP button.
6. Flip the chicken drumettes once cooked halfway through, then resume cooking.
7. During this time, mix soy sauce, honey, stock, vinegar, garlic, and crushed red pepper in a suitable saucepan and place it over medium-high heat to cook on a simmer.
8. Cook this sauce for 6 minutes with occasional stirring, then pour it into a medium-sized bowl.
9. Add air fried drumettes and toss well to coat with the honey sauce.
10. Garnish with chives and peanuts.
11. Serve warm and fresh.

**Nutrition:**

- (Per serving) Calories 268 | Fat 10.4g |Sodium 411mg | Carbs 0.4g | Fiber 0.1g | Sugar 0.1g | Protein 40.6g

## Broccoli And Cheese Stuffed Chicken

Servings: 4
Cooking Time: 20 Minutes

**Ingredients:**

- 60 g cream cheese, softened
- 70 g chopped fresh broccoli, steamed
- 120 g shredded sharp Cheddar cheese
- 4 (170 g) boneless, skinless chicken breasts
- 2 tablespoons mayonnaise
- ¼ teaspoon salt
- ¼ teaspoon garlic powder
- ⅛ teaspoon ground black pepper

**Directions:**

1. In a medium bowl, combine cream cheese, broccoli, and Cheddar. Cut a 4-inch pocket into each chicken breast. Evenly divide mixture between chicken breasts; stuff the pocket of each chicken breast with the mixture.
2. Spread ¼ tablespoon mayonnaise per side of each chicken breast, then sprinkle both sides of breasts with salt, garlic powder, and pepper.
3. Place stuffed chicken breasts into the two ungreased air fryer drawers so that the open seams face up. Adjust the temperature to 180ºC and air fry for 20 minutes, turning chicken halfway through cooking. When done, chicken will be golden and have an internal temperature of at least 76ºC. Serve warm.

## Spiced Chicken And Vegetables

Servings:1
Cooking Time:45

**Ingredients:**

- 2 large chicken breasts
- 2 teaspoons of olive oil
- 1 teaspoon of chili powder
- 1 teaspoon of paprika powder
- 1 teaspoon of onion powder
- ½ teaspoon of garlic powder
- 1/4 teaspoon of Cumin
- Salt and black pepper, to taste
- Vegetable Ingredients:
- 2 large potato, cubed
- 4 large carrots cut into bite-size pieces
- 1 tablespoon of olive oil
- Salt and black pepper, to taste

**Directions:**

1. Take chicken breast pieces and rub olive oil, salt, pepper, chili powder, onion powder, cumin, garlic powder, and paprika.
2. Season the vegetables with olive oil, salt, and black pepper.
3. Now put the chicken breast pieces in the zone 1 basket.
4. Put the vegetables into the zone 2 basket.
5. Now hit 1 for the first basket and set it to ROAST at 350 degrees F(175°C) , for 45 minutes.
6. For the second basket hit 2 and set time for 45 minutes, by selecting AIR FRY mode at 350 degrees F(175°C) .
7. To start cooking hit the smart finish button and press hit start.
8. Once the cooking cycle is done, serve, and enjoy.

**Nutrition:**

- (Per serving) Calories1510 | Fat 51.3g| Sodium 525mg | Carbs 163g | Fiber24.7 g | Sugar 21.4g | Protein 102.9

## Cornish Hen

Servings: 4
Cooking Time: 35 Minutes

**Ingredients:**

- 2 Cornish hens
- 2 tablespoons olive oil
- 2 teaspoons salt
- 1½ teaspoons Italian seasoning
- 1 teaspoon garlic powder
- 1 teaspoon paprika
- ½ teaspoon black pepper
- ½ teaspoon lemon zest

**Directions:**

1. Mix Italian seasoning with lemon zest, juice, black pepper, paprika, and garlic powder in a bowl.
2. Rub each hen with the seasoning mixture.
3. Tuck the hen wings in and place one in each air fryer basket.
4. Return the air fryer basket 1 to Zone 1, and basket 2 to Zone 2 of the Ninja Foodi 2-Basket Air Fryer.
5. Choose the "Air Fry" mode for Zone 1 and set the temperature to 375 degrees F(190°C) and 35 minutes of cooking time.
6. Select the "MATCH COOK" option to copy the settings for Zone 2.
7. Initiate cooking by pressing the START/PAUSE BUTTON.
8. Flip the hens once cooked halfway through.
9. Serve warm.

**Nutrition:**

- (Per serving) Calories 223 | Fat 11.7g |Sodium 721mg | Carbs 13.6g | Fiber 0.7g | Sugar 8g | Protein 15.7g

## Sweet-and-sour Chicken With Pineapple Cauliflower Rice

Servings:4
Cooking Time: 30 Minutes
**Ingredients:**

- FOR THE CHICKEN
- ¼ cup cornstarch, plus 2 teaspoons
- ¼ teaspoon kosher salt
- 2 large eggs
- 1 tablespoon sesame oil
- 1½ pounds boneless, skinless chicken breasts, cut into 1-inch pieces
- Nonstick cooking spray
- 6 tablespoons ketchup
- ¾ cup apple cider vinegar
- 1½ tablespoons soy sauce
- 1 tablespoon sugar
- FOR THE CAULIFLOWER RICE
- 1 cup finely diced fresh pineapple
- 1 red bell pepper, thinly sliced
- 1 small red onion, thinly sliced
- 1 tablespoon vegetable oil
- 2 cups frozen cauliflower rice, thawed
- 2 tablespoons soy sauce
- 1 teaspoon sesame oil
- 2 scallions, sliced

**Directions:**

1. To prep the chicken: Set up a breading station with two small shallow bowls. Combine ¼ cup of cornstarch and the salt in the first bowl. In the second bowl, beat the eggs with the sesame oil.
2. Dip the chicken pieces in the cornstarch mixture to coat, then into the egg mixture, then back into the cornstarch mixture to coat. Mist the coated pieces with cooking spray.
3. In a small bowl, whisk together the ketchup, vinegar, soy sauce, sugar, and remaining 2 teaspoons of cornstarch.
4. To prep the cauliflower rice: Blot the pineapple dry with a paper towel. In a large bowl, combine the pineapple, bell pepper, onion, and vegetable oil.
5. To cook the chicken and cauliflower rice: Install a crisper plate in each of the two baskets. Place the chicken in the Zone 1 basket and insert the basket in the unit. Place a piece of aluminum foil over the crisper plate in the Zone 2 basket and add the pineapple mixture. Insert the basket in the unit.
6. Select Zone 1, select AIR FRY, set the temperature to 400°F (205°C), and set the time to 30 minutes.
7. Select Zone 2, select AIR BROIL, set the temperature to 450°F (230°C), and set the time to 12 minutes. Select SMART FINISH.
8. Press START/PAUSE to begin cooking.
9. When the Zone 2 timer reads 4 minutes, press START/PAUSE. Remove the basket and stir in the cauliflower rice, soy sauce, and sesame oil. Reinsert the basket and press START/PAUSE to resume cooking.
10. When cooking is complete, the chicken will be golden brown and cooked through and the rice warmed through. Stir the scallions into the rice and serve.

**Nutrition:**

- (Per serving) Calories: 457; Total fat: 17g; Saturated fat: 2.5g; Carbohydrates: 31g; Fiber: 2.5g; Protein: 43g; Sodium: 1,526mg

## Italian Chicken & Potatoes

Servings: 4
Cooking Time: 24 Minutes
**Ingredients:**

- 450g chicken breast, boneless & diced
- 30ml olive oil
- ½ tsp lemon zest
- 2 tbsp fresh lemon juice
- 450g baby potatoes, quartered
- 1 tbsp Greek seasoning
- Pepper
- Salt

**Directions:**

1. Toss potatoes with ½ tablespoon Greek seasoning, 1 tablespoon oil, lemon zest, lemon juice, pepper, and salt in a bowl.
2. Insert a crisper plate in the Ninja Foodi air fryer baskets.
3. Add potatoes into the zone 1 basket.
4. In a bowl, toss chicken with the remaining oil and seasoning.
5. Add the chicken into the zone 2 basket.
6. Select zone 1, then select "air fry" mode and set the temperature to 390 degrees F(190°C) for 12 minutes. Press "match" to match zone 2 settings to zone 1. Press "start/stop" to begin.

**Nutrition:**

- (Per serving) Calories 262 | Fat 10.1g |Sodium 227mg | Carbs 15.5g | Fiber 2.9g | Sugar 0.2g | Protein 27.2g

## Air Fried Chicken Legs

Servings: 4
Cooking Time: 10 Minutes
**Ingredients:**

- 8 chicken legs
- 2 tablespoons olive oil
- 1 teaspoon salt
- 1 teaspoon black pepper
- 1 teaspoon smoked paprika
- 1 teaspoon garlic powder
- 1 teaspoon dried parsley

**Directions:**

1. Mix chicken with oil, herbs and spices in a bowl.
2. Divide the chicken legs in the air fryer baskets.
3. Return the air fryer basket 1 to Zone 1, and basket 2 to Zone 2 of the Ninja Foodi 2-Basket Air Fryer.
4. Choose the "Air Fry" mode for Zone 1 at 400 degrees F(205°C) and 10 minutes of cooking time.
5. Select the "MATCH COOK" option to copy the settings for Zone 2.
6. Initiate cooking by pressing the START/PAUSE BUTTON.
7. Flip the chicken once cooked halfway through.
8. Serve warm.

**Nutrition:**

- (Per serving) Calories 220 | Fat 13g |Sodium 542mg | Carbs 0.9g | Fiber 0.3g | Sugar 0.2g | Protein 25.6g

## Air Fried Chicken Potatoes With Sun-dried Tomato

Servings: 2
Cooking Time: 25 Minutes
**Ingredients:**

- 2 teaspoons minced fresh oregano, divided
- 2 teaspoons minced fresh thyme, divided
- 2 teaspoons extra-virgin olive oil, plus extra as needed
- 450 g fingerling potatoes, unpeeled
- 2 (340 g) bone-in split chicken breasts, trimmed
- 1 garlic clove, minced
- 15 g oil-packed sun-dried tomatoes, patted dry and chopped

- 1½ tablespoons red wine vinegar
- 1 tablespoon capers, rinsed and minced
- 1 small shallot, minced
- Salt and ground black pepper, to taste

**Directions:**

1. Preheat the zone 1 air fryer drawer to 180ºC.
2. Combine 1 teaspoon of oregano, 1 teaspoon of thyme, ¼ teaspoon of salt, ¼ teaspoon of ground black pepper, 1 teaspoons of olive oil in a large bowl. Add the potatoes and toss to coat well.
3. Combine the chicken with remaining thyme, oregano, and olive oil. Sprinkle with garlic, salt, and pepper. Toss to coat well.
4. Place the potatoes in the preheated air fryer drawer, then arrange the chicken on top of the potatoes.
5. Air fry for 25 minutes or until the internal temperature of the chicken reaches at least 76ºC and the potatoes are wilted. Flip the chicken and potatoes halfway through.
6. Meanwhile, combine the sun-dried tomatoes, vinegar, capers, and shallot in a separate large bowl. Sprinkle with salt and ground black pepper. Toss to mix well.
7. Remove the chicken and potatoes from the air fryer and allow to cool for 10 minutes. Serve with the sun-dried tomato mix.

## General Tso' s Chicken

Servings: 4

Cooking Time: 22 Minutes.

**Ingredients:**

- 1 egg, large
- ⅓ cup 2 teaspoons cornstarch,
- ¼ teaspoons salt
- ¼ teaspoons ground white pepper
- 7 tablespoons chicken broth
- 2 tablespoons soy sauce
- 2 tablespoons ketchup
- 2 teaspoons sugar
- 2 teaspoons unseasoned rice vinegar
- 1 ½ tablespoons canola oil
- 4 chile de árbol, chopped and seeds discarded
- 1 tablespoon chopped fresh ginger
- 1 tablespoon garlic, chopped
- 2 tablespoons green onion, sliced
- 1 teaspoon toasted sesame oil
- 1 lb. boneless chicken thighs, cut into 1 ¼ -inch chunks
- ½ teaspoon toasted sesame seeds

**Directions:**

1. Add egg to a large bowl and beat it with a fork.
2. Add chicken to the egg and coat it well.
3. Whisk ⅓ cup of cornstarch with black pepper and salt in a small bowl.
4. Add chicken to the cornstarch mixture and mix well to coat.
5. Divide the chicken in the two crisper plates and spray them cooking oi.
6. Return the crisper plates to the Ninja Foodi Dual Zone Air Fryer.
7. Choose the Air Fry mode for Zone 1 and set the temperature to 390 degrees F(200°C) and the time to 20 minutes.
8. Select the "MATCH" button to copy the settings for Zone 2.
9. Initiate cooking by pressing the START/STOP button.
10. Once done, remove the air fried chicken from the air fryer.
11. Whisk 2 teaspoons of cornstarch with soy sauce, broth, sugar, ketchup, and rice vinegar in a small bowl.
12. Add chilies and canola oil to a skillet and sauté for 1 minute.
13. Add garlic and ginger, then sauté for 30 seconds.
14. Stir in cornstarch sauce and cook until it bubbles and thickens.
15. Toss in cooked chicken and garnish with sesame oil, sesame seeds, and green onion.
16. Enjoy.

**Nutrition:**

- (Per serving) Calories 351 | Fat 16g |Sodium 777mg | Carbs 26g | Fiber 4g | Sugar 5g | Protein 28g

## Sesame Ginger Chicken

Servings: 4

Cooking Time: 30 Minutes

**Ingredients:**

- 4 ounces green beans
- 1 tablespoon canola oil
- 1½ pounds boneless, skinless chicken breasts
- 1/3 cup prepared sesame-ginger sauce
- Kosher salt, to taste
- Black pepper, to taste

**Directions:**

1. Toss the green beans with a teaspoon of salt and pepper in a medium mixing bowl.
2. Place a crisper plate in each drawer. Place the green beans in the zone 1 drawer and insert it into the unit. Place the chicken breasts in the zone 2 drawer and place it inside the unit.
3. Select zone 1, then AIR FRY, and set the temperature to 390 degrees F/ 200 degrees C with a 10-minute timer. Select zone 2, then AIR FRY, and set the temperature to 390 degrees F/ 200 degrees C with an 18-minute timer. Select SYNC. To begin cooking, press the START/STOP button.
4. Press START/STOP to pause the unit when the zone 2 timer reaches 9 minutes. Remove the chicken from the drawer and toss it in the sesame ginger sauce. To resume cooking, re-insert the drawer into the unit and press START/STOP.
5. When cooking is complete, serve the chicken breasts and green beans straight away.

**Nutrition:**

- (Per serving) Calories 143 | Fat 7g | Sodium 638mg | Carbs 11.6g | Fiber 1.4g | Sugar 8.5g | Protein 11.1g

## Greek Chicken Souvlaki

Servings: 3 To 4

Cooking Time: 15 Minutes

**Ingredients:**

- Chicken:
- Grated zest and juice of 1 lemon
- 2 tablespoons extra-virgin olive oil
- 1 tablespoon Greek souvlaki seasoning
- 450 g boneless, skinless chicken breast, cut into 2-inch chunks
- Vegetable oil spray
- For Serving:
- Warm pita bread or hot cooked rice
- Sliced ripe tomatoes
- Sliced cucumbers
- Thinly sliced red onion
- Kalamata olives
- Tzatziki

**Directions:**

1. For the chicken: In a small bowl, combine the lemon zest, lemon juice, olive oil, and souvlaki seasoning. Place the chicken in a gallon-size resealable plastic bag. Pour the marinade over chicken. Seal bag and massage to coat. Place the bag in a large bowl and marinate for 30 minutes, or cover and

refrigerate up to 24 hours, turning the bag occasionally. 2. Place the chicken a single layer in the zone 1 air fryer drawer. Cook at 180ºC for 10 minutes, turning the chicken and spraying with a little vegetable oil spray halfway through the cooking time. Increase the air fryer temperature to 200ºC for 5 minutes to allow the chicken to crisp and brown a little. 3. Transfer the chicken to a serving platter and serve with pita bread or rice, tomatoes, cucumbers, onion, olives and tzatziki.

## Buffalo Chicken

Servings: 4
Cooking Time: 22 Minutes
**Ingredients:**

- ½ cup plain fat-free Greek yogurt
- ¼ cup egg substitute
- 1 tablespoon plus 1 teaspoon hot sauce
- 1 cup panko breadcrumbs
- 1 tablespoon sweet paprika
- 1 tablespoon garlic pepper seasoning
- 1 tablespoon cayenne pepper
- 1-pound skinless, boneless chicken breasts, cut into 1-inch strips

**Directions:**

1. Combine the Greek yogurt, egg substitute, and hot sauce in a mixing bowl.
2. In a separate bowl, combine the panko breadcrumbs, paprika, garlic powder, and cayenne pepper.
3. Dip the chicken strips in the yogurt mixture, then coat them in the breadcrumb mixture.
4. Install a crisper plate in both drawers. Place the chicken strips into the drawers and then insert the drawers into the unit.
5. Select zone 1, select AIR FRY, set temperature to 390 degrees F/ 200 degrees C, and set time to 22 minutes. Select MATCH to match zone 2 settings to zone 1. Press the START/STOP button to begin cooking.
6. When cooking is complete, serve immediately.

**Nutrition:**

- (Per serving) Calories 234 | Fat 15.8g | Sodium 696mg | Carbs 22.1g | Fiber 1.1g | Sugar 1.7g | Protein 31.2g

## Chicken And Vegetable Fajitas

Servings: 6
Cooking Time: 23 Minutes
**Ingredients:**

- Chicken:
- 450 g boneless, skinless chicken thighs, cut crosswise into thirds
- 1 tablespoon vegetable oil
- 4½ teaspoons taco seasoning
- Vegetables:
- 50 g sliced onion
- 150 g sliced bell pepper
- 1 or 2 jalapeños, quartered lengthwise
- 1 tablespoon vegetable oil
- ½ teaspoon kosher salt
- ½ teaspoon ground cumin
- For Serving:
- Tortillas
- Sour cream
- Shredded cheese
- Guacamole
- Salsa

**Directions:**

1. For the chicken: In a medium bowl, toss together the chicken, vegetable oil, and taco seasoning to coat. 2. For the vegetables: In a separate bowl, toss together the onion, bell pepper, jalapeño, vegetable oil, salt, and cumin to coat. 3. Place the chicken in the air fryer basket. Set the air fryer to (190ºC for 10 minutes. Add the vegetables to the basket, toss everything together to blend the seasonings, and set the air fryer for 13 minutes more. Use a meat thermometer to ensure the chicken has reached an internal temperature of 75ºC. 4. Transfer the chicken and vegetables to a serving platter. Serve with tortillas and the desired fajita fixings.

## Italian Flavour Chicken Breasts With Roma Tomatoes

Servings: 8
Cooking Time: 60 Minutes
**Ingredients:**

- 1.4 kg chicken breasts, bone-in
- 1 teaspoon minced fresh basil
- 1 teaspoon minced fresh rosemary
- 2 tablespoons minced fresh parsley
- 1 teaspoon cayenne pepper
- ½ teaspoon salt
- ½ teaspoon freshly ground black pepper
- 4 medium Roma tomatoes, halved
- Cooking spray

**Directions:**

1. Preheat the air fryer to 190ºC. Spritz the two air fryer drawers with cooking spray.
2. Combine all the ingredients, except for the chicken breasts and tomatoes, in a large bowl. Stir to mix well.
3. Dunk the chicken breasts in the mixture and press to coat well.
4. Transfer the chicken breasts in the two preheated air fryer drawers.
5. Air fry for 25 minutes or until the internal temperature of the thickest part of the breasts reaches at least 76ºC. Flip the breasts halfway through the cooking time.
6. Remove the cooked chicken breasts from the drawer and adjust the temperature to 180ºC.
7. Place the tomatoes in the air fryer and spritz with cooking spray. Sprinkle with a touch of salt and cook for 10 minutes or until tender. Shake the drawer halfway through the cooking time.
8. Serve the tomatoes with chicken breasts on a large serving plate.

## Thai Curry Chicken Kabobs

Servings: 4
Cooking Time: 15 Minutes
**Ingredients:**

- 900g skinless chicken thighs
- 120ml Tamari
- 60ml coconut milk
- 3 tablespoons lime juice
- 3 tablespoons maple syrup
- 2 tablespoons Thai red curry

**Directions:**

1. Mix red curry paste, honey, lime juice, coconut milk, soy sauce in a bowl.
2. Add this sauce and chicken to a Ziplock bag.
3. Seal the bag and shake it to coat well.
4. Refrigerate the chicken for 2 hours then thread the chicken over wooden skewers.
5. Divide the skewers in the air fryer baskets.
6. Return the air fryer basket 1 to Zone 1, and basket 2 to Zone 2 of the Ninja Foodi 2-Basket Air Fryer.
7. Choose the "Air Fry" mode for Zone 1 at 350 degrees F(175°C) and 15 minutes of cooking time.

8. Select the "MATCH COOK" option to copy the settings for Zone 2.
9. Initiate cooking by pressing the START/PAUSE BUTTON.
10. Flip the skewers once cooked halfway through.
11. Serve warm.

**Nutrition:**

- (Per serving) Calories 353 | Fat 5g |Sodium 818mg | Carbs 53.2g | Fiber 4.4g | Sugar 8g | Protein 17.3g

## Hawaiian Chicken Bites

Servings: 4
Cooking Time: 15 Minutes

**Ingredients:**

- 120 ml pineapple juice
- 2 tablespoons apple cider vinegar
- ½ tablespoon minced ginger
- 120 g ketchup
- 2 garlic cloves, minced
- 110 g brown sugar
- 2 tablespoons sherry
- 120 ml soy sauce
- 4 chicken breasts, cubed
- Cooking spray

**Directions:**

1. Combine the pineapple juice, cider vinegar, ginger, ketchup, garlic, and sugar in a saucepan. Stir to mix well. Heat over low heat for 5 minutes or until thickened. Fold in the sherry and soy sauce.
2. Dunk the chicken cubes in the mixture. Press to submerge. Wrap the bowl in plastic and refrigerate to marinate for at least an hour.
3. Preheat the air fryer to 180ºC. Spritz the two air fryer drawers with cooking spray.
4. Remove the chicken cubes from the marinade. Shake the excess off and put in the preheated air fryer. Spritz with cooking spray.
5. Air fry for 15 minutes or until the chicken cubes are glazed and well browned. Shake the drawer at least three times during the frying.
6. Serve immediately.

## Chicken Thighs With Brussels Sprouts

Servings:2
Cooking Time:30

**Ingredients:**

- 2 tablespoons of honey
- 4 tablespoons of Dijon mustard
- Salt and black pepper, to tat
- 4 tablespoons of olive oil
- 1-1/2 cup Brussels sprouts
- 8 chicken thighs, skinless

**Directions:**

1. Take a bowl and add chicken thighs to it.
2. Add honey, Dijon mustard, salt, pepper, and 2 tablespoons of olive oil to the thighs.
3. Coat the chicken well and marinate it for 1 hour.
4. Now when start cooking season the Brussels sprouts with salt and black pepper along with remaining olive oil.
5. Put the chicken in the zone 1 basket.
6. Put the Brussels sprouts into the zone 2 basket.
7. Select ROAST function for chicken and set time to 30 minutes at 390 degrees F(200°C) .
8. Select AIR FRY function for Brussels sprouts and set the timer to 20 at 400 degrees F(205°C) .
9. Once done, serve and enjoy.

**Nutrition:**

- (Per serving) Calories1454 | Fat 72.2g| Sodium 869mg | Carbs 23g | Fiber 2.7g | Sugar 19g | Protein 172g

## "fried" Chicken With Warm Baked Potato Salad

Servings:4
Cooking Time: 40 Minutes

**Ingredients:**

- FOR THE "FRIED" CHICKEN
- 1 cup buttermilk
- 1 tablespoon kosher salt
- 4 bone-in, skin-on chicken drumsticks and/or thighs
- 2 cups all-purpose flour
- 1 tablespoon seasoned salt
- 1 tablespoon paprika
- Nonstick cooking spray
- FOR THE POTATO SALAD
- 1½ pounds baby red potatoes, halved
- 1 tablespoon vegetable oil
- ½ cup mayonnaise
- ⅓ cup plain reduced-fat Greek yogurt
- 1 tablespoon apple cider vinegar
- ½ teaspoon kosher salt
- ½ teaspoon freshly ground black pepper
- ¾ cup shredded Cheddar cheese
- 4 slices cooked bacon, crumbled
- 3 scallions, sliced

**Directions:**

1. To prep the chicken: In a large bowl, combine the buttermilk and salt. Add the chicken and turn to coat. Let rest for at least 30 minutes (for the best flavor, marinate the chicken overnight in the refrigerator).
2. In a separate large bowl, combine the flour, seasoned salt, and paprika.
3. Remove the chicken from the marinade and allow any excess marinade to drip off. Discard the marinade. Dip the chicken pieces in the flour, coating them thoroughly. Mist with cooking spray. Let the chicken rest for 10 minutes.
4. To prep the potatoes: In a large bowl, combine the potatoes and oil and toss to coat.
5. To cook the chicken and potatoes: Install a crisper plate in the Zone 1 basket. Place the chicken in the basket in a single layer and insert the basket in the unit. Place the potatoes in the Zone 2 basket and insert the basket in the unit.
6. Select Zone 1, select AIR FRY, set the temperature to 390°F (200°C), and set the time to 30 minutes.
7. Select Zone 2, select BAKE, set the temperature to 400°F (205°C), and set the time to 40 minutes. Select SMART FINISH.
8. Press START/PAUSE to begin cooking.
9. When cooking is complete, the chicken will be golden brown and cooked through (an instant-read thermometer should read 165°F (75°C)) and the potatoes will be fork-tender.
10. Rinse the potatoes under cold water for about 1 minute to cool them.
11. Place the potatoes in a large bowl and stir in the mayonnaise, yogurt, vinegar, salt, and black pepper. Gently stir in the Cheddar, bacon, and scallions. Serve warm with the "fried" chicken.

**Nutrition:**

- (Per serving) Calories: 639; Total fat: 38g; Saturated fat: 9.5g; Carbohydrates: 54g; Fiber: 4g; Protein: 21g; Sodium: 1,471mg

## Asian Chicken Drumsticks

Servings: 4
Cooking Time: 20 Minutes
**Ingredients:**

- 8 chicken drumsticks
- 1 lime juice
- 30ml rice wine
- 45ml fish sauce
- 2 tbsp garlic, minced
- 55g brown sugar
- ½ tsp Sriracha sauce
- 1 tsp black pepper
- 1 tsp sesame oil
- Salt

**Directions:**

1. Add chicken drumsticks and remaining ingredients into the bowl and mix well. Cover and place in refrigerator for 4 hours.
2. Insert a crisper plate in the Ninja Foodi air fryer baskets.
3. Place the marinated chicken drumsticks in both baskets.
4. Select zone 1, then select "air fry" mode and set the temperature to 360 degrees F(180°C) for 20 minutes. Press "match" to match zone 2 settings to zone 1. Press "start/stop" to begin.

**Nutrition:**

- (Per serving) Calories 225 | Fat 6.4g |Sodium 1223mg | Carbs 14.6g | Fiber 0.2g | Sugar 11.3g | Protein 26.3g

## Goat Cheese - stuffed Chicken Breast With Broiled Zucchini And Cherry Tomatoes

Servings:4
Cooking Time: 25 Minutes
**Ingredients:**

- FOR THE STUFFED CHICKEN BREASTS
- 2 ounces soft goat cheese
- 1 tablespoon minced fresh parsley
- ½ teaspoon minced garlic
- 4 boneless, skinless chicken breasts (6 ounces each)
- 1 tablespoon vegetable oil
- ½ teaspoon Italian seasoning
- ½ teaspoon kosher salt
- ½ teaspoon freshly ground black pepper
- FOR THE ZUCCHINI AND TOMATOES
- 1 pound zucchini, diced
- 1 cup cherry tomatoes, halved
- 1 tablespoon vegetable oil
- ½ teaspoon kosher salt
- ¼ teaspoon freshly ground black pepper

**Directions:**

1. To prep the stuffed chicken breasts: In a small bowl, combine the goat cheese, parsley, and garlic. Mix well.
2. Cut a deep slit into the fatter side of each chicken breast to create a pocket (taking care to not go all the way through). Stuff each breast with the goat cheese mixture. Use a toothpick to secure the opening of the chicken, if needed.
3. Brush the outside of the chicken breasts with the oil and season with the Italian seasoning, salt, and black pepper.
4. To prep the zucchini and tomatoes: In a large bowl, combine the zucchini, tomatoes, and oil. Mix to coat. Season with salt and black pepper.
5. To cook the chicken and vegetables: Install a crisper plate in each of the two baskets. Insert a broil rack in the Zone 2 basket over the crisper plate. Place the chicken in the Zone 1 basket and insert the basket in the unit. Place the vegetables on the broiler rack in the Zone 2 basket and insert the basket in the unit.
6. Select Zone 1, select AIR FRY, set the temperature to 390°F (200°C), and set the time to 25 minutes.
7. Select Zone 2, select AIR BROIL, set the temperature to 450°F (230°C), and set the time to 10 minutes. Select SMART FINISH.
8. Press START/PAUSE to begin cooking.
9. When cooking is complete, the chicken will be golden brown and cooked through (an instant-read thermometer should read 165°F (75°C)) and the zucchini will be soft and slightly charred. Serve hot.

**Nutrition:**

- (Per serving) Calories: 330; Total fat: 15g; Saturated fat: 4g; Carbohydrates: 5g; Fiber: 1.5g; Protein: 42g; Sodium: 409mg

## Bacon-wrapped Chicken

Servings: 2
Cooking Time: 28 Minutes.
**Ingredients:**

- Butter:
- ½ stick butter softened
- ½ garlic clove, minced
- ¼ teaspoon dried thyme
- ¼ teaspoon dried basil
- ⅛ teaspoon coarse salt
- 1 pinch black pepper, ground
- ⅓ lb. thick-cut bacon
- 1 ½ lbs. boneless skinless chicken thighs
- 2 teaspoons garlic, minced

**Directions:**

1. Mix garlic softened butter with thyme, salt, basil, and black pepper in a bowl.
2. Add butter mixture on a piece of wax paper and roll it up tightly to make a butter log.
3. Place the log in the refrigerator for 2 hours.
4. Spray one bacon strip on a piece of wax paper.
5. Place each chicken thigh on top of one bacon strip and rub it with garlic.
6. Make a slit in the chicken thigh and add a teaspoon of butter to the chicken.
7. Wrap the bacon around the chicken thigh.
8. Repeat those same steps with all the chicken thighs.
9. Place the bacon-wrapped chicken thighs in the two crisper plates.
10. Return the crisper plates to the Ninja Foodi Dual Zone Air Fryer.
11. Choose the Air Fry mode for Zone 1 and set the temperature to 390 degrees F(200°C) and the time to 28 minutes.
12. Select the "MATCH" button to copy the settings for Zone 2.
13. Initiate cooking by pressing the START/STOP button.
14. Flip the chicken once cooked halfway through, and resume cooking.
15. Serve warm.

**Nutrition:**

- (Per serving) Calories 380 | Fat 29g |Sodium 821mg | Carbs 34.6g | Fiber 0g | Sugar 0g | Protein 30g

## Whole Chicken

Servings: 8
Cooking Time: 20 Minutes
**Ingredients:**

- 1 whole chicken (about 2.8 pounds), cut in half
- 4 tablespoons olive oil
- 2 teaspoons paprika
- 1 teaspoon garlic powder

- 1 teaspoon onion powder
- Salt and pepper, to taste

**Directions:**

1. Mix the olive oil, paprika, garlic powder, and onion powder together in a bowl.
2. Place the chicken halves, breast side up, on a plate. Spread a teaspoon or two of the oil mix all over the halves using either your hands or a brush. Season with salt and pepper.
3. Flip the chicken halves over and repeat on the other side. You'll want to reserve a little of the oil mix for later, but other than that, use it liberally.
4. Install a crisper plate in both drawers. Place one half of the chicken in the zone 1 drawer and the other half in the zone 2 drawer, then insert the drawers into the unit.
5. Select zone 1, select AIR FRY, set temperature to 390 degrees F/ 200 degrees C, and set time to 20 minutes. Select MATCH to match zone 2 settings to zone 1. Press the START/STOP button to begin cooking.
6. When cooking is done, check the internal temperature of the chicken. It should read 165°F (75°C). If the chicken isn't done, add more cooking time.

**Nutrition:**

- (Per serving) Calories 131 | Fat 8g | Sodium 51mg | Carbs 0g | Fiber 0g | Sugar 0g | Protein 14g

## Lemon-pepper Chicken Thighs With Buttery Roasted Radishes

Servings:4

Cooking Time: 28 Minutes

**Ingredients:**

- FOR THE CHICKEN
- 4 bone-in, skin-on chicken thighs (6 ounces each)
- 1 teaspoon olive oil
- 2 teaspoons lemon pepper
- ¼ teaspoon kosher salt
- FOR THE RADISHES
- 1 bunch radishes (greens removed), halved through the stem
- 1 teaspoon olive oil
- ¼ teaspoon kosher salt
- ¼ teaspoon freshly ground black pepper
- 1 tablespoon unsalted butter, cut into small pieces
- 2 tablespoons chopped fresh parsley

**Directions:**

1. To prep the chicken: Brush both sides of the chicken thighs with olive oil, then season with lemon pepper and salt.
2. To prep the radishes: In a large bowl, combine the radishes, olive oil, salt, and black pepper. Stir well to coat the radishes.
3. To cook the chicken and radishes: Install a crisper plate in each of the two baskets. Place the chicken skin-side up in the Zone 1 basket and insert the basket in the unit. Place the radishes in the Zone 2 basket and insert the basket in the unit.
4. Select Zone 1, select AIR FRY, set the temperature to 390°F (200°C), and set the time to 28 minutes.
5. Select Zone 2, select ROAST, set the temperature to 400°F (205°C), and set the time to 15 minutes. Select SMART FINISH.
6. Press START/PAUSE to begin cooking.
7. When the Zone 2 timer reads 5 minutes, press START/PAUSE. Remove the basket, scatter the butter pieces over the radishes, and reinsert the basket. Press START/PAUSE to resume cooking.
8. When cooking is complete, the chicken should be cooked through (an instant-read thermometer should read at least 165°F (75°C)) and the radishes will be soft. Stir the parsley into the radishes and serve.

**Nutrition:**

- (Per serving) Calories: 271; Total fat: 29g; Saturated fat: 6g; Carbohydrates: 5g; Fiber: 1g; Protein: 23g; Sodium: 246mg

## Pecan-crusted Chicken Tenders

Servings: 4

Cooking Time: 12 Minutes

**Ingredients:**

- 2 tablespoons mayonnaise
- 1 teaspoon Dijon mustard
- 455 g boneless, skinless chicken tenders
- ½ teaspoon salt
- ¼ teaspoon ground black pepper
- 75 g chopped roasted pecans, finely ground

**Directions:**

1. In a small bowl, whisk mayonnaise and mustard until combined. Brush mixture onto chicken tenders on both sides, then sprinkle tenders with salt and pepper.
2. Place pecans in a medium bowl and press each tender into pecans to coat each side.
3. Place tenders into the two ungreased air fryer drawers in a single layer. Adjust the temperature to 190ºC and roast for 12 minutes, turning tenders halfway through cooking. Tenders will be golden brown and have an internal temperature of at least 76ºC when done. Serve warm.

## Coriander Lime Chicken Thighs

Servings: 4

Cooking Time: 22 Minutes

**Ingredients:**

- 4 bone-in, skin-on chicken thighs
- 1 teaspoon baking powder
- ½ teaspoon garlic powder
- 2 teaspoons chili powder
- 1 teaspoon cumin
- 2 medium limes
- 5 g chopped fresh coriander

**Directions:**

1. Pat chicken thighs dry and sprinkle with baking powder.
2. In a small bowl, mix garlic powder, chili powder, and cumin and sprinkle evenly over thighs, gently rubbing on and under chicken skin.
3. Cut one lime in half and squeeze juice over thighs. Place chicken into the zone 1 air fryer drawer.
4. Adjust the temperature to 190ºC and roast for 22 minutes.
5. Cut other lime into four wedges for serving and garnish cooked chicken with wedges and coriander.

## Chicken Shawarma

Servings: 4

Cooking Time: 15 Minutes

**Ingredients:**

- Shawarma Spice:
- 2 teaspoons dried oregano
- 1 teaspoon ground cinnamon
- 1 teaspoon ground cumin
- 1 teaspoon ground coriander
- 1 teaspoon kosher salt
- ½ teaspoon ground allspice
- ½ teaspoon cayenne pepper
- Chicken:
- 450 g boneless, skinless chicken thighs, cut into large bite-size chunks
- 2 tablespoons vegetable oil
- For Serving:
- Tzatziki
- Pita bread

**Directions:**

1. For the shawarma spice: In a small bowl, combine the oregano, cayenne, cumin, coriander, salt, cinnamon, and allspice. 2. For the chicken: In a large bowl, toss together the chicken, vegetable oil, and shawarma spice to coat. Marinate at room temperature for 30 minutes or cover and refrigerate for up to 24 hours. 3. Place the chicken in the zone 1 air fryer basket. Set the air fryer to 180°C for 15 minutes, or until the chicken reaches an internal temperature of 75°C. 4. Transfer the chicken to a serving platter. Serve with tzatziki and pita bread.

## Chicken Thighs In Waffles

Servings: 4
Cooking Time: 40 Minutes
**Ingredients:**

- For the chicken:
- 4 chicken thighs, skin on
- 240 ml low-fat buttermilk
- 65 g all-purpose flour
- ½ teaspoon garlic powder
- ½ teaspoon mustard powder
- 1 teaspoon kosher salt
- ½ teaspoon freshly ground black pepper
- 85 g honey, for serving
- Cooking spray
- For the waffles:
- 65 g all-purpose flour
- 65 g whole wheat pastry flour
- 1 large egg, beaten
- 240 ml low-fat buttermilk
- 1 teaspoon baking powder
- 2 tablespoons rapeseed oil
- ½ teaspoon kosher salt
- 1 tablespoon granulated sugar

**Directions:**

1. Combine the chicken thighs with buttermilk in a large bowl. Wrap the bowl in plastic and refrigerate to marinate for at least an hour. 2. Preheat the air fryer to 180°C. Spritz the two air fryer baskets with cooking spray. 3. Combine the flour, mustard powder, garlic powder, salt, and black pepper in a shallow dish. Stir to mix well. 4. Remove the thighs from the buttermilk and pat dry with paper towels. Sit the bowl of buttermilk aside. 5. Dip the thighs in the flour mixture first, then into the buttermilk, and then into the flour mixture. Shake the excess off. 6. Arrange the thighs in the two preheated air fryer baskets and spritz with cooking spray. Air fryer for 20 minutes or until an instant-read thermometer inserted in the thickest part of the chicken thighs registers at least 75°C. Flip the thighs halfway through. 7. Meanwhile, make the waffles: combine the ingredients for the waffles in a large bowl. Stir to mix well, then arrange the mixture in a waffle iron and cook until a golden and fragrant waffle forms. 8. Remove the waffles from the waffle iron and slice into 4 pieces. Remove the chicken thighs from the air fryer and allow to cool for 5 minutes. 9. Arrange each chicken thigh on each waffle piece and drizzle with 1 tablespoon of honey. Serve warm.

## Chicken With Bacon And Tomato & Bacon-wrapped Stuffed Chicken Breasts

Servings: 8
Cooking Time: 30 Minutes
**Ingredients:**

- Chicken with Bacon and Tomato:
- 4 medium-sized skin-on chicken drumsticks
- 1½ teaspoons herbs de Provence
- Salt and pepper, to taste
- 1 tablespoon rice vinegar
- 2 tablespoons olive oil
- 2 garlic cloves, crushed
- 340 g crushed canned tomatoes
- 1 small-size leek, thinly sliced
- 2 slices smoked bacon, chopped
- Bacon-Wrapped Stuffed Chicken Breasts:
- 80 g chopped frozen spinach, thawed and squeezed dry
- 55 g cream cheese, softened
- 20 g grated Parmesan cheese
- 1 jalapeño, seeded and chopped
- ½ teaspoon kosher salt
- 1 teaspoon black pepper
- 2 large boneless, skinless chicken breasts, butterflied and pounded to ½-inch thickness
- 4 teaspoons salt-free Cajun seasoning
- 6 slices bacon

**Directions:**

1. Make the Chicken with Bacon and Tomato :
2. Sprinkle the chicken drumsticks with herbs de Provence, salt and pepper; then, drizzle them with rice vinegar and olive oil.
3. Place into a baking pan and cook in the zone 1 basket at 180°C for 8 to 10 minutes. Pause the air fryer; stir in the remaining ingredients and continue to cook for 15 minutes longer; make sure to check them periodically. Bon appétit!
4. Make the Bacon-Wrapped Stuffed Chicken Breasts :
5. In a small bowl, combine the spinach, cream cheese, Parmesan cheese, jalapeño, salt, and pepper. Stir until well combined.
6. Place the butterflied chicken breasts on a flat surface. Spread the cream cheese mixture evenly across each piece of chicken. Starting with the narrow end, roll up each chicken breast, ensuring the filling stays inside. Season chicken with the Cajun seasoning, patting it in to ensure it sticks to the meat.
7. Wrap each breast in 3 slices of bacon. Place in the zone 2 air fryer basket. Set the air fryer to 180°C for 30 minutes. Use a meat thermometer to ensure the chicken has reached an internal temperature of 75°C.
8. Let the chicken stand 5 minutes before slicing each rolled-up breast in half to serve.

## Spice-rubbed Chicken Pieces

Servings:6
Cooking Time:40
**Ingredients:**

- 3 pounds chicken, pieces
- 1 teaspoon sweet paprika
- 1 teaspoon mustard powder
- 1 tablespoon brown sugar, dark
- Salt and black pepper, to taste
- 1 teaspoon Chile powder, New Mexico
- 1 teaspoon oregano, dried
- ¼ teaspoon allspice powder, ground

**Directions:**

1. Take a bowl and mix dark brown sugar, salt, paprika, mustard powder, oregano, Chile powder, black pepper, and all spice powder.
2. Mix well and rub this spice mixture all over the chicken.
3. Divide the chicken between two air fryer baskets.
4. Oil sprays the meat and then adds it to the air fryer.
5. Now press button1 and button 2 and set the time to 40 minutes at 350 degrees F(175°C) .
6. Now press start and once the cooking cycle completes, press pause for both the zones.
7. Take out the chicken and serve hot.

**Nutrition:**

- (Per serving) Calories353 | Fat 7.1g| Sodium400 mg | Carbs 2.2g | Fiber0.4 g | Sugar 1.6g | Protein66 g

## Fajita Chicken Strips & Barbecued Chicken With Creamy Coleslaw

Servings: 6
Cooking Time: 20 Minutes
**Ingredients:**

- Fajita Chicken Strips:
- 450 g boneless, skinless chicken tenderloins, cut into strips
- 3 bell peppers, any color, cut into chunks
- 1 onion, cut into chunks
- 1 tablespoon olive oil
- 1 tablespoon fajita seasoning mix
- Cooking spray
- Barbecued Chicken with Creamy Coleslaw:
- 270 g shredded coleslaw mix
- Salt and pepper
- 2 (340 g) bone-in split chicken breasts, trimmed
- 1 teaspoon vegetable oil
- 2 tablespoons barbecue sauce, plus extra for serving
- 2 tablespoons mayonnaise
- 2 tablespoons sour cream
- 1 teaspoon distilled white vinegar, plus extra for seasoning
- ¼ teaspoon sugar

**Directions:**

1. Make the Fajita Chicken Strips :
2. Preheat the air fryer to 190ºC.
3. In a large bowl, mix together the chicken, bell peppers, onion, olive oil, and fajita seasoning mix until completely coated.
4. Spray the zone 1 air fryer basket lightly with cooking spray.
5. Place the chicken and vegetables in the zone 1 air fryer basket and lightly spray with cooking spray.
6. Air fry for 7 minutes. Shake the basket and air fry for an additional 5 to 8 minutes, until the chicken is cooked through and the veggies are starting to char.
7. Serve warm.
8. Make the Barbecued Chicken with Creamy Coleslaw :
9. Preheat the air fryer to 180ºC.
10. Toss coleslaw mix and ¼ teaspoon salt in a colander set over bowl. Let sit until wilted slightly, about 30 minutes. Rinse, drain, and dry well with a dish towel.
11. Meanwhile, pat chicken dry with paper towels, rub with oil, and season with salt and pepper. Arrange breasts skin-side down in zone 2 air fryer basket, spaced evenly apart, alternating ends. Bake for 10 minutes. Flip breasts and brush skin side with barbecue sauce. Return basket to air fryer and bake until well browned and chicken registers 70ºC, 10 to 15 minutes.
12. Transfer chicken to serving platter, tent loosely with aluminum foil, and let rest for 5 minutes. While chicken rests, whisk mayonnaise, sour cream, vinegar, sugar, and pinch pepper together in a large bowl. Stir in coleslaw mix and season with salt, pepper, and additional vinegar to taste. Serve chicken with coleslaw, passing extra barbecue sauce separately.

## Chicken & Veggies

Servings: 4
Cooking Time: 10 Minutes
**Ingredients:**

- 450g chicken breast, boneless & cut into pieces
- 2 garlic cloves, minced
- 15ml olive oil
- 239g frozen mix vegetables
- 1 tbsp Italian seasoning
- ½ tsp chilli powder
- ½ tsp garlic powder
- Pepper
- Salt

**Directions:**

1. In a bowl, toss chicken with remaining ingredients until well coated.
2. Insert a crisper plate in the Ninja Foodi air fryer baskets.
3. Add chicken and vegetables in both baskets.
4. Select zone 1 then select "air fry" mode and set the temperature to 390 degrees F(200°C) for 10 minutes. Press "match" to match zone 2 settings to zone 1. Press "start/stop" to begin.

**Nutrition:**

- (Per serving) Calories 221 | Fat 7.6g |Sodium 126mg | Carbs 10.6g | Fiber 3.3g | Sugar 2.7g | Protein 26.3g

## Yummy Chicken Breasts

Servings:2
Cooking Time:25
**Ingredients:**

- 4 large chicken breasts, 6 ounces each
- 2 tablespoons of oil bay seasoning
- 1 tablespoon Montreal chicken seasoning
- 1 teaspoon of thyme
- 1/2 teaspoon of paprika
- Salt, to taste
- oil spray, for greasing

**Directions:**

1. Season the chicken breast pieces with the listed seasoning and let them rest for 40 minutes.
2. Grease both sides of the chicken breast pieces with oil spray.
3. Divide the chicken breast piece between both baskets.
4. Set zone 1 to AIRFRY mode at 400 degrees F(205°C) , for 15 minutes.
5. Select the MATCH button for another basket.
6. Select pause and take out the baskets and flip the chicken breast pieces, after 15 minutes.
7. Select the zones to 400 degrees F(205°C) for 10 more minutes using the MATCH cook button.
8. Once it's done serve.

**Nutrition:**

- (Per serving) Calories 711| Fat 27.7g| Sodium 895mg | Carbs 1.6g | Fiber 0.4g | Sugar 0.1g | Protein 106.3g

## Bbq Cheddar-stuffed Chicken Breasts

Servings: 2
Cooking Time: 25 Minutes
**Ingredients:**

- 3 strips cooked bacon, divided
- 2 ounces cheddar cheese, cubed, divided
- ¼ cup BBQ sauce, divided
- 2 (4-ounces) skinless, boneless chicken breasts
- Salt and ground black pepper, to taste

**Directions:**

1. In a mixing bowl, combine the cooked bacon, cheddar cheese, and 1 tablespoon BBQ sauce.
2. Make a horizontal 1-inch cut at the top of each chicken breast with a long, sharp knife, producing a little interior pouch.

Fill each breast with an equal amount of the bacon-cheese mixture. Wrap the remaining bacon strips around each chicken breast. Coat the chicken breasts with the leftover BBQ sauce and lay them in a baking dish.
3. Install a crisper plate in both drawers. Place half the chicken breasts in zone 1 and half in zone 2, then insert the drawers into the unit.
4. Select zone 1, select AIR FRY, set temperature to 390 degrees F/ 200 degrees C, and set time to 22 minutes. Select MATCH to match zone 2 settings to zone 1. Press the START/STOP button to begin cooking.
5. When the time reaches 11 minutes, press START/STOP to pause the unit. Remove the drawers and flip the chicken. Re-insert drawers into the unit and press START/STOP to resume cooking.
6. When cooking is complete, remove the chicken breasts.

**Nutrition:**

- (Per serving) Calories 379 | Fat 12.8g | Sodium 906mg | Carbs 11.1g | Fiber 0.4g | Sugar 8.3g | Protein 37.7g

## Turkey And Cranberry Quesadillas

Servings: 4
Cooking Time: 4 To 8 Minutes

**Ingredients:**

- 6 low-sodium whole-wheat tortillas
- 75 g shredded low-sodium low-fat Swiss cheese
- 105 g shredded cooked low-sodium turkey breast
- 2 tablespoons cranberry sauce
- 2 tablespoons dried cranberries
- ½ teaspoon dried basil
- Olive oil spray, for spraying the tortillas

**Directions:**

1. Preheat the air fryer to 200ºC.
2. Put 3 tortillas on a work surface.
3. Evenly divide the Swiss cheese, turkey, cranberry sauce, and dried cranberries among the tortillas. Sprinkle with the basil and top with the remaining tortillas.
4. Spray the outsides of the tortillas with olive oil spray.
5. One at a time, air fry the quesadillas in the air fryer for 4 to 8 minutes, or until crisp and the cheese is melted. Cut into quarters and serve.

## Brazilian Chicken Drumsticks

Servings: 6
Cooking Time: 47 Minutes.

**Ingredients:**

- 2 teaspoons cumin seeds
- 2 teaspoons dried parsley
- 2 teaspoons turmeric powder
- 2 teaspoons dried oregano leaves
- 2 teaspoons salt
- 1 teaspoon coriander seeds
- 1 teaspoon black peppercorns
- 1 teaspoon cayenne pepper
- ½ cup lime juice
- 4 tablespoons vegetable oil
- 3 lbs. chicken drumsticks

**Directions:**

1. Grind cumin, parsley, salt, coriander seeds, cayenne pepper, peppercorns, oregano, and turmeric in a food processor.
2. Add this mixture to lemon juice and oil in a bowl and mix well.
3. Rub the spice paste over the chicken drumsticks and let them marinate for 30 minutes.
4. Divide the chicken drumsticks in both the crisper plates.
5. Return the crisper plates to the Ninja Foodi Dual Zone Air Fryer.
6. Choose the Air Fry mode for Zone 1 and set the temperature to 390 degrees F(200°C) and the time to 47 minutes.
7. Select the "MATCH" button to copy the settings for Zone 2.
8. Initiate cooking by pressing the START/STOP button.
9. Flip the drumsticks when cooked halfway through, then resume cooking.
10. Serve warm.

**Nutrition:**

- (Per serving) Calories 456 | Fat 16.4g |Sodium 1321mg | Carbs 19.2g | Fiber 2.2g | Sugar 4.2g | Protein 55.2g

## Turkey Burger Patties

Servings: 4
Cooking Time: 14 Minutes

**Ingredients:**

- 1 egg white
- 453g ground turkey
- 30ml Worcestershire sauce
- ½ tsp dried basil
- ½ tsp dried oregano
- Pepper
- Salt

**Directions:**

1. In a bowl, mix ground turkey with remaining ingredients until well combined.
2. Insert a crisper plate in the Ninja Foodi air fryer baskets.
3. Make patties from the turkey mixture and place them in both baskets.
4. Select zone 1, then select "air fry" mode and set the temperature to 360 degrees F(180°C) for 14 minutes. Press "match" to match zone 2 settings to zone 1. Press "start/stop" to begin.

**Nutrition:**

- (Per serving) Calories 234 | Fat 12.5g |Sodium 251mg | Carbs 1.7g | Fiber 0.1g | Sugar 1.6g | Protein 32g

## Chicken Patties And One-dish Chicken Rice

Servings: 8
Cooking Time: 40 Minutes

**Ingredients:**

- Chicken Patties:
- 450 g chicken thigh mince
- 110 g shredded Mozzarella cheese
- 1 teaspoon dried parsley
- ½ teaspoon garlic powder
- ¼ teaspoon onion powder
- 1 large egg
- 60 g pork rinds, finely ground
- One-Dish Chicken and Rice:
- 190 g long-grain white rice, rinsed and drained
- 120 g cut frozen green beans (do not thaw)
- 1 tablespoon minced fresh ginger
- 3 cloves garlic, minced
- 1 tablespoon toasted sesame oil
- 1 teaspoon kosher salt

- 1 teaspoon black pepper
- 450 g chicken wings, preferably drumettes

**Directions:**

1. Make the Chicken Patties :
2. In a large bowl, mix chicken mince, Mozzarella, parsley, garlic powder, and onion powder. Form into four patties.
3. Place patties in the freezer for 15 to 20 minutes until they begin to firm up.
4. Whisk egg in a medium bowl. Place the ground pork rinds into a large bowl.
5. Dip each chicken patty into the egg and then press into pork rinds to fully coat. Place patties into the zone 1 air fryer drawer.
6. Adjust the temperature to 180ºC and air fry for 12 minutes.
7. Patties will be firm and cooked to an internal temperature of 76ºC when done. Serve immediately.
8. Make the One-Dish Chicken and Rice :
9. In a baking pan, combine the rice, green beans, ginger, garlic, sesame oil, salt, and pepper. Stir to combine. Place the chicken wings on top of the rice mixture.
10. Cover the pan with foil. Make a long slash in the foil to allow the pan to vent steam. Place the pan in the zone 2 air fryer drawer. Set the air fryer to 190ºC for 30 minutes.
11. Remove the foil. Set the air fryer to 200ºC for 10 minutes, or until the wings have browned and rendered fat into the rice and vegetables, turning the wings halfway through the cooking time.

## Spicy Chicken Sandwiches With "fried" Pickles

Servings:4

Cooking Time: 18 Minutes

**Ingredients:**

- FOR THE CHICKEN SANDWICHES
- 2 tablespoons all-purpose flour
- 2 large eggs
- 2 teaspoons Louisiana-style hot sauce
- 1 cup panko bread crumbs
- 1 teaspoon paprika
- ½ teaspoon garlic powder
- ¼ teaspoon salt
- ¼ teaspoon freshly ground black pepper
- ¼ teaspoon cayenne pepper (optional)
- 4 thin-sliced chicken cutlets (4 ounces each)
- 2 teaspoons vegetable oil
- 4 hamburger rolls
- FOR THE PICKLES
- 1 cup dill pickle chips, drained
- 1 large egg
- ½ cup panko bread crumbs
- Nonstick cooking spray
- ½ cup ranch dressing, for serving (optional)

**Directions:**

1. To prep the sandwiches: Set up a breading station with three small shallow bowls. Place the flour in the first bowl. In the second bowl, whisk together the eggs and hot sauce. Combine the panko, paprika, garlic powder, salt, black pepper, and cayenne pepper (if using) in the third bowl.
2. Bread the chicken cutlets in this order: First, dip them into the flour, coating both sides. Then, dip into the egg mixture. Finally, coat them in the panko mixture, gently pressing the breading into the chicken to help it adhere. Drizzle the cutlets with the oil.
3. To prep the pickles: Pat the pickles dry with a paper towel.
4. In a small shallow bowl, whisk the egg. Add the panko to a second shallow bowl.
5. Dip the pickles in the egg, then the panko. Mist both sides of the pickles with cooking spray.
6. To cook the chicken and pickles: Install a crisper plate in each of the two baskets. Place the chicken in the Zone 1 basket and insert the basket in the unit. Place the pickles in the Zone 2 basket and insert the basket in the unit.
7. Select Zone 1, select AIR FRY, set the temperature to 390°F (200°C), and set the time to 18 minutes.
8. Select Zone 2, select AIR FRY, set the temperature to 400°F (205°C), and set the time to 15 minutes. Select SMART FINISH.
9. Press START/PAUSE to begin cooking.
10. When both timers read 10 minutes, press START/PAUSE. Remove the Zone 1 basket and use silicone-tipped tongs to flip the chicken. Reinsert the basket. Remove the Zone 2 basket and shake to redistribute the pickles. Reinsert the basket and press START/PAUSE to resume cooking.
11. When cooking is complete, the breading will be crisp and golden brown and the chicken cooked through (an instant-read thermometer should read 75°F (190°C)). Place one chicken cutlet on each hamburger roll. Serve the "fried" pickles on the side with ranch dressing, if desired.

**Nutrition:**

- (Per serving) Calories: 418; Total fat: 12g; Saturated fat: 1.5g; Carbohydrates: 42g; Fiber: 2g; Protein: 36g; Sodium: 839mg

## Asian Chicken

Servings: 4

Cooking Time: 12 Minutes

**Ingredients:**

- 8 chicken thighs, boneless
- 4 garlic cloves, minced
- 85g honey
- 120ml soy sauce
- 1 tsp dried oregano
- 2 tbsp parsley, chopped
- 1 tbsp ketchup

**Directions:**

1. Add chicken and remaining ingredients in a bowl and mix until well coated. Cover and place in the refrigerator for 6 hours.
2. Insert a crisper plate in the Ninja Foodi air fryer baskets.
3. Remove the chicken from the marinade and place them in both baskets.
4. Select zone 1 then select "air fry" mode and set the temperature to 390 degrees F(200°C) for 12 minutes. Press "match" to match zone 2 settings to zone 1. Press "start/stop" to begin.

**Nutrition:**

- (Per serving) Calories 646 | Fat 21.7g |Sodium 2092mg | Carbs 22.2g | Fiber 0.6g | Sugar 18.9g | Protein 86.9g

## Chicken Parmesan With Roasted Lemon-parmesan Broccoli

Servings:4
Cooking Time: 18 Minutes

**Ingredients:**

- FOR THE CHICKEN PARMESAN
- 2 tablespoons all-purpose flour
- 2 large eggs
- 1 cup panko bread crumbs
- 2 tablespoons grated Parmesan cheese
- 2 teaspoons Italian seasoning
- 4 thin-sliced chicken cutlets (4 ounces each)
- 2 tablespoons vegetable oil
- ½ cup marinara sauce
- ½ cup shredded part-skim mozzarella cheese
- FOR THE BROCCOLI
- 4 cups broccoli florets
- 2 tablespoons olive oil, divided
- ¼ teaspoon kosher salt
- ¼ teaspoon freshly ground black pepper
- 2 teaspoons fresh lemon juice
- 2 tablespoons grated Parmesan cheese

**Directions:**

1. To prep the chicken Parmesan: Set up a breading station with 3 small shallow bowls. Place the flour in the first bowl. In the second bowl, beat the eggs. Combine the panko, Parmesan, and Italian seasoning in the third bowl.
2. Bread the chicken cutlets in this order: First, dip them into the flour, coating both sides. Then, dip into the beaten egg. Finally, place in the panko mixture, coating both sides of the cutlets. Drizzle the oil over the cutlets.
3. To prep the broccoli: In a large bowl, combine the broccoli, 1 tablespoon of olive oil, the salt, and black pepper.
4. To cook the chicken and broccoli: Install a crisper plate in the Zone 1 basket. Place the chicken in the basket and insert the basket in the unit. Place the broccoli in the Zone 2 basket and insert the basket in the unit.
5. Select Zone 1, select AIR FRY, set the temperature to 390°F (200°C), and set the time to 18 minutes.
6. Select Zone 2, select ROAST, set the temperature to 390°F (200°C), and set the time to 15 minutes. Select SMART FINISH.
7. Press START/PAUSE to begin cooking.
8. When the Zone 1 timer reads 10 minutes, press START/PAUSE. Remove the basket and use silicone-tipped tongs to flip the chicken. Reinsert the basket and press START/PAUSE to resume cooking.
9. When the Zone 1 timer reads 2 minutes, press START/PAUSE. Remove the basket and spoon 2 tablespoons of marinara sauce over each chicken cutlet. Sprinkle the mozzarella on top. Reinsert the basket and press START/PAUSE to resume cooking.
10. When cooking is complete, the cheese will be melted and the chicken cooked through (an instant-read thermometer should read 165°F (75°C)). Transfer the broccoli to a large bowl. Add the lemon juice and Parmesan and toss to coat. Serve the chicken and broccoli warm.

**Nutrition:**

- (Per serving) Calories: 462; Total fat: 22g; Saturated fat: 5g; Carbohydrates: 25g; Fiber: 2.5g; Protein: 37g; Sodium: 838mg

# Fish And Seafood Recipes

## Lemony Prawns And Courgette

Servings: 4
Cooking Time: 7 To 8 Minutes
**Ingredients:**
- 570 g extra-large raw prawns, peeled and deveined
- 2 medium courgettes (about 230 g each), halved lengthwise and cut into ½-inch-thick slices
- 1½ tablespoons olive oil
- ½ teaspoon garlic salt
- 1½ teaspoons dried oregano
- ⅛ teaspoon crushed red pepper flakes (optional)
- Juice of ½ lemon
- 1 tablespoon chopped fresh mint
- 1 tablespoon chopped fresh dill

**Directions:**
1. Preheat the air fryer to 176ºC.
2. In a large bowl, combine the prawns, courgette, oil, garlic salt, oregano, and pepper flakes and toss to coat.
3. Arrange a single layer of the prawns and courgette in the two air fryer drawers. Air fry for 7 to 8 minutes, shaking the drawer halfway, until the courgette is golden and the prawns are cooked through.
4. Transfer to a serving dish and tent with foil while you air fry the remaining prawns and courgette.
5. Top with the lemon juice, mint, and dill and serve.

## Two-way Salmon

Servings:2
Cooking Time:18
**Ingredients:**
- 2 salmon fillets, 8 ounces each
- 2 tablespoons of Cajun seasoning
- 2 tablespoons of jerk seasoning
- 1 lemon cut in half
- oil spray, for greasing

**Directions:**
1. First, drizzle lemon juice over the salmon and wash it with tap water.
2. Rinse and pat dry the fillets with a paper towel.
3. Now rub o fillet with Cajun seasoning and grease it with oil spray.
4. Take the second fillet and rub it with jerk seasoning.
5. Grease the second fillet of salmon with oil spray.
6. now put the salmon fillets in both the baskets.
7. Set the Zone 1 basket to 390 degrees F(200°C) for 16-18 minutes
8. Select MATCH button for zone 2 basket.
9. hit the start button to start cooking.
10. Once the cooking is done, serve the fish hot with mayonnaise.

**Nutrition:**
- (Per serving) Calories 238| Fat 11.8g| Sodium 488mg | Carbs 9g | Fiber 0g | Sugar8 g | Protein 35g

## Salmon With Fennel Salad

Servings: 4
Cooking Time: 17 Minutes.
**Ingredients:**
- 2 teaspoons fresh parsley, chopped
- 1 teaspoon fresh thyme, chopped
- 1 teaspoon salt
- 4 (6-oz) skinless center-cut salmon fillets
- 2 tablespoons olive oil
- 4 cups fennel, sliced
- ⅔ cup Greek yogurt
- 1 garlic clove, grated
- 2 tablespoons orange juice
- 1 teaspoon lemon juice
- 2 tablespoons fresh dill, chopped

**Directions:**
1. Preheat your Ninja Foodi Dual Zone Air Fryer to 200 degrees F(95°C) .
2. Mix ½ teaspoon of salt, thyme, and parsley in a small bowl.
3. Brush the salmon with oil first, then rub liberally rub the herb mixture.
4. Place 2 salmon fillets in each of the crisper plate.
5. Return the crisper plate to the Ninja Foodi Dual Zone Air Fryer.
6. Choose the Air Fry mode for Zone 1 and set the temperature to 390 degrees F(190°C) and the time to 17 minutes.
7. Select the "MATCH" button to copy the settings for Zone 2.
8. Initiate cooking by pressing the START/STOP button.
9. Meanwhile, mix fennel with garlic, yogurt, lemon juice, orange juice, remaining salt, and dill in a mixing bowl.
10. Serve the air fried salmon fillets with fennel salad.
11. Enjoy.

**Nutrition:**
- (Per serving) Calories 305 | Fat 15g |Sodium 482mg | Carbs 17g | Fiber 3g | Sugar 2g | Protein 35g

## Broiled Crab Cakes With Hush Puppies

Servings:4
Cooking Time: 15 Minutes
**Ingredients:**
- FOR THE CRAB CAKES
- 2 large eggs
- 2 tablespoons Dijon mustard
- 2 teaspoons Worcestershire sauce
- 1 teaspoon Old Bay seasoning
- ¼ teaspoon paprika
- ¼ cup cracker crumbs (about 9 crackers)
- 1 pound lump crab meat
- 2 teaspoons vegetable oil
- FOR THE HUSH PUPPIES
- ½ cup all-purpose flour
- ⅓ cup yellow cornmeal
- 3 tablespoons sugar
- ¼ teaspoon kosher salt
- ¼ teaspoon baking powder
- 1 large egg
- ½ cup whole milk
- Nonstick cooking spray

**Directions:**

1. To prep the crab cakes: In a large bowl, whisk together the eggs, mustard, Worcestershire, Old Bay, and paprika until smooth. Stir in the cracker crumbs until fully incorporated, then fold in the crab meat. Refrigerate the crab mixture for 30 minutes.
2. Divide the crab mixture into 8 equal portions. With damp hands, press each portion gently into a loose patty. Brush both sides of each patty with the oil.
3. To prep the hush puppies: In a large bowl, combine the flour, cornmeal, sugar, salt, and baking powder. Stir in the egg and milk to form a stiff batter.
4. Roll the batter into 8 balls. Spritz each hush puppy with cooking spray.
5. To cook the crab cakes and hush puppies: Install a crisper plate in each of the two baskets. Place the crab cakes in a single layer in the Zone 1 basket and insert the basket in the unit. Line the Zone 2 plate with aluminum foil and spray the foil with cooking spray. Arrange the hush puppies on the foil and insert the basket in the unit.
6. Select Zone 1, select AIR BROIL, set the temperature to 400°F (205°C), and set the timer to 15 minutes.
7. Select Zone 2, select AIR FRY, set the temperature to 400°F (205°C), and set the timer to 7 minutes. Select SMART FINISH.
8. Press START/PAUSE to begin cooking.
9. When cooking is complete, the crab cakes and hush puppies will be golden brown and cooked through. Serve hot.

**Nutrition:**

- (Per serving) Calories: 403; Total fat: 16g; Saturated fat: 2g; Carbohydrates: 40g; Fiber: 1g; Protein: 27g; Sodium: 872mg

## Foil Packet Salmon

Servings: 4
Cooking Time: 14 Minutes

**Ingredients:**

- 455g salmon fillets
- 4 cups green beans defrosted
- 4 tablespoons soy sauce
- 2 tablespoons honey
- 2 teaspoons sesame seeds
- 1 teaspoon garlic powder
- ½ teaspoon ginger powder
- ½ teaspoon salt
- ¼ teaspoon white pepper
- ¼ teaspoon red pepper flakes
- Salt, to taste
- Canola oil spray

**Directions:**

1. Make 4 foil packets and adjust the salmon fillets in each.
2. Divide the green beans in the foil packets and drizzle half of the spices on top.
3. Place one salmon piece on top of each and drizzle the remaining ingredients on top.
4. Pack the salmon with the foil and place two packets in each air fryer basket.
5. Return the air fryer basket 1 to Zone 1, and basket 2 to Zone 2 of the Ninja Foodi 2-Basket Air Fryer.
6. Choose the "Air Fry" mode for Zone 1 and set the temperature to 425 degrees F(215°C) and 14 minutes of cooking time.
7. Select the "MATCH COOK" option to copy the settings for Zone 2.
8. Initiate cooking by pressing the START/PAUSE BUTTON.
9. Serve warm.

**Nutrition:**

- (Per serving) Calories 305 | Fat 15g |Sodium 482mg | Carbs 17g | Fiber 3g | Sugar 2g | Protein 35g

## Bacon Halibut Steak

Servings: 4
Cooking Time: 10 Minutes

**Ingredients:**

- 680 g halibut steaks (170 g each fillet)
- 1 teaspoon avocado oil
- 1 teaspoon ground black pepper
- 110 g bacon, sliced

**Directions:**

1. Sprinkle the halibut steaks with avocado oil and ground black pepper.
2. Then wrap the fish in the bacon slices and put in the two air fryer baskets.
3. Cook the fish at 200ºC for 5 minutes per side.

## Scallops Gratiné With Parmesan

Servings: 2
Cooking Time: 9 Minutes

**Ingredients:**

- Scallops:
- 120 ml single cream
- 45 g grated Parmesan cheese
- 235 g thinly sliced spring onions
- 5 g chopped fresh parsley
- 3 cloves garlic, minced
- ½ teaspoon kosher or coarse sea salt
- ½ teaspoon black pepper
- 455 g sea scallops
- Topping:
- 30 g panko bread crumbs
- 20 g grated Parmesan cheese
- Vegetable oil spray
- For Serving:
- Lemon wedges
- Crusty French bread (optional)

**Directions:**

1. For the scallops: In a baking pan, combine the single cream, cheese, spring onions, parsley, garlic, salt, and pepper. Stir in the scallops. 2. For the topping: In a small bowl, combine the bread crumbs and cheese. Sprinkle evenly over the scallops. Spray the topping with vegetable oil spray. 3. Place the pan in the zone 1 air fryer drawer. Set the temperature to 164ºC for 6 minutes. Set the temperature to 204ºC for 3 minutes until the topping has browned. 4. To serve: Squeeze the lemon wedges over the gratin and serve with crusty French bread, if desired.

## Brown Sugar Garlic Salmon

Servings: 4
Cooking Time: 10 Minutes

**Ingredients:**

- 455g salmon
- Salt and black pepper, to taste
- 2 tablespoons brown sugar
- 1 teaspoon chili powder
- ½ teaspoon paprika
- 1 teaspoon Italian seasoning
- 1 teaspoon garlic powder

**Directions:**

1. Mix brown sugar with garlic powder, Italian seasoning, paprika, and chili powder in a bowl.

2. Rub this mixture over the salmon along with black pepper and salt.
3. Place the salmon in the air fryer baskets.
4. Return the air fryer basket 1 to Zone 1, and basket 2 to Zone 2 of the Ninja Foodi 2-Basket Air Fryer.
5. Choose the "Air Fry" mode for Zone 1 and set the temperature to 400 degrees F(205°C) and 10 minutes of cooking time.
6. Select the "MATCH COOK" option to copy the settings for Zone 2.
7. Initiate cooking by pressing the START/PAUSE BUTTON.
8. Flip the salmon once cooked halfway through.
9. Serve warm.

**Nutrition:**

- (Per serving) Calories 275 | Fat 1.4g |Sodium 582mg | Carbs 31.5g | Fiber 1.1g | Sugar 0.1g | Protein 29.8g

## Honey Sriracha Mahi Mahi

Servings: 4
Cooking Time: 7 Minutes

**Ingredients:**

- 3 pounds mahi-mahi
- 6 tablespoons honey
- 4 tablespoons sriracha
- Salt, to taste
- Cooking spray

**Directions:**

1. In a small bowl, mix the sriracha sauce and honey. Mix well.
2. Season the fish with salt and pour the honey mixture over it. Let it sit at room temperature for 20 minutes.
3. Place a crisper plate in each drawer. Put the fish in a single layer in each. Insert the drawers into the unit.
4. Select zone 1, then AIR FRY, then set the temperature to 400 degrees F/ 205 degrees C with a 7-minute timer. To match zone 2 settings to zone 1, choose MATCH. To begin, select START/STOP.
5. Remove the fish from the drawers after the timer has finished.

**Nutrition:**

- (Per serving) Calories 581 | Fat 22g | Sodium 495mg | Carbs 26g | Fiber 4g | Sugar 26g | Protein 68g

## Breaded Scallops

Servings: 4
Cooking Time: 12 Minutes.

**Ingredients:**

- ½ cup crushed buttery crackers
- ½ teaspoon garlic powder
- ½ teaspoon seafood seasoning
- 2 tablespoons butter, melted
- 1 pound sea scallops patted dry
- cooking spray

**Directions:**

1. Mix cracker crumbs, garlic powder, and seafood seasoning in a shallow bowl. Spread melted butter in another shallow bowl.
2. Dip each scallop in the melted butter and then roll in the breading to coat well.
3. Grease each Air fryer basket with cooking spray and place half of the scallops in each.
4. Return the crisper plate to the Ninja Foodi Dual Zone Air Fryer.
5. Select the Air Fry mode for Zone 1 and set the temperature to 390 degrees F(200°C) and the time to 12 minutes.
6. Press the "MATCH" button to copy the settings for Zone 2.
7. Initiate cooking by pressing the START/STOP button.
8. Flip the scallops with a spatula after 4 minutes and resume cooking.
9. Serve warm.

**Nutrition:**

- (Per serving) Calories 275 | Fat 1.4g |Sodium 582mg | Carbs 31.5g | Fiber 1.1g | Sugar 0.1g | Protein 29.8g

## Orange-mustard Glazed Salmon And Cucumber And Salmon Salad

Servings: 4
Cooking Time: 10 Minutes

**Ingredients:**

- Orange-Mustard Glazed Salmon:
- 1 tablespoon orange marmalade
- ¼ teaspoon grated orange zest plus 1 tablespoon juice
- 2 teaspoons whole-grain mustard
- 2 (230 g) skin-on salmon fillets, 1½ inches thick
- Salt and pepper, to taste
- Vegetable oil spray
- Cucumber and Salmon Salad:
- 455 g salmon fillet
- 1½ tablespoons olive oil, divided
- 1 tablespoon sherry vinegar
- 1 tablespoon capers, rinsed and drained
- 1 seedless cucumber, thinly sliced
- ¼ white onion, thinly sliced
- 2 tablespoons chopped fresh parsley
- Salt and freshly ground black pepper, to taste

**Directions:**

1. Make the Orange-Mustard Glazed Salmon :
2. Preheat the air fryer to 205ºC.
3. Make foil sling for air fryer basket by folding 1 long sheet of aluminum foil so it is 4 inches wide. Lay sheet of foil widthwise across zone 1 basket, pressing foil into and up sides of basket. Fold excess foil as needed so that edges of foil are flush with top of basket. Lightly spray foil and basket with vegetable oil spray.
4. Combine marmalade, orange zest and juice, and mustard in bowl. Pat salmon dry with paper towels and season with salt and pepper. Brush tops and sides of fillets evenly with glaze. Arrange fillets skin side down on sling in prepared zone 1 basket, spaced evenly apart. Air fry salmon until center is still translucent when checked with the tip of a paring knife and registers 50ºC , 10 to 14 minutes, using sling to rotate fillets halfway through cooking.
5. Using the sling, carefully remove salmon from air fryer. Slide fish spatula along underside of fillets and transfer to individual serving plates, leaving skin behind. Serve.
6. Make the Cucumber and Salmon Salad :
7. Preheat the air fryer to 205ºC.
8. Lightly coat the salmon with ½ tablespoon of the olive oil. Place skin-side down in the zone 2 air fryer basket and air fry for 8 to 10 minutes until the fish is opaque and flakes easily with a fork. Transfer the salmon to a plate and let cool to room temperature. Remove the skin and carefully flake the fish into bite-size chunks.
9. In a small bowl, whisk the remaining 1 tablespoon olive oil and the vinegar until thoroughly combined. Add the flaked fish, capers, cucumber, onion, and parsley. Season to taste with salt and freshly ground black pepper. Toss gently to coat. Serve immediately or cover and refrigerate for up to 4 hours.

## South Indian Fried Fish

Servings: 4
Cooking Time: 8 Minutes
**Ingredients:**

- 2 tablespoons olive oil
- 2 tablespoons fresh lime or lemon juice
- 1 teaspoon minced fresh ginger
- 1 clove garlic, minced
- 1 teaspoon ground turmeric
- ½ teaspoon kosher or coarse sea salt
- ¼ to ½ teaspoon cayenne pepper
- 455 g tilapia fillets (2 to 3 fillets)
- Olive oil spray
- Lime or lemon wedges (optional)

**Directions:**

1. In a large bowl, combine the oil, lime juice, ginger, garlic, turmeric, salt, and cayenne. Stir until well combined; set aside.
2. Cut each tilapia fillet into three or four equal-size pieces. Add the fish to the bowl and gently mix until all of the fish is coated in the marinade. Marinate for 10 to 15 minutes at room temperature.
3. Spray the air fryer basket with olive oil spray. Place the fish in the basket and spray the fish. Set the air fryer to 165°C for 3 minutes to partially cook the fish. Set the air fryer to 205°C for 5 minutes to finish cooking and crisp up the fish.
4. Carefully remove the fish from the basket. Serve hot, with lemon wedges if desired.

## Spicy Salmon Fillets

Servings: 6
Cooking Time: 8 Minutes
**Ingredients:**

- 900g salmon fillets
- ¾ tsp ground cumin
- 1 tbsp brown sugar
- 2 tbsp steak seasoning
- ¼ tsp cayenne pepper
- ½ tsp ground coriander

**Directions:**

1. Mix ground cumin, coriander, steak seasoning, brown sugar, and cayenne in a small bowl.
2. Rub salmon fillets with spice mixture.
3. Insert a crisper plate in the Ninja Foodi air fryer baskets.
4. Place the salmon fillets in both baskets.
5. Select zone 1, then select "bake" mode and set the temperature to 360 degrees F(180°C) for 10 minutes. Press "match" to match zone 2 settings to zone 1. Press "start/stop" to begin.

**Nutrition:**

- (Per serving) Calories 207 | Fat 9.4g |Sodium 68mg | Carbs 1.6g | Fiber 0.1g | Sugar 1.5g | Protein 29.4g

## Thai Prawn Skewers And Lemon-tarragon Fish En Papillote

Servings: 5
Cooking Time: 15 Minutes
**Ingredients:**

- Lemon-Tarragon Fish en Papillote:
- Salt and pepper, to taste
- 340 g extra-large prawns, peeled and deveined
- 1 tablespoon vegetable oil
- 1 teaspoon honey
- ½ teaspoon grated lime zest plus 1 tablespoon juice, plus lime wedges for serving
- 6 (6-inch) wooden skewers
- 3 tablespoons creamy peanut butter
- 3 tablespoons hot tap water
- 1 tablespoon chopped fresh coriander
- 1 teaspoon fish sauce
- Lemon-Tarragon Fish en Papillote:
- 2 tablespoons salted butter, melted
- 1 tablespoon fresh lemon juice
- ½ teaspoon dried tarragon, crushed, or 2 sprigs fresh tarragon
- 1 teaspoon kosher or coarse sea salt
- 85 g julienned carrots
- 435 g julienned fennel, or 1 stalk julienned celery
- 75 g thinly sliced red bell pepper
- 2 cod fillets, 170 g each, thawed if frozen
- Vegetable oil spray
- ½ teaspoon black pepper

**Directions:**

1. Make the Lemon-Tarragon Fish en Papillote :
2. Preheat the air fryer to 204°C.
3. Dissolve 2 tablespoons salt in 1 litre cold water in a large container. Add prawns, cover, and refrigerate for 15 minutes.
4. Remove prawns from brine and pat dry with paper towels. Whisk oil, honey, lime zest, and ¼ teaspoon pepper together in a large bowl. Add prawns and toss to coat. Thread prawns onto skewers, leaving about ¼ inch between each prawns .
5. Arrange 3 skewers in the zone 1 air fryer drawer, parallel to each other and spaced evenly apart. Arrange remaining 3 skewers on top, perpendicular to the bottom layer. Air fry until prawns are opaque throughout, 6 to 8 minutes, flipping and rotating skewers halfway through cooking.
6. Whisk peanut butter, hot tap water, lime juice, coriander, and fish sauce together in a bowl until smooth. Serve skewers with peanut dipping sauce and lime wedges.
7. Make the Lemon-Tarragon Fish en Papillote :
8. In a medium bowl, combine the butter, lemon juice, tarragon, and ½ teaspoon of the salt. Whisk well until you get a creamy sauce. Add the carrots, fennel, and bell pepper and toss to combine; set aside.
9. Cut two squares of baking paper each large enough to hold one fillet and half the vegetables. Spray the fillets with vegetable oil spray. Season both sides with the remaining ½ teaspoon salt and the black pepper.
10. Lay one fillet down on each baking paper square. Top each with half the vegetables. Pour any remaining sauce over the vegetables.
11. Fold over the baking paper and crimp the sides in small, tight folds to hold the fish, vegetables, and sauce securely inside the packet. Place the packets in the zone 2 air fryer drawer. Set the air fryer to 176°C for 15 minutes.
12. Transfer each packet to a plate. Cut open with scissors just before serving .

## Salmon Fritters With Courgette & Cajun And Lemon Pepper Cod

Servings: 6
Cooking Time: 12 Minutes
**Ingredients:**

- Salmon Fritters with Courgette:
- 2 tablespoons almond flour
- 1 courgette, grated
- 1 egg, beaten
- 170 g salmon fillet, diced
- 1 teaspoon avocado oil
- ½ teaspoon ground black pepper
- Cajun and Lemon Pepper Cod:
- 1 tablespoon Cajun seasoning
- 1 teaspoon salt
- ½ teaspoon lemon pepper

- ½ teaspoon freshly ground black pepper
- 2 cod fillets, 230 g each, cut to fit into the air fryer basket
- Cooking spray
- 2 tablespoons unsalted butter, melted
- 1 lemon, cut into 4 wedges

**Directions:**

1. Make the Salmon Fritters with Courgette :
2. Mix almond flour with courgette, egg, salmon, and ground black pepper.
3. Then make the fritters from the salmon mixture.
4. Sprinkle the zone 1 air fryer basket with avocado oil and put the fritters inside.
5. Cook the fritters at 190ºC for 6 minutes per side.
6. Make the Cajun and Lemon Pepper Cod :
7. Preheat the air fryer to 180ºC. Spritz the zone 2 air fryer basket with cooking spray.
8. Thoroughly combine the Cajun seasoning, salt, lemon pepper, and black pepper in a small bowl. Rub this mixture all over the cod fillets until completely coated.
9. Put the fillets in the air fryer basket and brush the melted butter over both sides of each fillet.
10. Bake in the preheated air fryer for 12 minutes, flipping the fillets halfway through, or until the fish flakes easily with a fork.
11. Remove the fillets from the basket and serve with fresh lemon wedges.

## Parmesan-crusted Fish Sticks With Baked Macaroni And Cheese

Servings:4

Cooking Time: 25 Minutes

**Ingredients:**

- FOR THE FISH STICKS
- 1 pound cod or haddock fillets
- ½ cup all-purpose flour
- 2 large eggs
- ¼ teaspoon kosher salt
- ¼ teaspoon freshly ground black pepper
- ¾ cup panko bread crumbs
- ¼ cup grated Parmesan cheese
- Nonstick cooking spray
- FOR THE MACARONI AND CHEESE
- 1½ cups elbow macaroni
- 1 cup whole milk
- ½ cup heavy (whipping) cream
- 8 ounces shredded Colby-Jack cheese
- 4 ounces cream cheese, at room temperature
- 1 teaspoon Dijon mustard
- ½ teaspoon kosher salt
- ½ teaspoon freshly ground black pepper

**Directions:**

1. To prep the fish sticks: Cut the fish into sticks about 3 inches long and ¾ inch wide.
2. Set up a breading station with three small shallow bowls. Place the flour in the first bowl. In the second bowl, whisk the eggs and season with the salt and black pepper. Combine the panko and Parmesan in the third bowl.
3. Bread the fish sticks in this order: First, dip them into the flour, coating all sides. Then, dip into the beaten egg. Finally, coat them in the panko mixture, gently pressing the bread crumbs into the fish. Spritz each fish stick all over with cooking spray.
4. To prep the macaroni and cheese: Place the macaroni in the Zone 2 basket. Add the milk, cream, Colby-Jack, cream cheese, mustard, salt, and black pepper. Stir well to combine, ensuring the pasta is completely submerged in the liquid.
5. To cook the fish sticks and macaroni and cheese: Install a crisper plate in the Zone 1 basket. Arrange the fish sticks in a single layer in the basket (use a rack or cook in batches if necessary) and insert the basket in the unit. Insert the Zone 2 basket in the unit.
6. Select Zone 1, select AIR FRY, set the temperature to 390°F (200°C), and set the timer to 18 minutes.
7. Select Zone 2, select BAKE, set the temperature to 360°F (180°C), and set the timer to 25 minutes. Select SMART FINISH.
8. Press START/PAUSE to begin cooking.
9. When the Zone 1 timer reads 3 minutes, press START/PAUSE. Remove the basket and use silicone-tipped tongs to gently flip over the fish sticks. Reinsert the basket and press START/PAUSE to resume cooking.
10. When cooking is complete, the fish sticks should be crisp and the macaroni tender.
11. Stir the macaroni and cheese and let stand for 5 minutes before serving. The sauce will thicken as it cools.

**Nutrition:**

- (Per serving) Calories: 903; Total fat: 51g; Saturated fat: 25g; Carbohydrates: 60g; Fiber: 2.5g; Protein: 48g; Sodium: 844mg

## Fish Fillets With Lemon-dill Sauce

Servings: 4

Cooking Time: 7 Minutes

**Ingredients:**

- 455 g snapper, grouper, or salmon fillets
- Sea salt and freshly ground black pepper, to taste
- 1 tablespoon avocado oil
- 60 g sour cream
- 60 g mayonnaise
- 2 tablespoons fresh dill, chopped, plus more for garnish
- 1 tablespoon freshly squeezed lemon juice
- ½ teaspoon grated lemon zest

**Directions:**

1. Pat the fish dry with paper towels and season well with salt and pepper. Brush with the avocado oil. 2. Set the air fryer to 204ºC. Place the fillets in the two air fryer drawers and air fry for 1 minute. 3. Lower the air fryer temperature to 164ºC and continue cooking for 5 minutes. Flip the fish and cook for 1 minute more or until an instant-read thermometer reads 64ºC. 4. While the fish is cooking, make the sauce by combining the sour cream, mayonnaise, dill, lemon juice, and lemon zest in a medium bowl. Season with salt and pepper and stir until combined. Refrigerate until ready to serve. 5. Serve the fish with the sauce, garnished with the remaining dill.

## Prawn Dejonghe Skewers

Servings: 4

Cooking Time: 15 Minutes

**Ingredients:**

- 2 teaspoons sherry, or apple cider vinegar
- 3 tablespoons unsalted butter, melted
- 120 g panko bread crumbs
- 3 cloves garlic, minced
- 8 g minced flat-leaf parsley, plus more for garnish
- 1 teaspoon kosher salt
- Pinch of cayenne pepper
- 680 g prawns, peeled and deveined
- Vegetable oil, for spraying
- Lemon wedges, for serving

**Directions:**

1. Stir the sherry and melted butter together in a shallow bowl or pie plate and whisk until combined. Set aside. Whisk

together the panko, garlic, parsley, salt, and cayenne pepper on a large plate or shallow bowl.

2. Thread the prawns onto metal skewers designed for the air fryer or bamboo skewers, 3 to 4 per skewer. Dip 1 prawns skewer in the butter mixture, then dredge in the panko mixture until each prawns is lightly coated. Place the skewer on a plate or rimmed baking sheet and repeat the process with the remaining skewers.
3. Preheat the air fryer to 175ºC. Arrange 4 skewers in the zone 1 air fryer basket. Spray the skewers with oil and air fry for 8 minutes, until the bread crumbs are golden brown and the prawns are cooked through. Transfer the cooked skewers to a serving plate and keep warm while cooking the remaining 4 skewers in the air fryer.
4. Sprinkle the cooked skewers with additional fresh parsley and serve with lemon wedges if desired.

## Sweet & Spicy Fish Fillets

Servings: 4
Cooking Time: 8 Minutes
**Ingredients:**

- 4 salmon fillets
- 1 tsp smoked paprika
- 1 tsp chilli powder
- ½ tsp red pepper flakes, crushed
- ½ tsp garlic powder
- 85g honey
- Pepper
- Salt

**Directions:**

1. In a small bowl, mix honey, garlic powder, chilli powder, paprika, red pepper flakes, pepper, and salt.
2. Brush fish fillets with honey mixture.
3. Insert a crisper plate in the Ninja Foodi air fryer baskets.
4. Place fish fillets in both baskets.
5. Select zone 1, then select "air fry" mode and set the temperature to 390 degrees F(200°C) for 8 minutes. Press "match" and then"start/stop" to begin.

**Nutrition:**

- (Per serving) Calories 305 | Fat 11.2g |Sodium 125mg | Carbs 18.4g | Fiber 0.6g | Sugar 17.5g | Protein 34.8g

## Smoked Salmon

Servings:4
Cooking Time:12
**Ingredients:**

- 2 pounds of salmon fillets, smoked
- 6 ounces cream cheese
- 4 tablespoons mayonnaise
- 2 teaspoons of chives, fresh
- 1 teaspoon of lemon zest
- Salt and freshly ground black pepper, to taste
- 2 tablespoons of butter

**Directions:**

1. Cut the salmon into very small and uniform bite-size pieces.
2. Mix cream cheese, chives, mayonnaise, black pepper, and lemon zest, in a small mixing bowl.
3. Let it sit aside for further use.
4. Coat the salmon pieces with salt and butter.
5. Divide the bite-size pieces into both zones of the air fryer.
6. Set it on AIRFRY mode at 400 degrees F(205°C) for 12 minutes.
7. Select MATCH for zone 2 basket.
8. Hit start, so the cooking start.
9. Once the salmon is done, top it with a bowl creamy mixture and serve.
10. Enjoy hot.

**Nutrition:**

- (Per serving) Calories 557| Fat 15.7 g| Sodium 371mg | Carbs 4.8 g | Fiber 0g | Sugar 1.1g | Protein 48 g

## Herb Lemon Mussels

Servings: 6
Cooking Time: 10 Minutes
**Ingredients:**

- 1kg mussels, steamed & half shell
- 1 tbsp thyme, chopped
- 1 tbsp parsley, chopped
- 1 tsp dried parsley
- 1 tsp garlic, minced
- 60ml olive oil
- 45ml lemon juice
- Pepper
- Salt

**Directions:**

1. In a bowl, mix mussels with the remaining ingredients.
2. Insert a crisper plate in the Ninja Foodi air fryer baskets.
3. Add the mussels to both baskets.
4. Select zone 1 then select "air fry" mode and set the temperature to 360 degrees F(180°C) for 10 minutes. Press "match" to match zone 2 settings to zone 1. Press "start/stop" to begin.

**Nutrition:**

- (Per serving) Calories 206 | Fat 11.9g |Sodium 462mg | Carbs 6.3g | Fiber 0.3g | Sugar 0.2g | Protein 18.2g

## Simple Buttery Cod & Salmon On Bed Of Fennel And Carrot

Servings: 4
Cooking Time: 13 To 14 Minutes
**Ingredients:**

- Simple Buttery Cod:
- 2 cod fillets, 110 g each
- 2 tablespoons salted butter, melted
- 1 teaspoon Old Bay seasoning
- ½ medium lemon, sliced
- Salmon on Bed of Fennel and Carrot:
- 1 fennel bulb, thinly sliced
- 1 large carrot, peeled and sliced
- 1 small onion, thinly sliced
- 60 ml low-fat sour cream
- ¼ teaspoon coarsely ground pepper
- 2 salmon fillets, 140 g each

**Directions:**

1. Make the Simple Buttery Cod :
2. Place cod fillets into a round baking dish. Brush each fillet with butter and sprinkle with Old Bay seasoning. Lay two lemon slices on each fillet. Cover the dish with foil and place into the zone 1 air fryer basket.
3. Adjust the temperature to 175ºC and bake for 8 minutes. Flip halfway through the cooking time. When cooked, internal temperature should be at least 65ºC. Serve warm.
4. Make the Salmon on Bed of Fennel and Carrot :
5. Combine the fennel, carrot, and onion in a bowl and toss.
6. Put the vegetable mixture into a baking pan. Roast in the zone 2 air fryer basket at 205ºC for 4 minutes or until the vegetables are crisp-tender.
7. Remove the pan from the air fryer. Stir in the sour cream and sprinkle the vegetables with the pepper.
8. Top with the salmon fillets.
9. Return the pan to the air fryer. Roast for another 9 to 10 minutes or until the salmon just barely flakes when tested with a fork.

## Tuna Steaks

Servings: 2
Cooking Time: 30 Minutes
**Ingredients:**

- 2 (6 ounce) boneless tuna steaks
- ¼ cup soy sauce
- 2 teaspoons honey
- 1 teaspoon grated ginger
- 1 teaspoon sesame oil
- ½ teaspoon rice vinegar

**Directions:**

1. Mix rice vinegar, sesame oil, ginger, honey and soy sauce in a bowl.
2. Pour this marinade over the tuna steaks and cover to marinate for 30 minutes.
3. Place the tuna steaks in the air fryer baskets in a single layer.
4. Return the air fryer basket 1 to Zone 1, and basket 2 to Zone 2 of the Ninja Foodi 2-Basket Air Fryer.
5. Choose the "Air Fry" mode for Zone 1 and set the temperature to 380 degrees F(195°C) and 4 minutes of cooking time.
6. Select the "MATCH COOK" option to copy the settings for Zone 2.
7. Initiate cooking by pressing the START/PAUSE BUTTON.
8. Serve warm.

**Nutrition:**

- (Per serving) Calories 348 | Fat 30g |Sodium 660mg | Carbs 5g | Fiber 0g | Sugar 0g | Protein 14g

## Flavorful Salmon Fillets

Servings: 2
Cooking Time:10 Minutes
**Ingredients:**

- 2 salmon fillets, boneless
- 1/2 tsp garlic powder
- 1/2 tsp ground cumin
- 1/2 tsp chili powder
- 2 tbsp fresh lemon juice
- 2 tbsp olive oil
- Pepper
- Salt

**Directions:**

1. In a small bowl, mix oil, lemon juice, chili powder, ground cumin, garlic powder, pepper, and salt.
2. Brush salmon fillets with oil mixture and place into the air fryer basket and cook at 400 F for 10 minutes.
3. Serve and enjoy.

## Buttered Mahi-mahi

Servings: 4
Cooking Time: 22 Minutes.
**Ingredients:**

- 4 (6-oz) mahi-mahi fillets
- Salt and black pepper ground to taste
- Cooking spray
- ⅔ cup butter

**Directions:**

1. Preheat your Ninja Foodi Dual Zone Air Fryer to 350 degrees F(175°C) .
2. Rub the mahi-mahi fillets with salt and black pepper.
3. Place two mahi-mahi fillets in each of the crisper plate.
4. Return the crisper plates to the Ninja Foodi Dual Zone Air Fryer.
5. Choose the Air Fry mode for Zone 1 and set the temperature to 390 degrees F(200°C) and the time to 17 minutes.
6. Select the "MATCH" button to copy the settings for Zone 2.
7. Initiate cooking by pressing the START/STOP button.
8. Add butter to a saucepan and cook for 5 minutes until slightly brown.
9. Remove the butter from the heat.
10. Drizzle butter over the fish and serve warm.

**Nutrition:**

- (Per serving) Calories 399 | Fat 16g |Sodium 537mg | Carbs 28g | Fiber 3g | Sugar 10g | Protein 35g

## Easy Herbed Salmon

Servings: 2
Cooking Time:5 Minutes
**Ingredients:**

- 2 salmon fillets
- 1 tbsp butter
- 2 tbsp olive oil
- 1/4 tsp paprika
- 1 tsp herb de Provence
- Pepper
- Salt

**Directions:**

1. Brush salmon fillets with oil and sprinkle with paprika, herb de Provence, pepper, and salt.
2. Place salmon fillets into the air fryer basket and cook at 390 F for 5 minutes.
3. Melt butter in a pan and pour over cooked salmon fillets.
4. Serve and enjoy.

## Fried Lobster Tails

Servings: 4
Cooking Time: 18 Minutes.
**Ingredients:**

- 4 (4-oz) lobster tails
- 8 tablespoons butter, melted
- 2 teaspoons lemon zest
- 2 garlic cloves, grated
- Salt and black pepper, ground to taste
- 2 teaspoons fresh parsley, chopped
- 4 wedges lemon

**Directions:**

1. Spread the lobster tails into Butterfly, slit the top to expose the lobster meat while keeping the tail intact.
2. Place two lobster tails in each of the crisper plate with their lobster meat facing up.
3. Mix melted butter with lemon zest and garlic in a bowl.
4. Brush the butter mixture on top of the lobster tails.
5. And drizzle salt and black pepper on top.
6. Return the crisper plate to the Ninja Foodi Dual Zone Air Fryer.
7. Choose the Air Fry mode for Zone 1 and set the temperature to 390 degrees F(200°C) and the time to 18 minutes.
8. Select the "MATCH" button to copy the settings for Zone 2.
9. Initiate cooking by pressing the START/STOP button.
10. Garnish with parsley and lemon wedges.
11. Serve warm.

**Nutrition:**

- (Per serving) Calories 257 | Fat 10.4g |Sodium 431mg | Carbs 20g | Fiber 0g | Sugar 1.6g | Protein 21g

## Nutty Prawns With Amaretto Glaze

Servings: 10 To 12
Cooking Time: 10 Minutes
**Ingredients:**
- 120 g plain flour
- ½ teaspoon baking powder
- 1 teaspoon salt
- 2 eggs, beaten
- 120 ml milk
- 2 tablespoons olive or vegetable oil
- 185 g sliced almonds
- 900 g large prawns (about 32 to 40 prawns), peeled and deveined, tails left on
- 470 ml amaretto liqueur

**Directions:**
1. Combine the flour, baking powder and salt in a large bowl. Add the eggs, milk and oil and stir until it forms a smooth batter. Coarsely crush the sliced almonds into a second shallow dish with your hands.
2. Dry the prawns well with paper towels. Dip the prawns into the batter and shake off any excess batter, leaving just enough to lightly coat the prawns. Transfer the prawns to the dish with the almonds and coat completely. Place the coated prawns on a plate or baking sheet and when all the prawns have been coated, freeze the prawns for an 1 hour, or as long as a week before air frying.
3. Preheat the air fryer to 204°C.
4. Transfer frozen prawns to the two air fryer drawers. Air fry for 6 minutes. Turn the prawns over and air fry for an additional 4 minutes.
5. While the prawns are cooking, bring the Amaretto to a boil in a small saucepan on the stovetop. Lower the heat and simmer until it has reduced and thickened into a glaze, about 10 minutes.
6. Remove the prawns from the air fryer and brush both sides with the warm amaretto glaze. Serve warm.

## Scallops

Servings: 4
Cooking Time: 5 Minutes
**Ingredients:**
- ½ cup Italian breadcrumbs
- ½ teaspoon garlic powder
- ¼ teaspoon salt
- ½ teaspoon black pepper
- 2 tablespoons butter, melted
- 1 pound sea scallops, rinsed and pat dry

**Directions:**
1. Combine the breadcrumbs, garlic powder, salt, and pepper in a small bowl. Pour the melted butter into another shallow bowl.
2. Dredge each scallop in the melted butter, then roll it in the breadcrumb mixture until well covered.
3. Place a crisper plate in each drawer. Put the scallops in a single layer in each drawer. Insert the drawers into the unit.
4. Select zone 1, then AIR FRY, then set the temperature to 360 degrees F/ 180 degrees C with a 5-minute timer. To match zone 2 settings to zone 1, choose MATCH. To begin, select START/STOP.
5. Press START/STOP to pause the unit when the timer reaches 3 minutes. Remove the drawers. Use tongs to carefully flip the scallops over. To resume cooking, re-insert the drawers into the unit and press START/STOP.
6. Remove the scallops from the drawers after the timer has finished.

**Nutrition:**
- (Per serving) Calories 81 | Fat 6g | Sodium 145mg | Carbs 3g | Fiber 4g | Sugar 1g | Protein 3g

## Salmon With Cauliflower

Servings: 4
Cooking Time: 25 Minutes
**Ingredients:**
- 455 g salmon fillet, diced
- 100 g cauliflower, shredded
- 1 tablespoon dried coriander
- 1 tablespoon coconut oil, melted
- 1 teaspoon ground turmeric
- 60 ml coconut cream

**Directions:**
1. Mix salmon with cauliflower, dried cilantro, ground turmeric, coconut cream, and coconut oil.
2. Transfer the salmon mixture into the air fryer and cook the meal at 176°C for 25 minutes. Stir the meal every 5 minutes to avoid the burning.

## Glazed Scallops

Servings: 6
Cooking Time: 13 Minutes.
**Ingredients:**
- 12 scallops
- 3 tablespoons olive oil
- Black pepper and salt to taste

**Directions:**
1. Rub the scallops with olive oil, black pepper, and salt.
2. Divide the scallops in the two crisper plates.
3. Return the crisper plate to the Ninja Foodi Dual Zone Air Fryer.
4. Choose the Air Fry mode for Zone 1 and set the temperature to 390 degrees F(200°C) and the time to 13 minutes.
5. Select the "MATCH" button to copy the settings for Zone 2.
6. Initiate cooking by pressing the START/STOP button.
7. Flip the scallops once cooked halfway through, and resume cooking.
8. Serve warm.

**Nutrition:**
- (Per serving) Calories 308 | Fat 24g |Sodium 715mg | Carbs 0.8g | Fiber 0.1g | Sugar 0.1g | Protein 21.9g

## Honey Pecan Shrimp

Servings: 4
Cooking Time: 10 Minutes
**Ingredients:**
- ¼ cup cornstarch
- ¾ teaspoon salt
- ¼ teaspoon black pepper
- 2 egg whites
- ⅔ cup pecans, chopped
- 455g shrimp, peeled, and deveined
- ¼ cup honey
- 2 tablespoons mayonnaise

**Directions:**
1. Mix cornstarch with ½ teaspoon black pepper, and ½ teaspoon salt in a bowl.
2. Mix pecans and ¼ teaspoon salt in another bowl.
3. Beat egg whites in another bowl.
4. Dredge the shrimp through the cornstarch mixture then dip in the egg whites.
5. Coat the shrimp with pecans mixture.
6. Divide the coated shrimp in the air fryer baskets.

7. Return the air fryer basket 1 to Zone 1, and basket 2 to Zone 2 of the Ninja Foodi 2-Basket Air Fryer.
8. Choose the "Air Fry" mode for Zone 1 at 330 degrees F(165°C) and 10 minutes of cooking time.
9. Select the "MATCH COOK" option to copy the settings for Zone 2.
10. Initiate cooking by pressing the START/PAUSE BUTTON.
11. Flip the shrimps once cooked halfway through.
12. Serve.

**Nutrition:**

- (Per serving) Calories 155 | Fat 4.2g |Sodium 963mg | Carbs 21.5g | Fiber 0.8g | Sugar 5.7g | Protein 8.1g

## Air Fryer Calamari

Servings: 4
Cooking Time: 7 Minutes

**Ingredients:**

- ½ cup all-purpose flour
- 1 large egg
- 59ml milk
- 2 cups panko bread crumbs
- 1 teaspoon sea salt
- 1 teaspoon black pepper
- 455g calamari rings
- nonstick cooking spray

**Directions:**

1. Beat egg with milk in a bowl.
2. Mix flour with black pepper and salt in a bowl.
3. Coat the calamari rings with the flour mixture then dip in the egg mixture and coat with the breadcrumbs.
4. Place the coated calamari in the air fryer baskets.
5. Return the air fryer basket 1 to Zone 1, and basket 2 to Zone 2 of the Ninja Foodi 2-Basket Air Fryer.
6. Choose the "Air Fry" mode for Zone 1 at 400 degrees F(205°C) and 7 minutes of cooking time.
7. Select the "MATCH COOK" option to copy the settings for Zone 2.
8. Initiate cooking by pressing the START/PAUSE BUTTON.
9. Flip the calamari rings once cooked half way through.
10. Serve warm.

**Nutrition:**

- (Per serving) Calories 336 | Fat 6g |Sodium 181mg | Carbs 1.3g | Fiber 0.2g | Sugar 0.4g | Protein 69.2g

## Pecan-crusted Catfish

Servings: 4
Cooking Time: 12 Minutes

**Ingredients:**

- 65 g pecans, finely crushed
- 1 teaspoon fine sea salt
- ¼ teaspoon ground black pepper
- 4 catfish fillets, 110g each
- For Garnish (Optional):
- Fresh oregano
- Pecan halves

**Directions:**

1. Spray the two air fryer drawers with avocado oil. Preheat the air fryer to 192ºC.
2. In a large bowl, mix the crushed pecan, salt, and pepper. One at a time, dredge the catfish fillets in the mixture, coating them well. Use your hands to press the pecan meal into the fillets. Spray the fish with avocado oil and place them in the two air fryer drawers.
3. Air fry the coated catfish for 12 minutes, or until it flakes easily and is no longer translucent in the center, flipping halfway through.
4. Garnish with oregano sprigs and pecan halves, if desired.
5. Store leftovers in an airtight container in the fridge for up to 3 days. Reheat in a preheated 176ºC air fryer for 4 minutes, or until heated through.

## Chilean Sea Bass With Olive Relish And Snapper With Tomato

Servings: 4
Cooking Time: 15 Minutes

**Ingredients:**

- Chilean Sea Bass with Olive Relish:
- Olive oil spray
- 2 (170 g) Chilean sea bass fillets or other firm-fleshed white fish
- 3 tablespoons extra-virgin olive oil
- ½ teaspoon ground cumin
- ½ teaspoon kosher or coarse sea salt
- ½ teaspoon black pepper
- 60 g pitted green olives, diced
- 10 g finely diced onion
- 1 teaspoon chopped capers
- Snapper with Tomato:
- 2 snapper fillets
- 1 shallot, peeled and sliced
- 2 garlic cloves, halved
- 1 bell pepper, sliced
- 1 small-sized serrano pepper, sliced
- 1 tomato, sliced
- 1 tablespoon olive oil
- ¼ teaspoon freshly ground black pepper
- ½ teaspoon paprika
- Sea salt, to taste
- 2 bay leaves

**Directions:**

1. Make the Chilean Sea Bass with Olive Relish :
2. Spray the zone 1 air fryer drawer with the olive oil spray. Drizzle the fillets with the olive oil and sprinkle with the cumin, salt, and pepper. Place the fish in the zone 1 air fryer drawer. Set the air fryer to 164ºC for 10 minutes, or until the fish flakes easily with a fork.
3. Meanwhile, in a small bowl, stir together the olives, onion, and capers.
4. Serve the fish topped with the relish.
5. Make the Snapper with Tomato :
6. Place two baking paper sheets on a working surface. Place the fish in the center of one side of the baking paper.
7. Top with the shallot, garlic, peppers, and tomato. Drizzle olive oil over the fish and vegetables. Season with black pepper, paprika, and salt. Add the bay leaves.
8. Fold over the other half of the baking paper. Now, fold the paper around the edges tightly and create a half moon shape, sealing the fish inside.
9. Cook in the zone 2 air fryer drawer at 200ºC for 15 minutes. Serve warm.

## Southwestern Fish Fillets

Servings: 4
Cooking Time: 16 Minutes

**Ingredients:**

- 455g trout fillets
- 1 tsp garlic powder
- 29g breadcrumbs

- 15ml olive oil
- 1 tsp chilli powder
- 1 tsp onion powder

**Directions:**

1. In a small bowl, mix breadcrumbs, garlic powder, onion powder, and chilli powder.
2. Brush fish fillets with oil and coat with breadcrumbs.
3. Insert a crisper plate in the Ninja Foodi air fryer baskets.
4. Place coated fish fillets in both baskets.
5. Select zone 1 then select "air fry" mode and set the temperature to 375 degrees F(190°C) for 16 minutes. Press "match" and "start/stop" to begin.

**Nutrition:**

- (Per serving) Calories 272 | Fat 13.5g |Sodium 120mg | Carbs 5g | Fiber 0.6g | Sugar 0.7g | Protein 31.1g

## Basil Cheese S · saltalmon

Servings: 4

Cooking Time:7 Minutes

**Ingredients:**

- 4 salmon fillets
- 1/4 cup parmesan cheese, grated
- 5 fresh basil leaves, minced
- 2 tbsp mayonnaise
- 1/2 lemon juice
- Pepper

**Directions:**

1. Preheat the air fryer to 400 F.
2. Brush salmon fillets with lemon juice and season with pepper and salt.
3. In a small bowl, mix mayonnaise, basil, and cheese.
4. Spray air fryer basket with cooking spray.
5. Place salmon fillets into the air fryer basket and brush with mayonnaise mixture and cook for 7 minutes.
6. Serve and enjoy.

## Parmesan Mackerel With Coriander And Garlic Butter Prawns Scampi

Servings: 6

Cooking Time: 8 Minutes

**Ingredients:**

- Parmesan Mackerel with Coriander:
- 340 g mackerel fillet
- 60 g Parmesan, grated
- 1 teaspoon ground coriander
- 1 tablespoon olive oil
- Garlic Butter Prawns Scampi:
- Sauce:
- 60 g unsalted butter
- 2 tablespoons fish stock or chicken broth
- 2 cloves garlic, minced
- 2 tablespoons chopped fresh basil leaves
- 1 tablespoon lemon juice
- 1 tablespoon chopped fresh parsley, plus more for garnish
- 1 teaspoon red pepper flakes
- Prawns:
- 455 g large prawns, peeled and deveined, tails removed
- Fresh basil sprigs, for garnish

**Directions:**

1. Make the Parmesan Mackerel with Coriander :
2. Sprinkle the mackerel fillet with olive oil and put it in the zone 1 air fryer drawer.
3. Top the fish with ground coriander and Parmesan.
4. Cook the fish at 200ºC for 7 minutes.
5. Make the Garlic Butter Prawns Scampi :
6. Preheat the zone 2 air fryer drawer to 176ºC.
7. Put all the ingredients for the sauce in a baking pan and stir to incorporate.
8. Transfer the baking pan to the zone 2 air fryer drawer and air fry for 3 minutes, or until the sauce is heated through.
9. Once done, add the prawns to the baking pan, flipping to coat in the sauce.
10. Return to the air fryer and cook for another 5 minutes, or until the prawns are pink and opaque. Stir the prawns twice during cooking.
11. Serve garnished with the parsley and basil sprigs.

## Tilapia With Mojo And Crispy Plantains

Servings:4

Cooking Time: 30 Minutes

**Ingredients:**

- FOR THE TILAPIA
- 4 tilapia fillets (6 ounces each)
- 2 tablespoons all-purpose flour
- Nonstick cooking spray
- ¼ cup freshly squeezed orange juice
- 3 tablespoons fresh lime juice
- 2 tablespoons olive oil
- 1 tablespoon minced garlic
- ½ teaspoon ground cumin
- ¼ teaspoon kosher salt
- FOR THE PLANTAINS
- 1 large green plantain
- 2 cups cold water
- 2 teaspoons kosher salt
- Nonstick cooking spray

**Directions:**

1. To prep the tilapia: Dust both sides of the tilapia fillets with the flour, then spritz with cooking spray.
2. In a small bowl, whisk together the orange juice, lime juice, oil, garlic, cumin, and salt. Set the mojo sauce aside.
3. To prep the plantains: Cut the ends from the plantain, then remove and discard the peel. Slice the plantain into 1-inch rounds.
4. In a large bowl, combine the water, salt, and plantains. Let soak for 15 minutes.
5. Drain the plantains and pat them dry with paper towels. Spray with cooking spray.
6. To cook the tilapia and plantains: Install a crisper plate in each of the two baskets. Place the tilapia in a single layer in the Zone 1 basket (work in batches if needed) and insert the basket in the unit. Place the plantains in the Zone 2 basket and insert the basket in the unit.
7. Select Zone 1, select AIR FRY, set the temperature to 390°F (200°C), and set the timer to 10 minutes.
8. Select Zone 2, select AIR FRY, set the temperature to 390°F (200°C), and set the timer to 30 minutes. Select SMART FINISH.
9. Press START/PAUSE to begin cooking.
10. When the Zone 2 timer reads 10 minutes, press START/PAUSE. Remove the basket and use silicone-tipped tongs to transfer the plantains, which should be tender, to a cutting board. Use the bottom of a heavy glass to smash each plantain flat. Spray both sides with cooking spray and place them back in the basket. Reinsert the basket and press START/PAUSE to resume cooking.
11. When the Zone 1 timer reads 5 minutes, press START/PAUSE. Remove the basket. Spoon half of the mojo sauce over the tilapia. Reinsert the basket and press START/PAUSE to resume cooking.

12. When cooking is complete, the fish should be cooked through and the plantains crispy. Serve the tilapia and plantains with the remaining mojo sauce for dipping.

**Nutrition:**

- (Per serving) Calories: 380; Total fat: 21g; Saturated fat: 2g; Carbohydrates: 20g; Fiber: 1g; Protein: 35g; Sodium: 217mg

## Fish Sandwich

Servings: 4

Cooking Time: 22 Minutes.

**Ingredients:**

- 4 small cod fillets, skinless
- Salt and black pepper, to taste
- 2 tablespoons flour
- ¼ cup dried breadcrumbs
- Spray oil
- 9 ounces of frozen peas
- 1 tablespoon creme fraiche
- 12 capers
- 1 squeeze of lemon juice
- 4 bread rolls, cut in halve

**Directions:**

1. First, coat the cod fillets with flour, salt, and black pepper.
2. Then coat the fish with breadcrumbs.
3. Divide the coated codfish in the two crisper plates and spray them with cooking spray.
4. Return the crisper plate to the Ninja Foodi Dual Zone Air Fryer.
5. Choose the Air Fry mode for Zone 1 and set the temperature to 390 degrees F(200°C) and the time to 17 minutes.
6. Select the "MATCH" button to copy the settings for Zone 2.
7. Initiate cooking by pressing the START/STOP button.
8. Meanwhile, boil peas in hot water for 5 minutes until soft.
9. Then drain the peas and transfer them to the blender.
10. Add capers, lemon juice, and crème fraiche to the blender.
11. Blend until it makes a smooth mixture.
12. Spread the peas crème mixture on top of 2 lower halves of the bread roll, and place the fish fillets on it.
13. Place the remaining bread slices on top.
14. Serve fresh.

**Nutrition:**

- (Per serving) Calories 348 | Fat 30g |Sodium 660mg | Carbs 5g | Fiber 0g | Sugar 0g | Protein 14g

## Tilapia Sandwiches With Tartar Sauce

Servings: 4

Cooking Time: 17 Minutes

**Ingredients:**

- 160 g mayonnaise
- 2 tablespoons dried minced onion
- 1 dill pickle spear, finely chopped
- 2 teaspoons pickle juice
- ¼ teaspoon salt
- ⅛ teaspoon freshly ground black pepper
- 40 g plain flour
- 1 egg, lightly beaten
- 200 g panko bread crumbs
- 2 teaspoons lemon pepper
- 4 (170 g) tilapia fillets
- Olive oil spray
- 4 soft sub rolls
- 4 lettuce leaves

**Directions:**

1. To make the tartar sauce, in a small bowl, whisk the mayonnaise, dried onion, pickle, pickle juice, salt, and pepper until blended. Refrigerate while you make the fish.
2. Scoop the flour onto a plate; set aside.
3. Put the beaten egg in a medium shallow bowl.
4. On another plate, stir together the panko and lemon pepper.
5. Preheat the air fryer to 205°C.
6. Dredge the tilapia fillets in the flour, in the egg, and press into the panko mixture to coat.
7. Once the unit is preheated, spray the zone 1 basket with olive oil and place a baking paper liner into the basket. Place the prepared fillets on the liner in a single layer. Lightly spray the fillets with olive oil.
8. cook for 8 minutes, remove the basket, carefully flip the fillets, and spray them with more olive oil. Reinsert the basket to resume cooking.
9. When the cooking is complete, the fillets should be golden and crispy and a food thermometer should register 65°C. Place each cooked fillet in a sub roll, top with a little bit of tartar sauce and lettuce, and serve.

## Crispy Fish Nuggets

Servings: 4

Cooking Time: 8 Minutes

**Ingredients:**

- 2 eggs
- 96g all-purpose flour
- 700g cod fish fillets, cut into pieces
- 1 tsp garlic powder
- 1 tbsp old bay seasoning
- Pepper
- Salt

**Directions:**

1. In a small bowl, whisk eggs.
2. Mix flour, garlic powder, old bay seasoning, pepper, and salt in a shallow dish.
3. Coat each fish piece with flour, then dip in egg and again coat with flour.
4. Insert a crisper plate in the Ninja Foodi air fryer baskets.
5. Place coated fish pieces in both baskets.
6. Select zone 1, then select "air fry" mode and set the temperature to 380 degrees F(195°C) for 8 minutes. Press "match" to match zone 2 settings to zone 1. Press "start/stop" to begin.

**Nutrition:**

- (Per serving) Calories 298 | Fat 3.9g |Sodium 683mg | Carbs 18.6g | Fiber 0.7g | Sugar 0.4g | Protein 44.1g

## Sesame Honey Salmon

Servings: 4

Cooking Time: 10minutes

**Ingredients:**

- 4 salmon fillets
- 85g honey
- 15ml sesame oil
- 1 tbsp garlic, minced
- 2 tbsp soy sauce
- 1 tbsp sriracha
- Pepper
- Salt

**Directions:**

1. In a bowl, coat fish fillets with oil, garlic, honey, sriracha, soy sauce, pepper, and salt. Cover and place in refrigerator for 30 minutes.
2. Insert a crisper plate in the Ninja Foodi air fryer baskets.
3. Place the marinated fish fillets in both baskets.

4. Select zone 1, then select "air fry" mode and set the temperature to 375 degrees F(190°C) for 10 minutes. Press "match" to match zone 2 settings to zone 1. Press "start/stop" to begin.

**Nutrition:**

- (Per serving) Calories 341 | Fat 14.4g |Sodium 596mg | Carbs 19.5g | Fiber 0.2g | Sugar 17.6g | Protein 35.2g

## Crumb-topped Sole

Servings: 4

Cooking Time: 7 Minutes

**Ingredients:**

- 3 tablespoons mayonnaise
- 3 tablespoons Parmesan cheese, grated
- 2 teaspoons mustard seeds
- ¼ teaspoon black pepper
- 4 (170g) sole fillets
- 1 cup soft bread crumbs
- 1 green onion, chopped
- ½ teaspoon ground mustard
- 2 teaspoons butter, melted
- Cooking spray

**Directions:**

1. Mix mayonnaise with black pepper, mustard seeds, and 2 tablespoons cheese in a bowl.
2. Place 2 sole fillets in each air fryer basket and top them with mayo mixture.
3. Mix breadcrumbs with rest of the ingredients in a bowl.
4. Drizzle this mixture over the sole fillets.
5. Return the air fryer basket 1 to Zone 1, and basket 2 to Zone 2 of the Ninja Foodi 2-Basket Air Fryer.
6. Choose the "Air Fry" mode for Zone 1 and set the temperature to 375 degrees F(190°C) and 7 minutes of cooking time.
7. Select the "MATCH COOK" option to copy the settings for Zone 2.
8. Initiate cooking by pressing the START/PAUSE BUTTON.
9. Serve warm.

**Nutrition:**

- (Per serving) Calories 308 | Fat 24g |Sodium 715mg | Carbs 0.8g | Fiber 0.1g | Sugar 0.1g | Protein 21.9g

## Lemon Pepper Salmon With Asparagus

Servings:2

Cooking Time:18

**Ingredients:**

- 1 cup of green asparagus
- 2 tablespoons of butter
- 2 fillets of salmon, 8 ounces each
- Salt and black pepper, to taste
- 1 teaspoon of lemon juice
- ½ teaspoon of lemon zest
- oil spray, for greasing

**Directions:**

1. Rinse and trim the asparagus.
2. Rinse and pat dry the salmon fillets.
3. Take a bowl and mix lemon juice, lemon zest, salt, and black pepper.
4. Brush the fish fillet with the rub and place it in the zone 1 basket.
5. Place asparagus in zone 2 basket.
6. Spray the asparagus with oil spray.
7. Set zone 1 to AIRFRY mode for 18 minutes at 390 degrees F(200°C) .
8. Set the zone 2 to 5 minutes at 390 degrees F(200°C) , at air fry mode.
9. Hit the smart finish button to finish at the same time.
10. Once done, serve and enjoy.

**Nutrition:**

- (Per serving) Calories 482| Fat 28g| Sodium209 mg | Carbs 2.8g | Fiber1.5 g | Sugar1.4 g | Protein 56.3g

## Pecan-crusted Catfish Nuggets With "fried" Okra

Servings:4

Cooking Time: 17 Minutes

**Ingredients:**

- FOR THE CATFISH NUGGETS
- 1 cup whole milk
- 1 pound fresh catfish nuggets (or cut-up fillets)
- 1 large egg
- 2 to 3 dashes Louisiana-style hot sauce (optional)
- ¼ cup finely chopped pecans
- ½ cup all-purpose flour
- Nonstick cooking spray
- Tartar sauce, for serving (optional)
- FOR THE OKRA
- ½ cup fine yellow cornmeal
- ¼ cup all-purpose flour
- ½ teaspoon garlic powder
- ½ teaspoon paprika
- 1 teaspoon kosher salt
- 1 large egg
- 8 ounces frozen cut okra, thawed
- Nonstick cooking spray

**Directions:**

1. To prep the catfish: Pour the milk into a large zip-top bag. Add the catfish and turn to coat. Set in the refrigerator to soak for at least 1 hour or up to overnight.
2. Remove the fish from the milk, shaking off any excess liquid.
3. In a shallow dish, whisk together the egg and hot sauce (if using). In a second shallow dish, combine the pecans and flour.
4. Dip each piece of fish into the egg mixture, then into the nut mixture to coat. Gently press the nut mixture to adhere to the fish. Spritz each nugget with cooking spray.
5. To prep the okra: Set up a breading station with two small shallow bowls. In the first bowl, stir together the cornmeal, flour, garlic powder, paprika, and salt. In the second bowl, whisk the egg.
6. Dip the okra first in the cornmeal mixture, then the egg, then back into the cornmeal. Spritz with cooking spray.
7. To cook the catfish and okra: Install a crisper plate in each of the two baskets. Place the fish in a single layer in the Zone 1 basket and insert the basket in the unit. Place the okra in the Zone 2 basket and insert the basket in the unit.
8. Select Zone 1, select AIR FRY, set the temperature to 390°F (200°C), and set the timer to 17 minutes.
9. Select Zone 2, select AIR FRY, set the temperature to 400°F (205°C), and set the timer to 12 minutes. Select SMART FINISH.
10. Press START/PAUSE to begin cooking.
11. When cooking is complete, the fish should be cooked through and the okra golden brown and crispy. Serve hot.

**Nutrition:**

- (Per serving) Calories: 414; Total fat: 24g; Saturated fat: 2.5g; Carbohydrates: 30g; Fiber: 3g; Protein: 23g; Sodium: 569mg

## Basil Cheese Salmon

Servings: 4
Cooking Time:7 Minutes

**Ingredients:**

- 4 salmon fillets
- 1/4 cup parmesan cheese, grated
- 5 fresh basil leaves, minced
- 2 tbsp mayonnaise
- 1/2 lemon juice
- Pepper
- Salt

**Directions:**

1. Preheat the air fryer to 400 F.
2. Brush salmon fillets with lemon juice and season with pepper and salt.
3. In a small bowl, mix mayonnaise, basil, and cheese.
4. Spray air fryer basket with cooking spray.
5. Place salmon fillets into the air fryer basket and brush with mayonnaise mixture and cook for 7 minutes.
6. Serve and enjoy.

## Chili Lime Tilapia

Servings: 4
Cooking Time: 10 Minutes

**Ingredients:**

- 340g tilapia fillets
- 2 teaspoons chili powder
- 1 teaspoon cumin
- 1 teaspoon garlic powder
- ½ teaspoon oregano
- ½ teaspoon sea salt
- ¼ teaspoon black pepper
- Lime zest from 1 lime
- Juice of ½ lime

**Directions:**

1. Mix chili powder and other spices with lime juice and zest in a bowl.
2. Rub this spice mixture over the tilapia fillets.
3. Place two fillets in each air basket.
4. Return the air fryer basket to the Ninja Foodi 2 Baskets Air Fryer.
5. Choose the "Air Fry" mode for Zone 1 at 400 degrees F(205°C) and 10 minutes of cooking time.
6. Select the "MATCH COOK" option to copy the settings for Zone 2.
7. Initiate cooking by pressing the START/PAUSE BUTTON.
8. Flip the tilapia fillets once cooked halfway through.
9. Serve warm.

**Nutrition:**

- (Per serving) Calories 275 | Fat 1.4g |Sodium 582mg | Carbs 31.5g | Fiber 1.1g | Sugar 0.1g | Protein 29.8g

## Italian Baked Cod

Servings: 4
Cooking Time: 12 Minutes

**Ingredients:**

- 4 cod fillets, 170 g each
- 2 tablespoons salted butter, melted
- 1 teaspoon Italian seasoning
- ¼ teaspoon salt
- 120 ml tomato-based pasta sauce

**Directions:**

1. Place cod into an ungreased round nonstick baking dish. Pour butter over cod and sprinkle with Italian seasoning and salt. Top with pasta sauce.
2. Place dish into the two air fryer drawers. Adjust the temperature to 176ºC and bake for 12 minutes. Fillets will be lightly browned, easily flake, and have an internal temperature of at least 64ºC when done. Serve warm.

## Country Prawns

Servings: 4
Cooking Time: 15 To 20 Minutes

**Ingredients:**

- 455 g large prawns, peeled and deveined, with tails on
- 455 g smoked sausage, cut into thick slices
- 2 corn cobs, quartered
- 1 courgette, cut into bite-sized pieces
- 1 red bell pepper, cut into chunks
- 1 tablespoon Old Bay seasoning
- 2 tablespoons olive oil
- Cooking spray

**Directions:**

1. Preheat the air fryer to 204ºC. Spray the air fryer drawer lightly with cooking spray.
2. In a large bowl, mix the prawns, sausage, corn, courgette, bell pepper, and Old Bay seasoning, and toss to coat with the spices. Add the olive oil and toss again until evenly coated.
3. Spread the mixture in the two air fryer drawers in a single layer.
4. Air fry for 15 to 20 minutes, or until cooked through, shaking the drawers every 5 minutes for even cooking.
5. Serve immediately.

## Delicious Haddock

Servings: 4
Cooking Time: 10 Minutes

**Ingredients:**

- 1 egg
- 455g haddock fillets
- 1 tsp seafood seasoning
- 136g flour
- 15ml olive oil
- 119g breadcrumbs
- Pepper
- Salt

**Directions:**

1. In a shallow dish, whisk egg. Add flour to a plate.
2. In a separate shallow dish, mix breadcrumbs, pepper, seafood seasoning, and salt.
3. Brush fish fillets with oil.
4. Coat each fish fillet with flour, then dip in egg and finally coat with breadcrumbs.
5. Insert a crisper plate in the Ninja Foodi air fryer baskets.
6. Place coated fish fillets in both baskets.
7. Select zone 1, then select "air fry" mode and set the temperature to 360 degrees F(180°C) for 10 minutes. Press "match" to match zone 2 settings to zone 1. Press "start/stop" to begin.

**Nutrition:**

- (Per serving) Calories 393 | Fat 7.4g |Sodium 351mg | Carbs 43.4g | Fiber 2.1g | Sugar 1.8g | Protein 35.7g

## Beer Battered Fish Fillet

Servings:2
Cooking Time:14

**Ingredients:**

- 1 cup all-purpose flour
- 4 tablespoons cornstarch
- 1 teaspoon baking soda
- 8 ounces beer
- 2 egg beaten

- ½ cup all-purpose flour
- 1 teaspoon smoked paprika
- 1 teaspoon salt
- 1/4 teaspoon freshly ground black pepper
- ¼ teaspoon of cayenne pepper
- 2 cod fillets, 1½-inches thick, cut into 4 pieces
- Oil spray, for greasing

**Directions:**

1. Take a large bowl and combine flour, baking soda, corn starch, and salt
2. In a separate bowl beat eggs along with the beer.
3. In a shallow dish mix paprika, salt, pepper, and cayenne pepper.
4. Dry the codfish fillets with a paper towel.
5. Dip the fish into the eggs and coat it with seasoned flour.
6. Then dip it in the seasoning.
7. Grease the fillet with oil spray.
8. Divide the fillet between both zones.
9. Set zone 1 to AIR FRY mode at 400 degrees F(205°C) for 14 minutes.
10. Select MACTH button for zone 2 basket.
11. Press start and let the AIR fry do its magic.
12. Once cooking is done, serve the fish.
13. Enjoy it hot.

**Nutrition:**

- (Per serving) Calories 1691| Fat 6.1g| Sodium 3976mg | Carbs105.1 g | Fiber 3.4g | Sugar15.6 g | Protein 270g

## Keto Baked Salmon With Pesto

Servings:2
Cooking Time:18

**Ingredients:**

- 4 salmon fillets, 2 inches thick
- 2 ounces green pesto
- Salt and black pepper
- ½ tablespoon of canola oil, for greasing
- 1-1/2 cup mayonnaise
- 2 tablespoons Greek yogurt
- Salt and black pepper, to taste

**Directions:**

1. Rub the salmon with pesto, salt, oil, and black pepper.
2. In a small bowl, whisk together all the green sauce ingredients.
3. Divide the fish fillets between both the baskets.
4. Set zone 1 to air fry mode for 18 minutes at 390 degrees F(200°C) .
5. Select MATCH button for Zone 2 basket.
6. Once the cooking is done, serve it with green sauce drizzle.
7. Enjoy.

**Nutrition:**

- (Per serving) Calories 1165 | Fat80.7 g| Sodium 1087 mg | Carbs 33.1g | Fiber 0.5g | Sugar11.5 g | Protein 80.6g

## Codfish With Herb Vinaigrette

Servings:2
Cooking Time:16

**Ingredients:**

- Vinaigrette Ingredients:
- 1/2 cup parsley leaves
- 1 cup basil leaves
- ½ cup mint leaves
- 2 tablespoons thyme leaves
- 1/4 teaspoon red pepper flakes
- 2 cloves of garlic
- 4 tablespoons of red wine vinegar
- ¼ cup of olive oil
- Salt, to taste
- Other Ingredients:
- 1.5 pounds fish fillets, cod fish
- 2 tablespoons olive oil
- Salt and black pepper, to taste
- 1 teaspoon of paprika
- 1teasbpoon of Italian seasoning

**Directions:**

1. Blend the entire vinaigrette ingredient in a high-speed blender and pulse into a smooth paste.
2. Set aside for drizzling overcooked fish.
3. Rub the fillets with salt, black pepper, paprika, Italian seasoning, and olive oil.
4. Divide it between two baskets of the air fryer.
5. Set the zone 1 to 16 minutes at 390 degrees F(200°C) , at AIR FRY mode.
6. Press the MATCH button for the second basket.
7. Once done, serve the fillets with the drizzle of blended vinaigrette

**Nutrition:**

- (Per serving) Calories 1219| Fat 81.8g| Sodium 1906mg | Carbs64.4 g | Fiber5.5 g | Sugar 0.4g | Protein 52.1g

## Tuna Patties

Servings: 6
Cooking Time: 10 Minutes

**Ingredients:**

- For the tuna patties:
- 1 tablespoon extra-virgin olive oil
- 1 tablespoon butter
- ½ cup chopped onion
- ½ red bell pepper, chopped
- 1 teaspoon minced garlic
- 2 (7-ounce) cans or 3 (5-ounce) cans albacore tuna fish in water, drained
- 1 tablespoon lime juice
- 1 celery stalk, chopped
- ¼ cup chopped fresh parsley
- 3 tablespoons grated parmesan cheese
- ½ teaspoon dried oregano
- ¼ teaspoon salt
- Black pepper, to taste
- 1 teaspoon sriracha
- ½ cup panko crumbs
- 2 whisked eggs
- For the crumb coating:
- ½ cup panko crumbs
- ¼ cup parmesan cheese
- Non-stick spray

**Directions:**

1. In a skillet, heat the oil and butter over medium-high heat.
2. Sauté the onions, red bell pepper, and garlic for 5 to 7 minutes.
3. Drain the tuna from the cans thoroughly. Put the tuna in a large mixing bowl. Add the lime juice.
4. Add the sautéed vegetables to the mixing bowl.
5. Add the celery, parsley, and cheese. Combine well.
6. Add the oregano, salt, and pepper to taste. Mix well.
7. Add a dash of sriracha for a spicy kick and mix well.
8. Add the panko crumbs and mix well.
9. Mix in the eggs until the mixture is well combined. You can add an extra egg if necessary, but the tuna is usually wet enough that it isn't required. Form 6 patties from the mixture.
10. Refrigerate for 30 to 60 minutes (or even overnight).
11. Remove from refrigerator and coat with a mixture of the ½ cup of panko crumbs and ¼ cup of parmesan cheese.

12. Spray the tops of the coated patties with some non-stick cooking spray.
13. Place a crisper place in each drawer. Put 3 patties in each drawer. Insert the drawers into the unit.
14. Select zone 1, then AIR FRY, then set the temperature to 390 degrees F/ 200 degrees C with a 10-minute timer. To match zone 2 settings to zone 1, choose MATCH. To begin, select START/STOP.
15. Remove and garnish with chopped parsley.

**Nutrition:**

- (Per serving) Calories 381 | Fat 16g | Sodium 1007mg | Carbs 23g | Fiber 2g | Sugar 4g | Protein 38g

## Scallops With Greens

Servings: 8
Cooking Time: 13 Minutes.

**Ingredients:**

- ¾ cup heavy whipping cream
- 1 tablespoon tomato paste
- 1 tablespoon chopped fresh basil
- 1 teaspoon garlic, minced
- ½ teaspoons salt
- ½ teaspoons pepper
- 12 ounces frozen spinach thawed
- 8 jumbo sea scallops
- Vegetable oil to spray

**Directions:**

1. Season the scallops with vegetable oil, salt, and pepper in a bowl
2. Mix cream with spinach, basil, garlic, salt, pepper, and tomato paste in a bowl.
3. Pour this mixture over the scallops and mix gently.
4. Divide the scallops in the Air Fryers Baskets without using the crisper plate.
5. Return the crisper plate to the Ninja Foodi Dual Zone Air Fryer.
6. Choose the Air Fry mode for Zone 1 and set the temperature to 390 degrees F(200°C) and the time to 13 minutes.
7. Select the "MATCH" button to copy the settings for Zone 2.
8. Initiate cooking by pressing the START/STOP button.
9. Serve right away

**Nutrition:**

- (Per serving) Calories 266 | Fat 6.3g |Sodium 193mg | Carbs 39.1g | Fiber 7.2g | Sugar 5.2g | Protein 14.8g

## Fish Tacos

Servings: 5
Cooking Time: 30 Minutes

**Ingredients:**

- 1 pound firm white fish such as cod, haddock, pollock, halibut, or walleye
- ¾ cup gluten-free flour blend
- 3 eggs
- 1 cup gluten-free panko breadcrumbs
- 1 teaspoon garlic powder
- 1 teaspoon onion powder
- 1 teaspoon cumin
- 1 teaspoon lemon pepper
- 1 teaspoon red chili flakes
- 1 teaspoon kosher salt, divided
- 1 teaspoon pepper, divided
- Cooking oil spray
- 1 package corn tortillas
- Toppings such as tomatoes, avocado, cabbage, radishes, jalapenos, salsa, or hot sauce (optional)

**Directions:**

1. Dry the fish with paper towels. (Make sure to thaw the fish if it's frozen.) Depending on the size of the fillets, cut the fish in half or thirds.
2. On both sides of the fish pieces, liberally season with salt and pepper.
3. Put the flour in a dish.
4. In a separate bowl, crack the eggs and whisk them together until well blended.
5. Put the panko breadcrumbs in another bowl. Add the garlic powder, onion powder, cumin, lemon pepper, and red chili flakes. Add salt and pepper to taste. Stir until everything is well blended.
6. Each piece of fish should be dipped in the flour, then the eggs, and finally in the breadcrumb mixture. Make sure that each piece is completely coated.
7. Put a crisper plate in each drawer. Arrange the fish pieces in a single layer in each drawer. Insert the drawers into the unit.
8. Select zone 1, then AIR FRY, then set the temperature to 360 degrees F/ 180 degrees C with a 20-minute timer. To match zone 2 settings to zone 1, choose MATCH. To begin, select START/STOP.
9. Remove the fish from the drawers after the timer has finished. Place the crispy fish on warmed tortillas.

**Nutrition:**

- (Per serving) Calories 534 | Fat 18g | Sodium 679mg | Carbs 63g | Fiber 8g | Sugar 3g | Protein 27g

## Fried Tilapia

Servings: 4
Cooking Time: 20 Minutes

**Ingredients:**

- 4 fresh tilapia fillets, approximately 6 ounces each
- 2 teaspoons olive oil
- 2 teaspoons chopped fresh chives
- 2 teaspoons chopped fresh parsley
- 1 teaspoon minced garlic
- Freshly ground pepper, to taste
- Salt to taste

**Directions:**

1. Pat the tilapia fillets dry with a paper towel.
2. Stir together the olive oil, chives, parsley, garlic, salt, and pepper in a small bowl.
3. Brush the mixture over the top of the tilapia fillets.
4. Place a crisper plate in each drawer. Add the fillets in a single layer to each drawer. Insert the drawers into the unit.
5. Select zone 1, then AIR FRY, then set the temperature to 360 degrees F/ 180 degrees C with a 20-minute timer. To match zone 2 settings to zone 1, choose MATCH. To begin, select START/STOP.
6. Remove the tilapia fillets from the drawers after the timer has finished.

**Nutrition:**

- (Per serving) Calories 140 | Fat 5.7g | Sodium 125mg | Carbs 1.5g | Fiber 0.4g | Sugar 0g | Protein 21.7g

## Fish And Chips

Servings:2
Cooking Time:22

**Ingredients:**

- 1 pound of potatoes, cut lengthwise
- 1 cup seasoned flour
- 2 eggs, organic
- 1/3 cup buttermilk
- 2 cup seafood fry mix
- ½ cup bread crumbs
- 2 codfish fillet, 6 ounces each

- Oil spray, for greasing

**Directions:**

1. take a bowl and whisk eggs in it along buttermilk.
2. In a separate bowl mix seafood fry mix and bread crumbs
3. Take a baking tray and spread flour on it
4. Dip the fillets first in egg wash, then in flour, and at the end coat it with breadcrumbs mixture.
5. Put the fish fillet in air fryer zone 1 basket.
6. Grease the fish fillet with oil spray.
7. Set zone 1 to AIR FRY mode at 400 degrees F(205°C) for 14 minutes.
8. Put potato chip in zone two baskets and lightly grease it with oil spray.
9. Set the zone 2 basket to AIRFRY mode at 400 degrees F(205°C) for 22 minutes.
10. Hit the smart finish button.
11. Once done, serve and enjoy.

**Nutrition:**

- (Per serving) Calories 992| Fat 22.3g| Sodium1406 mg | Carbs 153.6g | Fiber 10g | Sugar10 g | Protein 40g

## Shrimp Skewers

Servings: 4

Cooking Time: 10minutes

**Ingredients:**

- 453g shrimp
- 15ml lemon juice
- 15ml olive oil
- 1 tbsp old bay seasoning
- 1 tsp garlic, minced

**Directions:**

1. Toss shrimp with old bay seasoning, garlic, lemon juice, and olive oil in a bowl.
2. Thread shrimp onto the soaked skewers.
3. Insert a crisper plate in the Ninja Foodi air fryer baskets.
4. Place the shrimp skewers in both baskets.
5. Select zone 1, then select "air fry" mode and set the temperature to 390 degrees F(200°C) for 10 minutes. Press "match" to match zone 2 settings to zone 1. Press "start/stop" to begin.

**Nutrition:**

- (Per serving) Calories 167 | Fat 5.5g |Sodium 758mg | Carbs 2g | Fiber 0g | Sugar 0.1g | Protein 25.9g

# Vegetables And Sides Recipes

## Healthy Air Fried Veggies

Servings: 4
Cooking Time: 15 Minutes
**Ingredients:**

- 52g onion, sliced
- 71g broccoli florets
- 116g radishes, sliced
- 15ml olive oil
- 100g Brussels sprouts, cut in half
- 325g cauliflower florets
- 1 tsp balsamic vinegar
- ½ tsp garlic powder
- Pepper
- Salt

**Directions:**

1. In a bowl, toss veggies with oil, vinegar, garlic powder, pepper, and salt.
2. Insert a crisper plate in the Ninja Foodi air fryer baskets.
3. Add veggies in both baskets.
4. Select zone 1 then select "air fry" mode and set the temperature to 380 degrees F(195°C) for 15 minutes. Press "match" to match zone 2 settings to zone 1. Press "start/stop" to begin. Stir halfway through.

**Nutrition:**

- (Per serving) Calories 71 | Fat 3.8g |Sodium 72mg | Carbs 8.8g | Fiber 3.2g | Sugar 3.3g | Protein 2.5g

## Fried Olives

Servings: 6
Cooking Time: 9 Minutes.
**Ingredients:**

- 2 cups blue cheese stuffed olives, drained
- ½ cup all-purpose flour
- 1 cup panko breadcrumbs
- ½ teaspoon garlic powder
- 1 pinch oregano
- 2 eggs

**Directions:**

1. Mix flour with oregano and garlic powder in a bowl and beat two eggs in another bowl.
2. Spread panko breadcrumbs in a bowl.
3. Coat all the olives with the flour mixture, dip in the eggs and then coat with the panko breadcrumbs.
4. As you coat the olives, place them in the two crisper plates in a single layer, then spray them with cooking oil.
5. Return the crisper plates to the Ninja Foodi Dual Zone Air Fryer.
6. Choose the Air Fry mode for Zone 1 and set the temperature to 375 degrees F(190°C) and the time to 9 minutes.
7. Select the "MATCH" button to copy the settings for Zone 2.
8. Initiate cooking by pressing the START/STOP button.
9. Flip the olives once cooked halfway through, then resume cooking.
10. Serve.

**Nutrition:**

- (Per serving) Calories 166 | Fat 3.2g |Sodium 437mg | Carbs 28.8g | Fiber 1.8g | Sugar 2.7g | Protein 5.8g

## Bacon Wrapped Corn Cob

Servings: 4
Cooking Time: 10 Minutes
**Ingredients:**

- 4 trimmed corns on the cob
- 8 bacon slices

**Directions:**

1. Wrap the corn cobs with two bacon slices.
2. Place the wrapped cobs into the Ninja Foodi 2 Baskets Air Fryer baskets.
3. Return the air fryer basket 1 to Zone 1, and basket 2 to Zone 2 of the Ninja Foodi 2-Basket Air Fryer.
4. Choose the "Air Fry" mode for Zone 1 and set the temperature to 355 degrees F(180°C) and 10 minutes of cooking time.
5. Select the "MATCH COOK" option to copy the settings for Zone 2.
6. Initiate cooking by pressing the START/PAUSE BUTTON.
7. Flip the corn cob once cooked halfway through.
8. Serve warm.

**Nutrition:**

- (Per serving) Calories 350 | Fat 2.6g |Sodium 358mg | Carbs 64.6g | Fiber 14.4g | Sugar 3.3g | Protein 19.9g

## Air-fried Radishes

Servings: 6
Cooking Time: 15 Minutes
**Ingredients:**

- 1020g radishes, quartered
- 3 tablespoons olive oil
- 1 tablespoon fresh oregano, minced
- ¼ teaspoon salt
- ⅛ teaspoon black pepper

**Directions:**

1. Toss radishes with oil, black pepper, salt and oregano in a bowl.
2. Divide the radishes into the Ninja Foodi 2 Baskets Air Fryer baskets.
3. Return the air fryer basket 1 to Zone 1, and basket 2 to Zone 2 of the Ninja Foodi 2-Basket Air Fryer.
4. Choose the "Air Fry" mode for Zone 1 at 375 degrees F(190°C) and 15 minutes of cooking time.
5. Select the "MATCH COOK" option to copy the settings for Zone 2.
6. Initiate cooking by pressing the START/PAUSE BUTTON.
7. Toss the radishes once cooked halfway through.
8. Serve.

**Nutrition:**

- (Per serving) Calories 270 | Fat 14.6g |Sodium 394mg | Carbs 31.3g | Fiber 7.5g | Sugar 9.7g | Protein 6.4g

## Broccoli, Squash, & Pepper

Servings: 4
Cooking Time: 12 Minutes
**Ingredients:**

- 175g broccoli florets
- 1 red bell pepper, diced
- 1 tbsp olive oil
- ½ tsp garlic powder
- ¼ onion, sliced
- 1 zucchini, sliced
- 2 yellow squash, sliced
- Pepper
- Salt

**Directions:**

1. In a bowl, toss veggies with oil, garlic powder, pepper, and salt.
2. Insert a crisper plate in the Ninja Foodi air fryer baskets.
3. Add the vegetable mixture in both baskets.
4. Select zone 1 then select "air fry" mode and set the temperature to 390 degrees F(200°C) for 12 minutes. Press "match" to match zone 2 settings to zone 1. Press "start/stop" to begin. Stir halfway through.

**Nutrition:**

- (Per serving) Calories 75 | Fat 3.9g |Sodium 62mg | Carbs 9.6g | Fiber 2.8g | Sugar 4.8g | Protein 2.9g

## Brussels Sprouts

Servings:2
Cooking Time:20
**Ingredients:**

- 2 pounds Brussels sprouts
- 2 tablespoons avocado oil
- Salt and pepper, to taste
- 1 cup pine nuts, roasted

**Directions:**

1. Trim the bottom of Brussels sprouts.
2. Take a bowl and combine the avocado oil, salt, and black pepper.
3. Toss the Brussels sprouts well.
4. Divide it in both air fryer baskets.
5. For the zone 1 basket use AIR fry mode for 20 minutes at 390 degrees F(200°C) .
6. Select the MATCH button for the zone 2 basket.
7. Once the Brussels sprouts get crisp and tender, take out and serve.

**Nutrition:**

- (Per serving) Calories 672| Fat 50g| Sodium 115mg | Carbs 51g | Fiber 20.2g | Sugar 12.3g | Protein 25g

## Garlic-herb Fried Squash

Servings: 4
Cooking Time: 15 Minutes
**Ingredients:**

- 5 cups halved small pattypan squash (about 1¼ pounds)
- 1 tablespoon olive oil
- 2 garlic cloves, minced
- ½ teaspoon salt
- ¼ teaspoon dried oregano
- ¼ teaspoon dried thyme
- ¼ teaspoon pepper
- 1 tablespoon minced fresh parsley, for serving

**Directions:**

1. Place the squash in a large bowl.
2. Mix the oil, garlic, salt, oregano, thyme, and pepper; drizzle over the squash. Toss to coat.
3. Place a crisper plate in both drawers. Put the squash in a single layer in each drawer. Insert the drawers into the unit.
4. Select zone 1, then AIR FRY, then set the temperature to 360 degrees F/ 180 degrees C with a 6-minute timer. To match zone 2 settings to zone 1, choose MATCH. To begin, select START/STOP.
5. Remove the squash from the drawers after the timer has finished. Sprinkle with the parsley.

**Nutrition:**

- (Per serving) Calories 58 | Fat 3g | Sodium 296mg | Carbs 6g | Fiber 2g | Sugar 3g | Protein 2g

## Bacon Potato Patties

Servings: 2
Cooking Time: 15 Minutes
**Ingredients:**

- 1 egg
- 600g mashed potatoes
- 119g breadcrumbs
- 2 bacon slices, cooked & chopped
- 235g cheddar cheese, shredded
- 15g flour
- Pepper
- Salt

**Directions:**

1. In a bowl, mix mashed potatoes with remaining ingredients until well combined.
2. Make patties from potato mixture and place on a plate.
3. Place plate in the refrigerator for 10 minutes
4. Insert a crisper plate in the Ninja Foodi air fryer baskets.
5. Place the prepared patties in both baskets.
6. Select zone 1 then select "air fry" mode and set the temperature to 390 degrees F(200°C) for 15 minutes. Press "match" to match zone 2 settings to zone 1. Press "start/stop" to begin. Turn halfway through.

**Nutrition:**

- (Per serving) Calories 702 | Fat 26.8g |Sodium 1405mg | Carbs 84.8g | Fiber 2.7g | Sugar 3.8g | Protein 30.5g

## Green Tomato Stacks

Servings: 6
Cooking Time: 12 Minutes
**Ingredients:**

- ¼ cup mayonnaise
- ¼ teaspoon lime zest, grated
- 2 tablespoons lime juice
- 1 teaspoon minced fresh thyme
- ½ teaspoon black pepper
- ¼ cup all-purpose flour
- 2 large egg whites, beaten
- ¾ cup cornmeal
- ¼ teaspoon salt
- 2 medium green tomatoes
- 2 medium re tomatoes
- Cooking spray
- 8 slices Canadian bacon, warmed

**Directions:**

1. Mix mayonnaise with ¼ teaspoon black pepper, thyme, lime juice and zest in a bowl.
2. Spread flour in one bowl, beat egg whites in another bowl and mix cornmeal with ¼ teaspoon black pepper and salt in a third bowl.
3. Cut the tomatoes into 4 slices and coat each with the flour then dip in the egg whites.
4. Coat the tomatoes slices with the cornmeal mixture.
5. Place the slices in the air fryer baskets.

6. Return the air fryer basket 1 to Zone 1, and basket 2 to Zone 2 of the Ninja Foodi 2-Basket Air Fryer.
7. Choose the "Air Fry" mode for Zone 1 at 390 degrees F(200°C) and 12 minutes of cooking time.
8. Select the "MATCH COOK" option to copy the settings for Zone 2.
9. Initiate cooking by pressing the START/PAUSE BUTTON.
10. Flip the tomatoes once cooked halfway through.
11. Place the green tomato slices on the working surface.
12. Top them with bacon, and red tomato slice.
13. Serve.

**Nutrition:**

- (Per serving) Calories 113 | Fat 3g |Sodium 152mg | Carbs 20g | Fiber 3g | Sugar 1.1g | Protein 3.5g

## Green Salad With Crispy Fried Goat Cheese And Baked Croutons

Servings:4
Cooking Time: 10 Minutes

**Ingredients:**

- FOR THE GOAT CHEESE
- 1 (4-ounce) log soft goat cheese
- ½ cup panko bread crumbs
- 2 tablespoons vegetable oil
- FOR THE CROUTONS
- 2 slices Italian-style sandwich bread
- 2 tablespoons vegetable oil
- 1 tablespoon poultry seasoning
- ½ teaspoon kosher salt
- ¼ teaspoon freshly ground black pepper
- FOR THE SALAD
- 8 cups green leaf lettuce leaves
- ½ cup store-bought balsamic vinaigrette

**Directions:**

1. To prep the goat cheese: Cut the goat cheese into 8 round slices.
2. Spread the panko on a plate. Gently press the cheese into the panko to coat on both sides. Drizzle with the oil.
3. To prep the croutons: Cut the bread into cubes and place them in a large bowl. Add the oil, poultry seasoning, salt, and black pepper. Mix well to coat the bread cubes evenly.
4. To cook the goat cheese and croutons: Install a crisper plate in each of the two baskets. Place the goat cheese in the Zone 1 basket and insert the basket in the unit. Place the croutons in the Zone 2 basket and insert the basket in the unit.
5. Select Zone 1, select AIR FRY, set the temperature to 400°F (205°C), and set the timer to 6 minutes.
6. Select Zone 2, select BAKE, set the temperature to 390°F (200°C), and set the timer to 10 minutes. Select SMART FINISH.
7. Press START/PAUSE to begin cooking.
8. When cooking is complete, the goat cheese will be golden brown and the croutons crisp.
9. Remove the Zone 1 basket. Let the goat cheese cool in the basket for 5 minutes; it will firm up as it cools.
10. To assemble the salad: In a large bowl, combine the lettuce, vinaigrette, and croutons. Toss well. Divide the salad among four plates. Top each plate with 2 pieces of goat cheese.

**Nutrition:**

- (Per serving) Calories: 578; Total fat: 40g; Saturated fat: 14g; Carbohydrates: 39g; Fiber: 3.5g; Protein: 24g; Sodium: 815mg

## Beets With Orange Gremolata And Goat' s Cheese

Servings: 12
Cooking Time: 45 Minutes

**Ingredients:**

- 3 medium fresh golden beets (about 1 pound)
- 3 medium fresh beets (about 1 pound)
- 2 tablespoons lime juice
- 2 tablespoons orange juice
- ½ teaspoon fine sea salt
- 1 tablespoon minced fresh parsley
- 1 tablespoon minced fresh sage
- 1 garlic clove, minced
- 1 teaspoon grated orange zest
- 3 tablespoons crumbled goat's cheese
- 2 tablespoons sunflower kernels

**Directions:**

1. Scrub the beets and trim the tops by 1 inch.
2. Place the beets on a double thickness of heavy-duty foil (about 24 x 12 inches). Fold the foil around the beets, sealing tightly.
3. Place a crisper plate in both drawers. Put the beets in a single layer in each drawer. Insert the drawers into the unit.
4. Select zone 1, then AIR FRY, then set the temperature to 360 degrees F/ 180 degrees C with a 45-minute timer. To match zone 2 settings to zone 1, choose MATCH. To begin, select START/STOP.
5. Remove the beets from the drawers after the timer has finished. Peel, halve, and slice them when they're cool enough to handle. Place them in a serving bowl.
6. Toss in the lime juice, orange juice, and salt to coat. Sprinkle the beets with the parsley, sage, garlic, and orange zest. The sunflower kernels and goat's cheese go on top.

**Nutrition:**

- (Per serving) Calories 481 | Fat 20g | Sodium 1162mg | Carbs 56g | Fiber 4g | Sugar 9g | Protein 19g

## Fried Asparagus

Servings: 4
Cooking Time: 6 Minutes

**Ingredients:**

- ¼ cup mayonnaise
- 4 teaspoons olive oil
- 1½ teaspoons grated lemon zest
- 1 garlic clove, minced
- ½ teaspoon pepper
- ¼ teaspoon seasoned salt
- 1-pound fresh asparagus, trimmed
- 2 tablespoons shredded parmesan cheese
- Lemon wedges (optional)

**Directions:**

1. In a large bowl, combine the first 6 ingredients.
2. Add the asparagus; toss to coat.
3. Put a crisper plate in both drawers. Put the asparagus in a single layer in each drawer. Top with the parmesan cheese. Place the drawers into the unit.
4. Select zone 1, then AIR FRY, then set the temperature to 375 degrees F/ 190 degrees C with a 6-minute timer. To match zone 2 settings to zone 1, choose MATCH. To begin, select START/STOP.
5. Remove the asparagus from the drawers after the timer has finished.

**Nutrition:**

- (Per serving) Calories 156 | Fat 15g | Sodium 214mg | Carbs 3g | Fiber 1g | Sugar 1g | Protein 2g

## Kale And Spinach Chips

Servings:2
Cooking Time:6
**Ingredients:**
- 2 cups spinach, torn in pieces and stem removed
- 2 cups kale, torn in pieces, stems removed
- 1 tablespoon of olive oil
- Sea salt, to taste
- 1/3 cup Parmesan cheese

**Directions:**
1. Take a bowl and add spinach to it.
2. Take another bowl and add kale to it.
3. Now, season both of them with olive oil, and sea salt.
4. Add kale to zone 1 basket and spinach to zone 2 basket.
5. Select the zone 1 air fry mode at 350 degrees F(175°C) for 6 minutes.
6. Set zone 2 to AIR FRY mode at 350 for 5 minutes.
7. Once done, take out the crispy chips and sprinkle Parmesan cheese on top.
8. Serve and Enjoy.

**Nutrition:**
- (Per serving) Calories 166| Fat 11.1g| Sodium 355mg | Carbs 8.1g | Fiber1.7 g | Sugar 0.1g | Protein 8.2g

## Balsamic Vegetables

Servings: 4
Cooking Time: 13 Minutes
**Ingredients:**
- 125g asparagus, cut woody ends
- 88g mushrooms, halved
- 1 tbsp Dijon mustard
- 3 tbsp soy sauce
- 27g brown sugar
- 57ml balsamic vinegar
- 32g olive oil
- 1 zucchini, sliced
- 1 yellow squash, sliced
- 170g grape tomatoes
- Pepper
- Salt

**Directions:**
1. In a bowl, mix asparagus, tomatoes, oil, mustard, soy sauce, mushrooms, zucchini, squash, brown sugar, vinegar, pepper, and salt.
2. Cover the bowl and place it in the refrigerator for 45 minutes.
3. Insert a crisper plate in the Ninja Foodi air fryer baskets.
4. Add the vegetable mixture in both baskets.
5. Select zone 1, then select "air fry" mode and set the temperature to 390 degrees F(200°C) for 12 minutes. Press "match" to match zone 2 settings to zone 1. Press "start/stop" to begin. Stir halfway through.

**Nutrition:**
- (Per serving) Calories 184 | Fat 13.3g |Sodium 778mg | Carbs 14.7g | Fiber 3.6g | Sugar 9.5g | Protein 5.5g

## Spanakopita Rolls With Mediterranean Vegetable Salad

Servings:4
Cooking Time: 15 Minutes
**Ingredients:**
- FOR THE SPANAKOPITA ROLLS
- 1 (10-ounce) package chopped frozen spinach, thawed
- 4 ounces feta cheese, crumbled
- 2 large eggs
- 1 teaspoon dried oregano
- ½ teaspoon freshly ground black pepper
- 12 sheets phyllo dough, thawed
- Nonstick cooking spray
- FOR THE ROASTED VEGETABLES
- 1 medium eggplant, diced
- 1 small red onion, cut into 8 wedges
- 1 red bell pepper, sliced
- 2 tablespoons olive oil
- FOR THE SALAD
- 1 (15-ounce) can chickpeas, drained and rinsed
- ¼ cup chopped fresh parsley
- ¼ cup olive oil
- ¼ cup red wine vinegar
- 2 garlic cloves, minced
- ½ teaspoon dried oregano
- ¼ teaspoon kosher salt
- ¼ teaspoon freshly ground black pepper

**Directions:**
1. To prep the spanakopita rolls: Squeeze as much liquid from the spinach as you can and place the spinach in a large bowl. Add the feta, eggs, oregano, and black pepper. Mix well.
2. Lay one sheet of phyllo on a clean work surface and mist it with cooking spray. Place another sheet of phyllo directly on top of the first sheet and mist it with cooking spray. Repeat with a third sheet.
3. Spoon one-quarter of the spinach mixture along one short side of the phyllo. Fold the long sides in over the spinach, then roll up it like a burrito.
4. Repeat this process with the remaining phyllo sheets and spinach mixture to form 4 rolls.
5. To prep the vegetables: In a large bowl, combine the eggplant, onion, bell pepper, and oil. Mix well.
6. To cook the rolls and vegetables: Install a crisper plate in each of the two baskets. Place the spanakopita rolls seam-side down in the Zone 1 basket, and spritz the rolls with cooking spray. Place the vegetables in the Zone 2 basket and insert both baskets in the unit.
7. Select Zone 1, select AIR FRY, set the temperature to 375°F (190°C), and set the timer to 10 minutes.
8. Select Zone 2, select ROAST, set the temperature to 375°F (190°C), and set the timer to 15 minutes. Select SMART FINISH.
9. Press START/PAUSE to begin cooking.
10. When the Zone 1 timer reads 3 minutes, press START/PAUSE. Remove the basket and use silicone-tipped tongs or a spatula to flip the spanakopita rolls. Reinsert the basket and press START/PAUSE to resume cooking.
11. When cooking is complete, the rolls should be crisp and golden brown and the vegetables tender.
12. To assemble the salad: Transfer the roasted vegetables to a large bowl. Stir in the chickpeas and parsley.
13. In a small bowl, whisk together the oil, vinegar, garlic, oregano, salt, and black pepper. Pour the dressing over the vegetables and toss to coat. Serve warm.

**Nutrition:**
- (Per serving) Calories: 739; Total fat: 51g; Saturated fat: 8g; Carbohydrates: 67g; Fiber: 11g; Protein: 21g; Sodium: 806mg

## Stuffed Sweet Potatoes

Servings: 4
Cooking Time: 55 Minutes
**Ingredients:**
- 2 medium sweet potatoes
- 1 teaspoon olive oil
- 1 cup cooked chopped spinach, drained

- 1 cup shredded cheddar cheese, divided
- 2 cooked bacon strips, crumbled
- 1 green onion, chopped
- ¼ cup fresh cranberries, coarsely chopped
- 1⁄3 cup chopped pecans, toasted
- 2 tablespoons butter
- ¼ teaspoon kosher salt
- ¼ teaspoon pepper

**Directions:**

1. Brush the sweet potatoes with the oil.
2. Place a crisper plate in both drawers. Add one sweet potato to each drawer. Place the drawers in the unit.
3. Select zone 1, then AIR FRY, then set the temperature to 360 degrees F/ 180 degrees C with a 40-minute timer. To match zone 2 settings to zone 1, choose MATCH. To begin, select START/STOP.
4. Remove the sweet potatoes from the drawers after the timer has finished. Cut them in half lengthwise. Scoop out the pulp, leaving a ¼-inch thick shell.
5. Put the pulp in a large bowl and stir in the spinach, ¾ cup of cheese, bacon, onion, pecans, cranberries, butter, salt, and pepper.
6. Spoon the mixture into the potato shells, mounding the mixture slightly.
7. Place a crisper plate in each drawer. Put one filled potato into each drawer and insert them into the unit.
8. Select zone 1, then AIR FRY, then set the temperature to 360 degrees F/ 180 degrees C with a 10-minute timer. To match zone 2 settings to zone 1, choose MATCH. To begin, select START/STOP.
9. Sprinkle with the remaining ¼ cup of cheese. Cook using the same settings until the cheese is melted (about 1 to 2 minutes).

**Nutrition:**

- (Per serving) Calories 376 | Fat 25g | Sodium 489mg | Carbs 28g | Fiber 10g | Sugar 5g | Protein 12g

## Hasselback Potatoes

Servings: 4
Cooking Time: 15 Minutes.

**Ingredients:**

- 4 medium Yukon Gold potatoes
- 3 tablespoons melted butter
- 1 tablespoon olive oil
- 3 garlic cloves, crushed
- ½ teaspoon ground paprika
- Salt and black pepper ground, to taste
- 1 tablespoon chopped fresh parsley

**Directions:**

1. Slice each potato from the top to make ¼-inch slices without cutting its ½-inch bottom, keeping the potato's bottom intact.
2. Mix butter with olive oil, garlic, and paprika in a small bowl.
3. Brush the garlic mixture on top of each potato and add the mixture into the slits.
4. Season them with salt and black pepper.
5. Place 2 seasoned potatoes in each of the crisper plate
6. Return the crisper plate to the Ninja Foodi Dual Zone Air Fryer.
7. Choose the Air Fry mode for Zone 1 and set the temperature to 375 degrees F and the time to 25 minutes.
8. Select the "MATCH" button to copy the settings for Zone 2.
9. Initiate cooking by pressing the START/STOP button.
10. Brushing the potatoes again with butter mixture after 15 minutes, then resume cooking.
11. Garnish with parsley.
12. Serve warm.

**Nutrition:**

- (Per serving) Calories 350 | Fat 2.6g |Sodium 358mg | Carbs 64.6g | Fiber 14.4g | Sugar 3.3g | Protein 19.9g

## Fresh Mix Veggies In Air Fryer

Servings:4
Cooking Time:12

**Ingredients:**

- 1 cup cauliflower florets
- 1 cup of carrots, peeled chopped
- 1 cup broccoli florets
- 2 tablespoons of avocado oil
- Salt, to taste
- ½ teaspoon of chili powder
- ½ teaspoon of garlic powder
- ½ teaspoon of herbs de Provence
- 1 cup parmesan cheese

**Directions:**

1. Take a bowl, and add all the veggies to it.
2. Toss and then season the veggies with salt, chili powder, garlic powder, and herbs de Provence.
3. Toss it all well and then drizzle avocado oil.
4. Make sure the ingredients are coated well.
5. Now distribute the veggies among both baskets of the air fryer.
6. Turn on the start button and set it to AIR FRY mode at 390 degrees F(200°C) for 10-12 minutes.
7. For the zone 2 basket setting, press the MATCH button.
8. After 8 minutes of cooking, select the pause button and then take out the baskets and sprinkle Parmesan cheese on top of the veggies.
9. Then let the cooking cycle complete for the next 3-4 minutes.
10. Once done, serve.

**Nutrition:**

- (Per serving) Calories161 | Fat 9.3g| Sodium434 mg | Carbs 7.7g | Fiber 2.4g | Sugar 2.5g | Protein 13.9

## Cheesy Potatoes With Asparagus

Servings:2
Cooking Time:35

**Ingredients:**

- 1-1/2 pounds of russet potato, wedges or cut in half
- 2 teaspoons mixed herbs
- 2 teaspoons chili flakes
- 2 cups asparagus
- 1 cup chopped onion
- 1 tablespoon Dijon mustard
- 1/4 cup fresh cream
- 1 teaspoon olive oil
- 2 tablespoons of butter
- 1/2 teaspoon salt and black pepper
- Water as required
- 1/2 cup Parmesan cheese

**Directions:**

1. Take a bowl and add asparagus and sweet potato wedges to it.
2. Season it with salt, black pepper, and olive oil.
3. Now add the potato wedges to the zone 1 air fryer basket and asparagus to the zone 2 basket.
4. Set basket1 to AIRFRY mode at 390 degrees F(200°C) for 12 minutes.

5. Set the zone 2 basket at 390 degrees F(200°C) , for 30-35 minutes.
6. Meanwhile, take a skillet and add butter and sauté onion in it for a few minutes.
7. Then add salt and Dijon mustard and chili flakes, Parmesan cheese, and fresh cream.
8. Once the air fry mode is done, take out the potato and asparagus.
9. Drizzle the skillet ingredients over the potatoes and serve with asparagus.

**Nutrition:**

- (Per serving) Calories 251| Fat11g | Sodium 279mg | Carbs 31.1g | Fiber 5g | Sugar 4.1g | Protein9 g

## Buffalo Seitan With Crispy Zucchini Noodles

Servings:4
Cooking Time: 12 Minutes

**Ingredients:**

- FOR THE BUFFALO SEITAN
- 1 (8-ounce) package precooked seitan strips
- 1 teaspoon garlic powder, divided
- ½ teaspoon onion powder
- ¼ teaspoon smoked paprika
- ¼ cup Louisiana-style hot sauce
- 2 tablespoons vegetable oil
- 1 tablespoon tomato paste
- ¼ teaspoon freshly ground black pepper
- FOR THE ZUCCHINI NOODLES
- 3 large egg whites
- 1¼ cups all-purpose flour
- 1 teaspoon kosher salt, divided
- 12 ounces seltzer water or club soda
- 5 ounces zucchini noodles
- Nonstick cooking spray

**Directions:**

1. To prep the Buffalo seitan: Season the seitan strips with ½ teaspoon of garlic powder, the onion powder, and smoked paprika.
2. In a large bowl, whisk together the hot sauce, oil, tomato paste, remaining ½ teaspoon of garlic powder, and the black pepper. Set the bowl of Buffalo sauce aside.
3. To prep the zucchini noodles: In a medium bowl, use a handheld mixer to beat the egg whites until stiff peaks form.
4. In a large bowl, combine the flour and ½ teaspoon of salt. Mix in the seltzer to form a thin batter. Fold in the beaten egg whites.
5. Add the zucchini to the batter and gently mix to coat.
6. To cook the seitan and zucchini noodles: Install a crisper plate in each of the two baskets. Place the seitan in the Zone 1 basket and insert the basket in the unit. Lift the noodles from the batter one at a time, letting the excess drip off, and place them in the Zone 2 basket. Insert the basket in the unit.
7. Select Zone 1, select BAKE, set the temperature to 370°F (185°C), and set the timer to 12 minutes.
8. Select Zone 2, select AIR FRY, set the temperature to 400°F (205°C), and set the timer to 12 minutes. Select SMART FINISH.
9. Press START/PAUSE to begin cooking.
10. When the Zone 1 timer reads 2 minutes, press START/PAUSE. Remove the basket and transfer the seitan to the bowl of Buffalo sauce. Turn to coat, then return the seitan to the basket. Reinsert the basket and press START/PAUSE to resume cooking.
11. When cooking is complete, the seitan should be warmed through and the zucchini noodles crisp and light golden brown.
12. Sprinkle the zucchini noodles with the remaining ½ teaspoon of salt. If desired, drizzle extra Buffalo sauce over the seitan. Serve hot.

**Nutrition:**

- (Per serving) Calories: 252; Total fat: 15g; Saturated fat: 1g; Carbohydrates: 22g; Fiber: 1.5g; Protein: 13g; Sodium: 740mg

## Balsamic-glazed Tofu With Roasted Butternut Squash

Servings:4
Cooking Time: 40 Minutes

**Ingredients:**

- FOR THE BALSAMIC TOFU
- 2 tablespoons balsamic vinegar
- 1 tablespoon maple syrup
- 1 teaspoon soy sauce
- 1 teaspoon Dijon mustard
- 1 (14-ounce) package firm tofu, drained and cut into large cubes
- 1 tablespoon canola oil
- FOR THE BUTTERNUT SQUASH
- 1 small butternut squash
- 1 tablespoon canola oil
- 1 teaspoon light brown sugar
- ¼ teaspoon kosher salt
- ¼ teaspoon freshly ground black pepper

**Directions:**

1. To prep the balsamic tofu: In a large bowl, whisk together the vinegar, maple syrup, soy sauce, and mustard. Add the tofu and stir to coat. Cover and marinate for at least 20 minutes (or up to overnight in the refrigerator).
2. To prep the butternut squash: Peel the squash and cut in half lengthwise. Remove and discard the seeds. Cut the squash crosswise into ½-inch-thick slices.
3. Brush the squash pieces with the oil, then sprinkle with the brown sugar, salt, and black pepper.
4. To cook the tofu and squash: Install a crisper plate in each of the two baskets. Place the tofu in the Zone 1 basket, drizzle with the oil, and insert the basket in the unit. Place the squash in the Zone 2 basket and insert the basket in the unit.
5. Select Zone 1, select AIR FRY, set the temperature to 400°F (205°C), and set the timer to 10 minutes.
6. Select Zone 2, select ROAST, set the temperature to 400°F (205°C), and set the timer to 40 minutes. Select SMART FINISH.
7. Press START/PAUSE to begin cooking.
8. When cooking is complete, the tofu will have begun to crisp and brown around the edges and the squash should be tender. Serve hot.

**Nutrition:**

- (Per serving) Calories: 253; Total fat: 11g; Saturated fat: 1g; Carbohydrates: 30g; Fiber: 4.5g; Protein: 11g; Sodium: 237mg

## Pepper Poppers

Servings: 24
Cooking Time: 20 Minutes

**Ingredients:**

- 8 ounces cream cheese, softened
- ¾ cup shredded cheddar cheese
- ¾ cup shredded Monterey Jack cheese
- 6 bacon strips, cooked and crumbled
- ¼ teaspoon salt
- ¼ teaspoon garlic powder
- ¼ teaspoon chili powder

- ¼ teaspoon smoked paprika
- 1-pound fresh jalapeño peppers, halved lengthwise and deseeded
- ½ cup dry breadcrumbs
- Sour cream, French onion dip, or ranch salad dressing (optional)

**Directions:**

1. In a large bowl, combine the cheeses, bacon, and seasonings; mix well. Spoon 1½ to 2 tablespoons of the mixture into each pepper half. Roll them in the breadcrumbs.
2. Place a crisper plate in each drawer. Put the prepared peppers in a single layer in each drawer. Insert the drawers into the unit.
3. Select zone 1, then AIR FRY, then set the temperature to 360 degrees F/ 180 degrees C with a 20-minute timer. To match zone 2 settings to zone 1, choose MATCH. To begin, select START/STOP.
4. Remove the peppers from the drawers after the timer has finished.

**Nutrition:**

- (Per serving) Calories 81 | Fat 6g | Sodium 145mg | Carbs 3g | Fiber 4g | Sugar 1g | Protein 3g

## Caprese Panini With Zucchini Chips

Servings:4
Cooking Time: 20 Minutes

**Ingredients:**

- FOR THE PANINI
- 4 tablespoons pesto
- 8 slices Italian-style sandwich bread
- 1 tomato, diced
- 6 ounces fresh mozzarella cheese, shredded
- ¼ cup mayonnaise
- FOR THE ZUCCHINI CHIPS
- ½ cup all-purpose flour
- 2 large eggs
- ¼ teaspoon freshly ground black pepper
- ⅛ teaspoon kosher salt
- ½ cup panko bread crumbs
- ¼ cup grated Parmesan cheese
- 1 teaspoon Italian seasoning
- 1 medium zucchini, cut into ¼-inch-thick rounds
- 2 tablespoons vegetable oil

**Directions:**

1. To prep the panini: Spread 1 tablespoon of pesto each on 4 slices of the bread. Layer the diced tomato and shredded mozzarella on the other 4 slices of bread. Top the tomato/cheese mixture with the pesto-coated bread, pesto-side down, to form 4 sandwiches.
2. Spread the outside of each sandwich (both bread slices) with a thin layer of the mayonnaise.
3. To prep the zucchini chips: Set up a breading station with three small shallow bowls. Place the flour in the first bowl. In the second bowl, beat together the eggs, salt, and black pepper. Place the panko, Parmesan, and Italian seasoning in the third bowl.
4. Bread the zucchini in this order: First, dip the slices into the flour, coating both sides. Then, dip into the beaten egg. Finally, coat in the panko mixture. Drizzle the zucchini on both sides with the oil.
5. To cook the panini and zucchini chips: Install a crisper plate in each of the two baskets. Place 2 sandwiches in the Zone 1 basket and insert the basket in the unit. Place half of the zucchini chips in a single layer in the Zone 2 basket and insert the basket in the unit.
6. Select Zone 1, select AIR FRY, set the temperature to 375°F (190°C), and set the timer to 20 minutes.
7. Select Zone 2, select AIR FRY, set the temperature to 400°F (205°C), and set the timer to 20 minutes. Select SMART FINISH.
8. Press START/PAUSE to begin cooking.
9. When the Zone 1 timer reads 15 minutes, press START/PAUSE. Remove the basket, and use silicone-tipped tongs or a spatula to flip the sandwiches. Reinsert the basket and press START/PAUSE to resume cooking.
10. When both timers read 10 minutes, press START/PAUSE. Remove the Zone 1 basket and transfer the sandwiches to a plate. Place the remaining 2 sandwiches into the basket and insert the basket in the unit. Remove the Zone 2 basket and transfer the zucchini chips to a serving plate. Place the remaining zucchini chips in the basket. Reinsert the basket and press START/PAUSE to resume cooking.
11. When the Zone 1 timer reads 5 minutes, press START/PAUSE. Remove the basket and flip the sandwiches. Reinsert the basket and press START/PAUSE to resume cooking.
12. When cooking is complete, the panini should be toasted and the zucchini chips golden brown and crisp.
13. Cut each panini in half. Serve hot with zucchini chips on the side.

**Nutrition:**

- (Per serving) Calories: 751; Total fat: 39g; Saturated fat: 9.5g; Carbohydrates: 77g; Fiber: 3.5g; Protein: 23g; Sodium: 1,086mg

## Lemon Herb Cauliflower

Servings: 4
Cooking Time: 10 Minutes

**Ingredients:**

- 384g cauliflower florets
- 1 tsp lemon zest, grated
- 1 tbsp thyme, minced
- 60ml olive oil
- 1 tbsp rosemary, minced
- ¼ tsp red pepper flakes, crushed
- 30ml lemon juice
- 25g parsley, minced
- ½ tsp salt

**Directions:**

1. In a bowl, toss cauliflower florets with the remaining ingredients until well coated.
2. Insert a crisper plate in the Ninja Foodi air fryer baskets.
3. Add cauliflower florets into both baskets.
4. Select zone 1, then select "air fry" mode and set the temperature to 360 degrees F(180°C) for 10 minutes. Press "match" and "start/stop" to begin.

**Nutrition:**

- (Per serving) Calories 166 | Fat 14.4g |Sodium 340mg | Carbs 9.5g | Fiber 4.6g | Sugar 3.8g | Protein 3.3g

## Chickpea Fritters

Servings: 6
Cooking Time: 6 Minutes

**Ingredients:**

- 237ml plain yogurt
- 2 tablespoons sugar
- 1 tablespoon honey
- ½ teaspoon salt
- ½ teaspoon black pepper
- ½ teaspoon crushed red pepper flakes
- 1 can (28g) chickpeas, drained
- 1 teaspoon ground cumin

- ½ teaspoon salt
- ½ teaspoon garlic powder
- ½ teaspoon ground ginger
- 1 large egg
- ½ teaspoon baking soda
- ½ cup fresh coriander, chopped
- 2 green onions, sliced

**Directions:**

1. Mash chickpeas with rest of the ingredients in a food processor.
2. Layer the two air fryer baskets with a parchment paper.
3. Drop the batter in the baskets spoon by spoon.
4. Return the air fryer basket 1 to Zone 1, and basket 2 to Zone 2 of the Ninja Foodi 2-Basket Air Fryer.
5. Choose the "Air Fry" mode for Zone 1 at 400 degrees F(205°C) and 6 minutes of cooking time.
6. Select the "MATCH COOK" option to copy the settings for Zone 2.
7. Initiate cooking by pressing the START/PAUSE BUTTON.
8. Flip the fritters once cooked halfway through.
9. Serve warm.

**Nutrition:**

- (Per serving) Calories 284 | Fat 7.9g |Sodium 704mg | Carbs 38.1g | Fiber 1.9g | Sugar 1.9g | Protein 14.8g

## Garlic Potato Wedges In Air Fryer

Servings:2
Cooking Time:23

**Ingredients:**

- 4 medium potatoes, peeled and cut into wedges
- 4 tablespoons of butter
- 1 teaspoon of chopped cilantro
- 1 cup plain flour
- 1 teaspoon of garlic, minced
- Salt and black pepper, to taste

**Directions:**

1. Soak the potatoes wedges in cold water for about 30 minutes.
2. Then drain and pat dry with a paper towel.
3. Boil water in a large pot and boil the wedges just for 3 minutes.
4. Then take it out on a paper towel.
5. Now in a bowl mix garlic, melted butter, salt, pepper, cilantro and whisk it well.
6. Add the flour to a separate bowl and add salt and black pepper.
7. Then add water to the flour so it gets runny in texture.
8. Now, coat the potatoes with flour mixture and add it to two foil tins.
9. Put foil tins in both the air fryer basket.
10. Now, set time for zone 1 basket using AIRFRY mode at 390 degrees F(200°C) for 20 minutes.
11. Select the MATCH button for the zone 2 basket.
12. Once done, serve and enjoy.

**Nutrition:**

- (Per serving) Calories 727| Fat 24.1g| Sodium 191mg | Carbs 115.1g | Fiber 12g | Sugar 5.1g | Protein14 g

## Lime Glazed Tofu

Servings: 6
Cooking Time: 14 Minutes.

**Ingredients:**

- ⅔ cup coconut aminos
- 2 (14-oz) packages extra-firm, water-packed tofu, drained
- 6 tablespoons toasted sesame oil
- ⅔ cup lime juice

**Directions:**

1. Pat dry the tofu bars and slice into half-inch cubes.
2. Toss all the remaining ingredients in a small bowl.
3. Marinate for 4 hours in the refrigerator. Drain off the excess water.
4. Divide the tofu cubes in the two crisper plates.
5. Return the crisper plates to the Ninja Foodi Dual Zone Air Fryer.
6. Choose the Air Fry mode for Zone 1 and set the temperature to 400 degrees F(205°C) and the time to 14 minutes.
7. Select the "MATCH" button to copy the settings for Zone 2.
8. Initiate cooking by pressing the START/STOP button.
9. Toss the tofu once cooked halfway through, then resume cooking.
10. Serve warm.

**Nutrition:**

- (Per serving) Calories 284 | Fat 7.9g |Sodium 704mg | Carbs 38.1g | Fiber 1.9g | Sugar 1.9g | Protein 14.8g

## Fried Patty Pan Squash

Servings: 6
Cooking Time: 15 Minutes

**Ingredients:**

- 5 cups small pattypan squash, halved
- 1 tablespoon olive oil
- 2 garlic cloves, minced
- ½ teaspoon salt
- ¼ teaspoon dried oregano
- ¼ teaspoon dried thyme
- ¼ teaspoon pepper
- 1 tablespoon minced parsley

**Directions:**

1. Rub the squash with oil, garlic and the rest of the ingredients.
2. Spread the squash in the air fryer baskets.
3. Return the air fryer basket 1 to Zone 1, and basket 2 to Zone 2 of the Ninja Foodi 2-Basket Air Fryer.
4. Choose the "Air Fry" mode for Zone 1 at 375 degrees F(190°C) and 15 minutes of cooking time.
5. Select the "MATCH COOK" option to copy the settings for Zone 2.
6. Initiate cooking by pressing the START/PAUSE BUTTON.
7. Flip the squash once cooked halfway through.
8. Garnish with parsley.
9. Serve warm.

**Nutrition:**

- (Per serving) Calories 208 | Fat 5g |Sodium 1205mg | Carbs 34.1g | Fiber 7.8g | Sugar 2.5g | Protein 5.9g

## Quinoa Patties

Servings: 4
Cooking Time: 32 Minutes.

**Ingredients:**

- 1 cup quinoa red
- 1½ cups water
- 1 teaspoon salt
- black pepper, ground
- 1½ cups rolled oats
- 3 eggs beaten
- ¼ cup minced white onion
- ½ cup crumbled feta cheese
- ¼ cup chopped fresh chives
- Salt and black pepper, to taste

- Vegetable or canola oil
- 4 hamburger buns
- 4 arugulas
- 4 slices tomato sliced
- Cucumber yogurt dill sauce
- 1 cup cucumber, diced
- 1 cup Greek yogurt
- 2 teaspoons lemon juice
- ¼ teaspoon salt
- Black pepper, ground
- 1 tablespoon chopped fresh dill
- 1 tablespoon olive oil

**Directions:**

1. Add quinoa to a saucepan filled with cold water, salt, and black pepper, and place it over medium-high heat.
2. Cook the quinoa to a boil, then reduce the heat, cover, and cook for 20 minutes on a simmer.
3. Fluff and mix the cooked quinoa with a fork and remove it from the heat.
4. Spread the quinoa in a baking stay.
5. Mix eggs, oats, onion, herbs, cheese, salt, and black pepper.
6. Stir in quinoa, then mix well. Make 4 patties out of this quinoa cheese mixture.
7. Divide the patties in the two crisper plates and spray them with cooking oil.
8. Return the crisper plates to the Ninja Foodi Dual Zone Air Fryer.
9. Choose the Air Fry mode for Zone 1 and set the temperature to 390 degrees F(200°C) and the time to 13 minutes.
10. Select the "MATCH" button to copy the settings for Zone 2.
11. Initiate cooking by pressing the START/STOP button.
12. Flip the patties once cooked halfway through, and resume cooking.
13. Meanwhile, prepare the cucumber yogurt dill sauce by mixing all of its ingredients in a mixing bowl.
14. Place each quinoa patty in a burger bun along with arugula leaves.
15. Serve with yogurt dill sauce.

**Nutrition:**

- (Per serving) Calories 231 | Fat 9g |Sodium 271mg | Carbs 32.8g | Fiber 6.4g | Sugar 7g | Protein 6.3g

## Veggie Burgers With "fried" Onion Rings

Servings:4
Cooking Time: 25 Minutes

**Ingredients:**

- FOR THE VEGGIE BURGERS
- 1 (15-ounce) can black beans, drained and rinsed
- ½ cup panko bread crumbs
- 1 large egg
- ¼ cup finely chopped red bell pepper
- ¼ cup frozen corn, thawed
- 1 tablespoon olive oil
- ½ teaspoon garlic powder
- ½ teaspoon ground cumin
- ¼ teaspoon smoked paprika
- Nonstick cooking spray
- 4 hamburger buns
- ¼ cup barbecue sauce, for serving
- FOR THE ONION RINGS
- 1 large sweet onion
- ½ cup all-purpose flour
- 2 large eggs
- 1 cup panko bread crumbs
- ½ teaspoon kosher salt
- Nonstick cooking spray

**Directions:**

1. To prep the veggie burgers: In a large bowl, mash the beans with a potato masher or a fork. Stir in the panko, egg, bell pepper, corn, oil, garlic powder, cumin, and smoked paprika. Mix well.
2. Shape the mixture into 4 patties. Spritz both sides of each patty with cooking spray.
3. To prep the onion rings: Cut the onion into ½-inch-thick rings.
4. Set up a breading station with three small shallow bowls. Place the flour in the first bowl. In the second bowl, beat the eggs. Place the panko and salt in the third bowl.
5. Bread the onions rings in this order: First, dip them into the flour, coating both sides. Then, dip into the beaten egg. Finally, coat them in the panko. Spritz each with cooking spray.
6. To cook the burgers and onion rings: Install a crisper plate in each of the two baskets. Place 2 veggie burgers in the Zone 1 basket. Place the onion rings in the Zone 2 basket and insert both baskets in the unit.
7. Select Zone 1, select AIR FRY, set the temperature to 390°F (200°C), and set the timer to 25 minutes.
8. Select Zone 2, select AIR FRY, set the temperature to 375°F (190°C), and set the timer to 10 minutes. Select SMART FINISH.
9. Press START/PAUSE to begin cooking.
10. When the Zone 1 timer reads 10 minutes, press START/PAUSE. Remove the basket and use a silicone spatula to flip the burgers. Reinsert the basket and press START/PAUSE to resume cooking.
11. When the Zone 1 timer reads 10 minutes, press START/PAUSE. Remove the basket and transfer the burgers to a plate. Place the 2 remaining burgers in the basket. Reinsert the basket and press START/PAUSE to resume cooking.
12. When both timers read 5 minutes, press START/PAUSE. Remove the Zone 1 basket and flip the burgers, then reinsert the basket. Remove the Zone 2 basket and shake vigorously to rearrange the onion rings and separate any that have stuck together. Reinsert the basket and press START/PAUSE to resume cooking.
13. When cooking is complete, the veggie burgers should be cooked through and the onion rings golden brown.
14. Place 1 burger on each bun. Top with barbecue sauce and serve with onion rings on the side.

**Nutrition:**

- (Per serving) Calories: 538; Total fat: 16g; Saturated fat: 2g; Carbohydrates: 83g; Fiber: 10g; Protein: 19g; Sodium: 914mg

## Flavourful Mexican Cauliflower

Servings: 4
Cooking Time: 12 Minutes

**Ingredients:**

- 1 medium cauliflower head, cut into florets
- ½ tsp turmeric
- 1 tsp onion powder
- 2 tsp garlic powder
- 2 tsp parsley
- 1 lime juice
- 30ml olive oil
- 1 tsp chilli powder
- 1 tsp cumin
- Pepper
- Salt

**Directions:**

1. In a bowl, toss cauliflower florets with onion powder, garlic powder, parsley, oil, chilli powder, turmeric, cumin, pepper, and salt.
2. Insert a crisper plate in the Ninja Foodi air fryer baskets.
3. Add cauliflower florets in both baskets.
4. Select zone 1, then select "air fry" mode and set the temperature to 390 degrees F(200°C) for 12 minutes. Press "match" to match zone 2 settings to zone 1. Press "start/stop" to begin. Stir halfway through.
5. Drizzle lime juice over cauliflower florets.

**Nutrition:**

- (Per serving) Calories 108 | Fat 7.4g |Sodium 91mg | Carbs 10g | Fiber 4.1g | Sugar 4.1g | Protein 3.4g

## Zucchini Cakes

Servings: 6
Cooking Time: 32 Minutes.

**Ingredients:**

- 2 medium zucchinis, grated
- 1 cup corn kernel
- 1 medium potato cooked
- 2 tablespoons chickpea flour
- 2 garlic minced
- 2 teaspoons olive oil
- Salt and black pepper
- For Serving:
- Yogurt tahini sauce

**Directions:**

1. Mix grated zucchini with a pinch of salt in a colander and leave them for 15 minutes.
2. Squeeze out their excess water.
3. Mash the cooked potato in a large-sized bowl with a fork.
4. Add zucchini, corn, garlic, chickpea flour, salt, and black pepper to the bowl.
5. Mix these fritters' ingredients together and make 2 tablespoons-sized balls out of this mixture and flatten them lightly.
6. Divide the fritters in the two crisper plates in a single layer and spray them with cooking.
7. Return the crisper plates to the Ninja Foodi Dual Zone Air Fryer.
8. Choose the Air Fry mode for Zone 1 and set the temperature to 390 degrees F(200°C) and the time to 17 minutes.
9. Select the "MATCH" button to copy the settings for Zone 2.
10. Initiate cooking by pressing the START/STOP button.
11. Flip the fritters once cooked halfway through, then resume cooking.
12. Serve.

**Nutrition:**

- (Per serving) Calories 270 | Fat 14.6g |Sodium 394mg | Carbs 31.3g | Fiber 7.5g | Sugar 9.7g | Protein 6.4g

## Sweet Potatoes With Honey Butter

Servings: 4
Cooking Time: 40 Minutes.

**Ingredients:**

- 4 sweet potatoes, scrubbed
- 1 teaspoon oil
- Honey Butter
- 4 tablespoons unsalted butter
- 1 tablespoon Honey
- 2 teaspoons hot sauce
- ¼ teaspoon salt

**Directions:**

1. Rub the sweet potatoes with oil and place two potatoes in each crisper plate.
2. Return the crisper plate to the Ninja Foodi Dual Zone Air Fryer.
3. Choose the Air Fry mode for Zone 1 and set the temperature to 400 degrees F(205°C) and the time to 40 minutes.
4. Select the "MATCH" button to copy the settings for Zone 2.
5. Initiate cooking by pressing the START/STOP button.
6. Flip the potatoes once cooked halfway through, then resume cooking.
7. Mix butter with hot sauce, honey, and salt in a bowl.
8. When the potatoes are done, cut a slit on top and make a well with a spoon
9. Pour the honey butter in each potato jacket.
10. Serve.

**Nutrition:**

- (Per serving) Calories 288 | Fat 6.9g |Sodium 761mg | Carbs 46g | Fiber 4g | Sugar 12g | Protein 9.6g

## Garlic-rosemary Brussels Sprouts

Servings: 4
Cooking Time: 8 Minutes

**Ingredients:**

- 3 tablespoons olive oil
- 2 garlic cloves, minced
- ½ teaspoon salt
- ¼ teaspoon black pepper
- 455g Brussels sprouts, halved
- ½ cup panko bread crumbs
- 1-½ teaspoons rosemary, minced

**Directions:**

1. Toss the Brussels sprouts with crumbs and the rest of the ingredients in a bowl.
2. Divide the sprouts into the Ninja Foodi 2 Baskets Air Fryer baskets.
3. Return the air fryer basket 1 to Zone 1, and basket 2 to Zone 2 of the Ninja Foodi 2-Basket Air Fryer.
4. Choose the "Air Fry" mode for Zone 1 at 350 degrees F(175°C) and 8 minutes of cooking time.
5. Select the "MATCH COOK" option to copy the settings for Zone 2.
6. Initiate cooking by pressing the START/PAUSE BUTTON.
7. Toss the Brussels sprouts once cooked halfway through.
8. Serve warm.

**Nutrition:**

- (Per serving) Calories 231 | Fat 9g |Sodium 271mg | Carbs 32.8g | Fiber 6.4g | Sugar 7g | Protein 6.3g

## Acorn Squash Slices

Servings: 6
Cooking Time: 10 Minutes

**Ingredients:**

- 2 medium acorn squashes
- ⅔ cup packed brown sugar
- ½ cup butter, melted

**Directions:**

1. Cut the squash in half, remove the seeds and slice into ½ inch slices.
2. Place the squash slices in the air fryer baskets.
3. Drizzle brown sugar and butter over the squash slices.
4. Return the air fryer basket 1 to Zone 1, and basket 2 to Zone 2 of the Ninja Foodi 2-Basket Air Fryer.

5. Choose the "Air Fry" mode for Zone 1 and set the temperature to 350 degrees F(175°C) and 10 minutes of cooking time.
6. Select the "MATCH COOK" option to copy the settings for Zone 2.
7. Initiate cooking by pressing the START/PAUSE BUTTON.
8. Flip the squash once cooked halfway through.
9. Serve.

**Nutrition:**

- (Per serving) Calories 206 | Fat 3.4g |Sodium 174mg | Carbs 35g | Fiber 9.4g | Sugar 5.9g | Protein 10.6g

## Breaded Summer Squash

Servings: 4
Cooking Time: 10 Minutes

**Ingredients:**

- 4 cups yellow summer squash, sliced
- 3 tablespoons olive oil
- ½ teaspoon salt
- ½ teaspoon pepper
- ⅛ teaspoon cayenne pepper
- ¾ cup panko bread crumbs
- ¾ cup grated Parmesan cheese

**Directions:**

1. Mix crumbs, cheese, cayenne pepper, black pepper, salt and oil in a bowl.
2. Coat the squash slices with the breadcrumb mixture.
3. Place these slices in the air fryer baskets.
4. Return the air fryer basket 1 to Zone 1, and basket 2 to Zone 2 of the Ninja Foodi 2-Basket Air Fryer.
5. Choose the "Air Fry" mode for Zone 1 at 350 degrees F(175°C) and 10 minutes of cooking time.
6. Select the "MATCH COOK" option to copy the settings for Zone 2.
7. Initiate cooking by pressing the START/PAUSE BUTTON.
8. Flip the squash slices once cooked half way through.
9. Serve warm.

**Nutrition:**

- (Per serving) Calories 193 | Fat 1g |Sodium 395mg | Carbs 38.7g | Fiber 1.6g | Sugar 0.9g | Protein 6.6g

## Fried Artichoke Hearts

Servings: 6
Cooking Time: 10 Minutes.

**Ingredients:**

- 3 cans Quartered Artichokes, drained
- ½ cup mayonnaise
- 1 cup panko breadcrumbs
- ⅓ cup grated Parmesan
- salt and black pepper to taste
- Parsley for garnish

**Directions:**

1. Mix mayonnaise with salt and black pepper and keep the sauce aside.
2. Spread panko breadcrumbs in a bowl.
3. Coat the artichoke pieces with the breadcrumbs.
4. As you coat the artichokes, place them in the two crisper plates in a single layer, then spray them with cooking oil.
5. Return the crisper plates to the Ninja Foodi Dual Zone Air Fryer.
6. Choose the Air Fry mode for Zone 1 and set the temperature to 375 degrees F(190°C) and the time to 10 minutes.
7. Select the "MATCH" button to copy the settings for Zone 2.
8. Initiate cooking by pressing the START/STOP button.
9. Flip the artichokes once cooked halfway through, then resume cooking.
10. Serve warm with mayo sauce.

**Nutrition:**

- (Per serving) Calories 193 | Fat 1g |Sodium 395mg | Carbs 38.7g | Fiber 1.6g | Sugar 0.9g | Protein 6.6g

## Saucy Carrots

Servings: 6
Cooking Time: 25 Minutes.

**Ingredients:**

- 1 lb. cup carrots, cut into chunks
- 1 tablespoon sesame oil
- ½ tablespoon ginger, minced
- ½ tablespoon soy sauce
- ½ teaspoon garlic, minced
- ½ tablespoon scallions, chopped, for garnish
- ½ teaspoon sesame seeds for garnish

**Directions:**

1. Toss all the ginger carrots ingredients, except the sesame seeds and scallions, in a suitable bowl.
2. Divide the carrots in the two crisper plates in a single layer.
3. Return the crisper plates to the Ninja Foodi Dual Zone Air Fryer.
4. Choose the Air Fry mode for Zone 1 and set the temperature to 390 degrees F(200°C) and the time to 25 minutes.
5. Select the "MATCH" button to copy the settings for Zone 2.
6. Initiate cooking by pressing the START/STOP button.
7. Toss the carrots once cooked halfway through.
8. Garnish with sesame seeds and scallions.
9. Serve warm.

**Nutrition:**

- (Per serving) Calories 206 | Fat 3.4g |Sodium 174mg | Carbs 35g | Fiber 9.4g | Sugar 5.9g | Protein 10.6g

## Rosemary Asparagus & Potatoes

Servings: 6
Cooking Time: 30 Minutes

**Ingredients:**

- 125g asparagus, trimmed & cut into pieces
- 2 tsp garlic powder
- 2 tbsp rosemary, chopped
- 30ml olive oil
- 679g baby potatoes, quartered
- ½ tsp red pepper flakes
- Pepper
- Salt

**Directions:**

1. Insert a crisper plate in the Ninja Foodi air fryer baskets.
2. Toss potatoes with 1 tablespoon of oil, pepper, and salt in a bowl until well coated.
3. Add potatoes into in zone 1 basket.
4. Toss asparagus with remaining oil, red pepper flakes, pepper, garlic powder, and rosemary in a mixing bowl.
5. Add asparagus into the zone 2 basket.
6. Select zone 1, then select "air fry" mode and set the temperature to 390 degrees F(200°C) for 20 minutes. Select zone 2, then select "air fry" mode and set the temperature to 390 degrees F(200°C) for 10 minutes. Press "match" mode, then press "start/stop" to begin.

**Nutrition:**

- (Per serving) Calories 121 | Fat 5g |Sodium 40mg | Carbs 17.1g | Fiber 4.2g | Sugar 1g | Protein 4g

# Satay-style Tempeh With Corn Fritters

Servings:4
Cooking Time: 15 Minutes

**Ingredients:**

- FOR THE TEMPEH
- 1 (8-ounce) package tempeh
- 3 tablespoons fresh lemon juice, divided
- 2 tablespoons soy sauce, divided
- 2 garlic cloves, chopped
- ½ teaspoon ground turmeric
- 2 tablespoons vegetable oil
- ¾ cup canned full-fat coconut milk
- 4 tablespoons peanut butter
- 1 teaspoon light brown sugar
- ½ teaspoon red pepper flakes
- 1 scallion, chopped
- FOR THE CORN FRITTERS
- 2 cups frozen corn, thawed and drained
- 2 scallions, thinly sliced
- ¼ cup chopped fresh cilantro
- ¼ teaspoon kosher salt
- 2 large eggs
- ½ cup all-purpose flour
- 2 tablespoons vegetable oil

**Directions:**

1. To prep the tempeh: Slice the tempeh into ¼-inch-thick slabs.
2. In a large bowl, combine 2 tablespoons of lemon juice, 1 tablespoon of soy sauce, the garlic, turmeric, and oil.
3. Add the tempeh to the marinade and toss to coat the pieces. Let marinate for 15 minutes.
4. In a medium bowl, whisk together the coconut milk, peanut butter, remaining 1 tablespoon of lemon juice, remaining 1 tablespoon of soy sauce, brown sugar, red pepper flakes, and scallion. Set aside.
5. To prep the corn fritters: In a large bowl, combine the corn, scallions, cilantro, and salt. Mix in the eggs and flour until everything is well combined.
6. To cook the tempeh and fritters: Install a broil rack in the Zone 1 basket. Arrange the tempeh in a single layer on the rack and insert the basket in the unit. Install a crisper plate in the Zone 2 basket. Spoon 2 tablespoons of corn fritter batter into each corner of the basket and drizzle with oil. Flatten slightly with the back of the spoon and insert the basket in the unit.
7. Select Zone 1, select AIR BROIL, set the temperature to 400°F (205°C), and set the timer to 8 minutes.
8. Select Zone 2, select AIR FRY, set the temperature to 375°F (190°C), and set the timer to 15 minutes. Select SMART FINISH.
9. Press START/PAUSE to begin cooking.
10. When the Zone 2 timer reads 5 minutes, press START/PAUSE. Remove the basket and use silicone-tipped tongs or a spatula to flip the corn fritters. Reinsert the basket and press START/PAUSE to resume cooking.
11. When cooking is complete, the tempeh will be golden brown and the corn fritters set in the center and browned on the edges.
12. Serve the tempeh with the peanut sauce for dipping and the corn fritters on the side.

**Nutrition:**

- (Per serving) Calories: 578; Total fat: 40g; Saturated fat: 14g; Carbohydrates: 39g; Fiber: 3.5g; Protein: 24g; Sodium: 815mg

# Desserts Recipes

## Chocó Lava Cake

Servings: 4
Cooking Time: 10 Minutes
**Ingredients:**

- 3 eggs
- 3 egg yolks
- 70g dark chocolate, chopped
- 168g cups powdered sugar
- 96g all-purpose flour
- 1 tsp vanilla
- 113g butter
- ½ tsp salt

**Directions:**

1. Add chocolate and butter to a bowl and microwave for 30 seconds. Remove from oven and stir until smooth.
2. Add eggs, egg yolks, sugar, flour, vanilla, and salt into the melted chocolate and stir until well combined.
3. Pour batter into the four greased ramekins.
4. Insert a crisper plate in Ninja Foodi air fryer baskets.
5. Place ramekins in both baskets.
6. Select zone 1 then select "air fry" mode and set the temperature to 390 degrees F(200°C) for 10 minutes. Press "match" to match zone 2 settings to zone 1. Press "start/stop" to begin.

**Nutrition:**

- (Per serving) Calories 687 | Fat 37.3g |Sodium 527mg | Carbs 78.3g | Fiber 1.5g | Sugar 57.4g | Protein 10.7g

## Victoria Sponge Cake

Servings: 8
Cooking Time: 16 Minutes
**Ingredients:**

- Sponge Cake Ingredients
- 400g self-rising flour
- 450g caster sugar
- 50g lemon curd
- 200g butter
- 4 medium eggs
- 1 tablespoon vanilla essence
- 480ml skimmed milk
- 1 tablespoon olive oil
- 4 tablespoons strawberry jam
- Strawberry buttercream
- 115g butter
- 210g icing sugar
- ½ teaspoon strawberry food coloring
- 1 tablespoon single cream
- 1 teaspoon vanilla essence
- 1 teaspoon maple syrup

**Directions:**

1. Mix sugar and butter in a bowl using a hand mixer.
2. Beat eggs with oil, and vanilla in a bowl with the mixer until creamy.
3. Stir in milk, flour and curd then mix well.
4. Add butter mixture then mix well.
5. Divide this mixture in two 4 inches greased cake pans.
6. Place one pan in each air fryer basket.
7. Return the air fryer basket 1 to Zone 1, and basket 2 to Zone 2 of the Ninja Foodi 2-Basket Air Fryer.
8. Choose the "Air Fry" mode for Zone 1 and set the temperature to 375 degrees F(190°C) and 16 minutes of cooking time.
9. Select the "MATCH COOK" option to copy the settings for Zone 2.
10. Initiate cooking by pressing the START/PAUSE BUTTON.
11. Meanwhile, blend the buttercream ingredients in a mixer until fluffy.
12. Place one cake on a plate and top it with the buttercream.
13. Top it jam and then with the other cake.
14. Serve.

**Nutrition:**

- (Per serving) Calories 284 | Fat 16g |Sodium 252mg | Carbs 31.6g | Fiber 0.9g | Sugar 6.6g | Protein 3.7g

## Walnuts Fritters

Servings: 6
Cooking Time: 15 Minutes.
**Ingredients:**

- 1 cup all-purpose flour
- ½ cup walnuts, chopped
- ¼ cup white sugar
- ¼ cup milk
- 1 egg
- 1 ½ teaspoons baking powder
- 1 pinch salt
- Cooking spray
- 2 tablespoons white sugar
- ½ teaspoon ground cinnamon
- Glaze:
- ½ cup confectioners' sugar
- 1 tablespoon milk
- ½ teaspoon caramel extract
- ¼ teaspoons ground cinnamon

**Directions:**

1. Layer both crisper plate with parchment paper.
2. Grease the parchment paper with cooking spray.
3. Whisk flour with milk, ¼ cup of sugar, egg, baking powder, and salt in a small bowl.
4. Separately mix 2 tablespoons of sugar with cinnamon in another bowl, toss in walnuts and mix well to coat.
5. Stir in flour mixture and mix until combined.
6. Drop the fritters mixture using a cookie scoop into the two crisper plate.
7. Return the crisper plate to the Ninja Foodi Dual Zone Air Fryer.
8. Choose the Air Fry mode for Zone 1 and set the temperature to 375 degrees F(190°C) and the time to 15 minutes.
9. Select the "MATCH" button to copy the settings for Zone 2.
10. Initiate cooking by pressing the START/STOP button.
11. Flip the fritters once cooked halfway through, then resume cooking.

12. Meanwhile, whisk milk, caramel extract, confectioners' sugar, and cinnamon in a bowl.
13. Transfer fritters to a wire rack and allow them to cool.
14. Drizzle with a glaze over the fritters.

**Nutrition:**

- (Per serving) Calories 391 | Fat 24g |Sodium 142mg | Carbs 38.5g | Fiber 3.5g | Sugar 21g | Protein 6.6g

## Citrus Mousse

Servings: 4
Cooking Time: 12 Minutes

**Ingredients:**

- 8 ounces cream cheese, softened
- 1 cup heavy cream
- 4 tablespoons fresh lime juice
- 4 tablespoons maple syrup
- Pinch of salt

**Directions:**

1. For mousse: Press "Zone 1" and "Zone 2" and then rotate the knob for each zone to select "Bake".
2. Set the temperature to 350 degrees F/ 175 degrees C for both zones and then set the time for 5 minutes to preheat.
3. In a bowl, add all the ingredients and mix until well combined.
4. Transfer the mixture into 4 ramekins.
5. After preheating, arrange 2 ramekins into the basket of each zone.
6. Slide each basket into Air Fryer and set the time for 12 minutes.
7. After cooking time is completed, remove the ramekins from Air Fryer.
8. Set the ramekins aside to cool.
9. Refrigerate the ramekins for at least 3 hours before serving.

## Fried Cheesecake Bites

Servings: 16 Bites
Cooking Time: 2 Minutes

**Ingredients:**

- 225 g cream cheese, softened
- 50 g powdered sweetener, plus 2 tablespoons, divided
- 4 tablespoons heavy cream, divided
- ½ teaspoon vanilla extract
- 50 g almond flour

**Directions:**

1. In a stand mixer fitted with a paddle attachment, beat the cream cheese, 50 g of the sweetener, 2 tablespoons of the heavy cream, and the vanilla until smooth. Using a small ice-cream scoop, divide the mixture into 16 balls and arrange them on a rimmed baking sheet lined with baking paper. Freeze for 45 minutes until firm.
2. Line the two air fryer drawers with baking paper and preheat the air fryer to 176°C.
3. In a small shallow bowl, combine the almond flour with the remaining 2 tablespoons of sweetener.
4. In another small shallow bowl, place the remaining 2 tablespoons cream.
5. One at a time, dip the frozen cheesecake balls into the cream and then roll in the almond flour mixture, pressing lightly to form an even coating. Arrange the balls in a single layer in the two air fryer drawers, leaving room between them. Air fry for 2 minutes until the coating is lightly browned.

## Soft Pecan Brownies

Servings: 6
Cooking Time: 20 Minutes

**Ingredients:**

- ½ cup blanched finely ground almond flour
- ½ cup powdered erythritol
- 2 tablespoons unsweetened cocoa powder
- ½ teaspoon baking powder
- ¼ cup unsalted butter, softened
- 1 large egg
- ¼ cup chopped pecans
- ¼ cup low-carb, sugar-free chocolate chips

**Directions:**

1. Stir erythritol, almond flour, baking powder and cocoa powder in a large bowl. Add in egg and butter, mix well.
2. Fold in chocolate chips and pecans. Pour mixture into 6&quot| round baking pan. Put pan into the air fryer basket.
3. Set the temperature to 300°F (150°C), then set the timer for 20 minutes.
4. A toothpick inserted in center will come out clean when completely cooked. Let it rest for 20 minutes to fully cool and firm up. Serve immediately.

## Homemade Mini Cheesecake

Servings: 2
Cooking Time: 15 Minutes

**Ingredients:**

- ½ cup walnuts
- 2 tablespoons salted butter
- 2 tablespoons granular erythritol
- 4 ounces full-fat cream cheese, softened
- 1 large egg
- ½ teaspoon vanilla extract
- ⅛ cup powdered erythritol

**Directions:**

1. Place butter, granular erythritol, and walnuts in a food processor. Pulse until all the ingredients stick together to form a dough.
2. Place dough into 4&quot| springform pan then put the pan into the air fryer basket.
3. Set the temperature to 400°F (205°C), then set the timer for 5 minutes.
4. When timer goes off, remove the crust and allow it rest.
5. Stir cream cheese with vanilla extract, powdered erythritol and egg until smooth in a medium bowl.
6. Pour mixture on top of baked walnut crust and then put into the air fryer basket.
7. Set the temperature to 300°F (150°C), then set the timer for 10 minutes.
8. Once cooked fully, allow to cool for 2 hours before serving.

## Churros

Servings: 8
Cooking Time: 10 Minutes

**Ingredients:**

- 1 cup water
- 1/3 cup unsalted butter, cut into cubes
- 2 tablespoons granulated sugar
- ¼ teaspoon salt
- 1 cup all-purpose flour
- 2 large eggs
- 1 teaspoon vanilla extract
- Cooking oil spray
- For the cinnamon-sugar coating:
- ½ cup granulated sugar
- ¾ teaspoon ground cinnamon

**Directions:**

1. Add the water, butter, sugar, and salt to a medium pot. Bring to a boil over medium-high heat.
2. Reduce the heat to medium-low and stir in the flour. Cook, stirring constantly with a rubber spatula until the dough is smooth and comes together.

3. Remove the dough from the heat and place it in a mixing bowl. Allow 4 minutes for cooling.
4. In a mixing bowl, beat the eggs and vanilla extract with an electric hand mixer or stand mixer until the dough comes together. The finished product will resemble gluey mashed potatoes. Press the lumps together into a ball with your hands, then transfer to a large piping bag with a large star-shaped tip. Pipe out the churros.
5. Install a crisper plate in both drawers. Place half the churros in the zone 1 drawer and half in zone 2's, then insert the drawers into the unit.
6. Select zone 1, select AIR FRY, set temperature to 390 degrees F/ 200 degrees C, and set time to 12 minutes. Select MATCH to match zone 2 settings to zone 1. Press the START/STOP button to begin cooking.
7. In a shallow bowl, combine the granulated sugar and cinnamon.
8. Immediately transfer the baked churros to the bowl with the sugar mixture and toss to coat.

**Nutrition:**

- (Per serving) Calories 204 | Fat 9g | Sodium 91mg | Carbs 27g | Fiber 0.3g | Sugar 15g | Protein 3g

## Lemon Raspberry Muffins

Servings: 6
Cooking Time: 15 Minutes

**Ingredients:**

- 220 g almond flour
- 75 g powdered sweetener
- 1¼ teaspoons baking powder
- ⅓ teaspoon ground allspice
- ⅓ teaspoon ground star anise
- ½ teaspoon grated lemon zest
- ¼ teaspoon salt
- 2 eggs
- 240 ml sour cream
- 120 ml coconut oil
- 60 g raspberries

**Directions:**

1. Preheat the air fryer to 176ºC. Line a muffin pan with 6 paper cases.
2. In a mixing bowl, mix the almond flour, sweetener, baking powder, allspice, star anise, lemon zest, and salt.
3. In another mixing bowl, beat the eggs, sour cream, and coconut oil until well mixed. Add the egg mixture to the flour mixture and stir to combine. Mix in the raspberries.
4. Scrape the batter into the prepared muffin cups, filling each about three-quarters full.
5. Bake for 15 minutes, or until the tops are golden and a toothpick inserted in the middle comes out clean.
6. Allow the muffins to cool for 10 minutes in the muffin pan before removing and serving.

## Chocolate Cookies

Servings: 18
Cooking Time: 7 Minutes

**Ingredients:**

- 96g flour
- 57g butter, softened
- 15ml milk
- 7.5g cocoa powder
- 80g chocolate chips
- ½ tsp vanilla
- 35g sugar
- ¼ tsp baking soda
- Pinch of salt

**Directions:**

1. In a bowl, mix flour, cocoa powder, sugar, baking soda, vanilla, butter, milk, and salt until well combined.
2. Add chocolate chips and mix well.
3. Insert a crisper plate in Ninja Foodi air fryer baskets.
4. Make cookies from the mixture and place in both baskets.
5. Select zone 1 then select "air fry" mode and set the temperature to 360 degrees F(180°C) for 7 minutes. Press "match" to match zone 2 settings to zone 1. Press "start/stop" to begin.

**Nutrition:**

- (Per serving) Calories 82 | Fat 4.1g |Sodium 47mg | Carbs 10.7g | Fiber 0.4g | Sugar 6.2g | Protein 1g

## Coconut Muffins And Dark Chocolate Lava Cake

Servings: 9
Cooking Time: 25 Minutes

**Ingredients:**

- Coconut Muffins:
- 55 g coconut flour
- 2 tablespoons cocoa powder
- 3 tablespoons granulated sweetener
- 1 teaspoon baking powder
- 2 tablespoons coconut oil
- 2 eggs, beaten
- 50 g desiccated coconut
- Dark Chocolate Lava Cake:
- Olive oil cooking spray
- 30 g whole wheat flour
- 1 tablespoon unsweetened dark chocolate cocoa powder
- ⅛ teaspoon salt
- ½ teaspoon baking powder
- 60 ml raw honey
- 1 egg
- 2 tablespoons olive oil

**Directions:**

1. Make the Coconut Muffins :
2. In the mixing bowl, mix all ingredients.
3. Then pour the mixture into the molds of the muffin and transfer in the zone 1 air fryer basket.
4. Cook the muffins at 175ºC for 25 minutes.
5. Make the Dark Chocolate Lava Cake :
6. Preheat the air fryer to 190ºC. Lightly coat the insides of four ramekins with olive oil cooking spray.
7. In a medium bowl, combine the flour, cocoa powder, salt, baking powder, honey, egg, and olive oil.
8. Divide the batter evenly among the ramekins.
9. Place the filled ramekins inside the zone 2 air fryer basket and bake for 10 minutes.
10. Remove the lava cakes from the air fryer and slide a knife around the outside edge of each cake. Turn each ramekin upside down on a saucer and serve.

## Apple Hand Pies

Servings: 8
Cooking Time: 21 Minutes.

**Ingredients:**

- 8 tablespoons butter, softened
- 12 tablespoons brown sugar
- 2 teaspoons cinnamon, ground
- 4 medium Granny Smith apples, diced
- 2 teaspoons cornstarch
- 4 teaspoons cold water
- 1 (14-oz) package pastry, 9-inch crust pie
- Cooking spray
- 1 tablespoon grapeseed oil

- ½ cup powdered sugar
- 2 teaspoons milk

**Directions:**

1. Toss apples with brown sugar, butter, and cinnamon in a suitable skillet.
2. Place the skillet over medium heat and stir cook for 5 minutes.
3. Mix cornstarch with cold water in a small bowl.
4. Add cornstarch mixture into the apple and cook for 1 minute until it thickens.
5. Remove this filling from the heat and allow it to cool.
6. Unroll the pie crust and spray on a floured surface.
7. Cut the dough into 16 equal rectangles.
8. Wet the edges of the 8 rectangles with water and divide the apple filling at the center of these rectangles.
9. Place the other 8 rectangles on top and crimp the edges with a fork, then make 2-3 slashes on top.
10. Place 4 small pies in each of the crisper plate.
11. Return the crisper plate to the Ninja Foodi Dual Zone Air Fryer.
12. Choose the Air Fry mode for Zone 1 and set the temperature to 390 degrees F(200°C) and the time to 17 minutes.
13. Select the "MATCH" button to copy the settings for Zone 2.
14. Initiate cooking by pressing the START/STOP button.
15. Flip the pies once cooked halfway through, and resume cooking.
16. Meanwhile, mix sugar with milk.
17. Pour this mixture over the apple pies.
18. Serve fresh.

**Nutrition:**

- (Per serving) Calories 284 | Fat 16g |Sodium 252mg | Carbs 31.6g | Fiber 0.9g | Sugar 6.6g | Protein 3.7g

## Grilled Peaches

Servings: 2
Cooking Time: 5 Minutes

**Ingredients:**

- 2 yellow peaches, peeled and cut into wedges
- ¼ cup graham cracker crumbs
- ¼ cup brown sugar
- ¼ cup butter diced into tiny cubes
- Whipped cream or ice cream

**Directions:**

1. Toss peaches with crumbs, brown sugar, and butter in a bowl.
2. Spread the peaches in one air fryer basket.
3. Return the air fryer basket to the Ninja Foodi 2 Baskets Air Fryer.
4. Choose the "Air Fry" mode for Zone 1 and set the temperature to 350 degrees F(175°C) and 5 minutes of cooking time.
5. Initiate cooking by pressing the START/PAUSE BUTTON.
6. Serve the peaches with a scoop of ice cream.

**Nutrition:**

- (Per serving) Calories 327 | Fat 14.2g |Sodium 672mg | Carbs 47.2g | Fiber 1.7g | Sugar 24.8g | Protein 4.4g

## Moist Chocolate Espresso Muffins

Servings: 8
Cooking Time: 18 Minutes

**Ingredients:**

- 1 egg
- 177ml milk
- ½ tsp baking soda
- ½ tsp espresso powder
- ½ tsp baking powder
- 50g cocoa powder
- 78ml vegetable oil
- 1 tsp apple cider vinegar
- 1 tsp vanilla
- 150g brown sugar
- 150g all-purpose flour
- ½ tsp salt

**Directions:**

1. In a bowl, whisk egg, vinegar, oil, brown sugar, vanilla, and milk.
2. Add flour, cocoa powder, baking soda, baking powder, espresso powder, and salt and stir until well combined.
3. Pour batter into the silicone muffin moulds.
4. Insert a crisper plate in Ninja Foodi air fryer baskets.
5. Place muffin moulds in both baskets.
6. Select zone 1 then select "bake" mode and set the temperature to 320 degrees F(160°C) for 18 minutes. Press match cook to match zone 2 settings to zone 1. Press "start/stop" to begin.

**Nutrition:**

- (Per serving) Calories 222 | Fat 11g |Sodium 251mg | Carbs 29.6g | Fiber 2g | Sugar 14.5g | Protein 4g

## "air-fried" Oreos Apple Fries

Servings:4
Cooking Time: 10 Minutes

**Ingredients:**

- FOR THE "FRIED" OREOS
- 1 teaspoon vegetable oil
- 1 cup all-purpose flour
- 1 tablespoon granulated sugar
- 1 tablespoon baking powder
- ½ teaspoon baking soda
- ¼ teaspoon kosher salt
- 1 large egg
- ¼ cup unsweetened almond milk
- ½ teaspoon vanilla extract
- 8 Oreo cookies
- Nonstick cooking spray
- 1 tablespoon powdered sugar (optional)
- FOR THE APPLE FRIES
- 1 teaspoon vegetable oil
- 1 cup all-purpose flour
- 1 tablespoon granulated sugar
- 1 tablespoon baking powder
- ½ teaspoon baking soda
- ¼ teaspoon kosher salt
- 1 large egg
- ¼ cup unsweetened almond milk
- ½ teaspoon vanilla extract
- 2 Granny Smith apples
- 2 tablespoons cornstarch
- ½ teaspoon apple pie spice
- Nonstick cooking spray
- 1 tablespoon powdered sugar (optional)

**Directions:**

1. To prep the "fried" Oreos: Brush a crisper plate with the oil and install it in the Zone 1 basket.
2. In a large bowl, combine the flour, granulated sugar, baking powder, baking soda, and salt. Mix in the egg, almond milk, and vanilla to form a thick batter.

3. Using a fork or slotted spoon, dip each cookie into the batter, coating it fully. Let the excess batter drip off, then place the cookies in the prepared basket in a single layer. Spritz each with cooking spray.
4. To prep the apple fries: Brush a crisper plate with the oil and install it in the Zone 2 basket.
5. In a large bowl, combine the flour, granulated sugar, baking powder, baking soda, and salt. Mix in the egg, almond milk, and vanilla to form a thick batter.
6. Core the apples and cut them into ½-inch-thick French fry shapes. Dust lightly with the cornstarch and apple pie spice.
7. Using a fork or slotted spoon, dip each apple into the batter, coating it fully. Let the excess batter drip off, then place the apples in the prepared basket in a single layer. Spritz with cooking spray.
8. To cook the "fried" Oreos and apple fries: Insert both baskets in the unit.
9. Select Zone 1, select AIR FRY, set the temperature to 400°F (205°C), and set the timer to 8 minutes.
10. Select Zone 2, select AIR FRY, set the temperature to 400°F (205°C), and set the timer to 10 minutes. Select SMART FINISH.
11. Press START/PAUSE to begin cooking.
12. When cooking is complete, the batter will be golden brown and crisp. If desired, dust the cookies and apples with the powdered sugar before serving.

**Nutrition:**

- (Per serving) Calories: 464; Total fat: 21g; Saturated fat: 3.5g; Carbohydrates: 66g; Fiber: 2.5g; Protein: 7g; Sodium: 293mg

## Cinnamon-sugar "churros" With Caramel Sauce

Servings:4
Cooking Time: 10 Minutes

**Ingredients:**

- FOR THE "CHURROS"
- 1 sheet frozen puff pastry, thawed
- Butter-flavored cooking spray
- 1 tablespoon granulated sugar
- 1 teaspoon ground cinnamon
- FOR THE CARAMEL SAUCE
- ½ cup packed light brown sugar
- 2 tablespoons unsalted butter, cut into small pieces
- ¼ cup heavy (whipping) cream
- 2 teaspoons vanilla extract
- ⅛ teaspoon kosher salt

**Directions:**

1. To prep the "churros": Cut the puff pastry crosswise into 4 rectangles. Fold each piece in half lengthwise to make a long thin "churro."
2. To prep the caramel sauce: Measure the brown sugar, butter, cream, and vanilla into an ovenproof ramekin or bowl (no need to stir).
3. To cook the "churros" and caramel sauce: Install a crisper plate in the Zone 1 basket. Place the "churros" in the basket and insert the basket in the unit. Place the ramekin in the Zone 2 basket and insert the basket in the unit.
4. Select Zone 1, select AIR FRY, set the temperature to 330°F (165°C), and set the timer to 10 minutes.
5. Select Zone 2, select BAKE, set the temperature to 350°F (175°C), and set the timer to 10 minutes. Select SMART FINISH.
6. Press START/PAUSE to begin cooking.
7. When the Zone 2 timer reads 5 minutes, press START/PAUSE. Remove the basket and stir the caramel. Reinsert the basket and press START/PAUSE to resume cooking.
8. When cooking is complete, the "churros" will be golden brown and cooked through and the caramel sauce smooth.
9. Spritz each "churro" with cooking spray and sprinkle generously with the granulated sugar and cinnamon.
10. Stir the salt into the caramel sauce. Let cool for 5 to 10 minutes before serving. Note that the caramel will thicken as it cools.

**Nutrition:**

- (Per serving) Calories: 460; Total fat: 26g; Saturated fat: 14g; Carbohydrates: 60g; Fiber: 1.5g; Protein: 5g; Sodium: 254mg

## Baked Brazilian Pineapple

Servings: 4
Cooking Time: 10 Minutes

**Ingredients:**

- 95 g brown sugar
- 2 teaspoons ground cinnamon
- 1 small pineapple, peeled, cored, and cut into spears
- 3 tablespoons unsalted butter, melted

**Directions:**

1. In a small bowl, mix the brown sugar and cinnamon until thoroughly combined.
2. Brush the pineapple spears with the melted butter. Sprinkle the cinnamon-sugar over the spears, pressing lightly to ensure it adheres well.
3. Place the spears in the two air fryer drawers in a single layer. Set the air fryer to 204ºC and cook for 10 minutes. Halfway through the cooking time, brush the spears with butter.
4. The pineapple spears are done when they are heated through, and the sugar is bubbling. Serve hot.

## Homemade Mint Pie And Strawberry Pecan Pie

Servings: 8
Cooking Time: 25 Minutes

**Ingredients:**

- Homemade Mint Pie:
- 1 tablespoon instant coffee
- 2 tablespoons almond butter, softened
- 2 tablespoons granulated sweetener
- 1 teaspoon dried mint
- 3 eggs, beaten
- 1 teaspoon dried spearmint
- 4 teaspoons coconut flour
- Cooking spray
- Strawberry Pecan Pie:
- 190 g whole shelled pecans
- 1 tablespoon unsalted butter, softened
- 240 ml heavy whipping cream
- 12 medium fresh strawberries, hulled
- 2 tablespoons sour cream

**Directions:**

1. Make the Homemade Mint Pie:
2. Spray the zone 1 air fryer drawer with cooking spray.
3. Then mix all ingredients in the mixer bowl.
4. When you get a smooth mixture, transfer it in the zone 1 air fryer drawer. Flatten it gently. Cook the pie at 185ºC for 25 minutes.
5. Make the Strawberry Pecan Pie:
6. Place pecans and butter into a food processor and pulse ten times until a dough forms. Press dough into the bottom of an ungreased round nonstick baking dish.

7. Place dish into the zone 2 air fryer drawer. Adjust the temperature to 160ºC and set the timer for 10 minutes. Crust will be firm and golden when done. Let cool 20 minutes.
8. In a large bowl, whisk cream until fluffy and doubled in size, about 2 minutes.
9. In a separate large bowl, mash strawberries until mostly liquid. Fold strawberries and sour cream into whipped cream.
10. Spoon mixture into cooled crust, cover, and place in refrigerator for at least 30 minutes to set. Serve chilled.

## Gluten-free Spice Cookies

Servings: 4
Cooking Time: 12 Minutes
**Ingredients:**
- 4 tablespoons unsalted butter, at room temperature
- 2 tablespoons agave nectar
- 1 large egg
- 2 tablespoons water
- 240 g almond flour
- 100 g granulated sugar
- 2 teaspoons ground ginger
- 1 teaspoon ground cinnamon
- ½ teaspoon freshly grated nutmeg
- 1 teaspoon baking soda
- ¼ teaspoon kosher, or coarse sea salt

**Directions:**
1. Line the bottom of the air fryer basket with baking paper cut to fit.
2. In a large bowl, using a hand mixer, beat together the butter, agave, egg, and water on medium speed until light and fluffy.
3. Add the almond flour, sugar, ginger, cinnamon, nutmeg, baking soda, and salt. Beat on low speed until well combined.
4. Roll the dough into 2-tablespoon balls and arrange them on the baking paper in the basket. Set the air fryer to 165ºC, and cook for 12 minutes, or until the tops of cookies are lightly browned.
5. Transfer to a wire rack and let cool completely. Store in an airtight container for up to a week.

## Butter Cake

Servings: 6
Cooking Time: 20 Minutes
**Ingredients:**
- 1 egg
- 3 tablespoons butter, softened
- ½ cup milk
- 1 tablespoon icing sugar
- ½ cup caster sugar
- 1½ cup plain flour
- A pinch of salt

**Directions:**
1. In a bowl, add the butter and sugar. Whisk until creamy.
2. Now, add the egg and whisk until fluffy.
3. Add the flour and salt. Mix well with the milk.
4. Place the mixture evenly into the greased cake pan.
5. Press "Zone 1" and "Zone 2" and then rotate the knob for each zone to select "Air Fry".
6. Set the temperature to 350 degrees F/ 175 degrees C for both zones and then set the time for 5 minutes to preheat.
7. After preheating, arrange the pan into the basket of each zone.
8. Slide each basket into Air Fryer and set the time for 15 minutes.
9. After cooking time is completed, remove the pan from Air Fryer.
10. Set aside to cool.
11. Serve and enjoy!

## Pecan Brownies And Cinnamon-sugar Almonds

Servings: 10
Cooking Time: 20 Minutes
**Ingredients:**
- Pecan Brownies:
- 50 g blanched finely ground almond flour
- 55 g powdered sweetener
- 2 tablespoons unsweetened cocoa powder
- ½ teaspoon baking powder
- 55 g unsalted butter, softened
- 1 large egg
- 35 g chopped pecans
- 40 g low-carb, sugar-free chocolate chips
- Cinnamon-Sugar Almonds:
- 150 g whole almonds
- 2 tablespoons salted butter, melted
- 1 tablespoon granulated sugar
- ½ teaspoon ground cinnamon

**Directions:**
1. Make the Pecan Brownies :
2. In a large bowl, mix almond flour, sweetener, cocoa powder, and baking powder. Stir in butter and egg.
3. Fold in pecans and chocolate chips. Scoop mixture into a round baking pan. Place pan into the zone 1 air fryer basket.
4. Adjust the temperature to 150ºC and bake for 20 minutes.
5. When fully cooked a toothpick inserted in center will come out clean. Allow 20 minutes to fully cool and firm up.
6. Make the Cinnamon-Sugar Almonds :
7. In a medium bowl, combine the almonds, butter, sugar, and cinnamon. Mix well to ensure all the almonds are coated with the spiced butter.
8. Transfer the almonds to the zone 2 air fryer basket and shake so they are in a single layer. Set the air fryer to 150ºC, and cook for 8 minutes, stirring the almonds halfway through the cooking time.
9. Let cool completely before serving.

## Air Fried Beignets

Servings: 6
Cooking Time: 17 Minutes.
**Ingredients:**
- Cooking spray
- ¼ cup white sugar
- ⅛ cup water
- ½ cup all-purpose flour
- 1 large egg, separated
- 1 ½ teaspoons butter, melted
- ½ teaspoon baking powder
- ½ teaspoon vanilla extract
- 1 pinch salt
- 2 tablespoons confectioners' sugar, or to taste

**Directions:**
1. Beat flour with water, sugar, egg yolk, baking powder, butter, vanilla extract, and salt in a large bowl until lumps-free.
2. Beat egg whites in a separate bowl and beat using an electric hand mixer until it forms soft peaks.
3. Add the egg white to the flour batter and mix gently until fully incorporated.
4. Divide the dough into small beignets and place them in the crisper plate.
5. Return the crisper plate to the Ninja Foodi Dual Zone Air Fryer.

6. Choose the Air Fry mode for Zone 1 and set the temperature to 390 degrees F(200°C) and the time to 17 minutes.
7. Select the "MATCH" button to copy the settings for Zone 2.
8. Initiate cooking by pressing the START/STOP button.
9. And cook for another 4 minutes. Dust the cooked beignets with sugar.
10. Serve.

**Nutrition:**

- (Per serving) Calories 327 | Fat 14.2g |Sodium 672mg | Carbs 47.2g | Fiber 1.7g | Sugar 24.8g | Protein 4.4g

## Easy Mini Chocolate Chip Pan Cookie

Servings: 4
Cooking Time: 7 Minutes

**Ingredients:**

- ½ cup blanched finely ground almond flour
- ¼ cup powdered erythritol
- 2 tablespoons unsalted butter, softened
- 1 large egg
- ½ teaspoon unflavored gelatin
- ½ teaspoon baking powder
- ½ teaspoon vanilla extract
- 2 tablespoons low-carb, sugar-free chocolate chips

**Directions:**

1. Combine erythritol and almond flour in a large bowl. Add in egg, gelatin, and butter , stir well.
2. Stir in vanilla and baking powder and then fold in chocolate chips. Spoon batter into 6&quot| round baking pan. Put pan into the air fryer basket.
3. Set the temperature to 300°F (150°C), then set the timer for 7 minutes.
4. The top of the cookie will be golden brown and a toothpick inserted in center will come out clean when fully cooked. Allow to rest for more than 10 minutes.

## Spiced Apple Cake

Servings: 6
Cooking Time: 30 Minutes

**Ingredients:**

- Vegetable oil
- 2 diced & peeled Gala apples
- 1 tablespoon fresh lemon juice
- 55 g unsalted butter, softened
- 65 g granulated sugar
- 2 large eggs
- 155 g plain flour
- 1½ teaspoons baking powder
- 1 tablespoon apple pie spice
- ½ teaspoon ground ginger
- ¼ teaspoon ground cardamom
- ¼ teaspoon ground nutmeg
- ½ teaspoon kosher, or coarse sea salt
- 60 ml whole milk
- Icing sugar, for dusting

**Directions:**

1. Grease a 0.7-liter Bundt, or tube pan with oil; set aside.
2. In a medium bowl, toss the apples with the lemon juice until well coated; set aside.
3. In a large bowl, combine the butter and sugar. Beat with an electric hand mixer on medium speed until the sugar has dissolved. Add the eggs and beat until fluffy. Add the flour, baking powder, apple pie spice, ginger, cardamom, nutmeg, salt, and milk. Mix until the batter is thick but pourable.
4. Pour the batter into the prepared pan. Top batter evenly with the apple mixture. Place the pan in the zone 1 air fryer drawer. Set the temperature to 176ºC and cook for 30 minutes, or until a toothpick inserted in the center of the cake comes out clean. Close the air fryer and let the cake rest for 10 minutes. Turn the cake out onto a wire rack and cool completely.
5. Right before serving, dust the cake with icing sugar.

## Fudge Brownies

Servings:4
Cooking Time:16

**Ingredients:**

- 1/2 cup all-purpose flour
- 1/4 cup unsweetened cocoa powder
- 3/4 teaspoon kosher salt
- 2 large eggs, whisked
- 1 tablespoon almond milk
- 1/2 cup brown sugar
- 1/2 cup packed white sugar
- 1/2 tablespoon vanilla extract
- 8 ounces of semisweet chocolate chips, melted
- 2/4 cup unsalted butter, melted

**Directions:**

1. Take a medium bowl, and use a hand beater to whisk together eggs, milk, both the sugars and vanilla.
2. In a separate microwave-safe bowl, mix melted butter and chocolate and microwave it for 30 seconds to melt the chocolate.
3. Add all the listed dry ingredients to the chocolate mixture.
4. Now incorporate the egg bowl ingredient into the batter.
5. Spray a reasonable size round baking pan that fits in baskets of air fryer
6. Grease the pan with cooking spray.
7. Now pour the batter into the pan, put the crisper plate in baskets.
8. Add the pans and insert the basket into the unit.
9. Select the AIR FRY mode and adjust the setting the temperature to 300 degrees F(150°C) , for 30 minutes.
10. Check it after 35 minutes and if not done, cook for 10 more minutes
11. Once it's done, take it out and let it get cool before serving.
12. Enjoy.

**Nutrition:**

- (Per serving) Calories 760| Fat43.3 g| Sodium644 mg | Carbs 93.2g | Fiber5.3 g | Sugar 70.2g | Protein 6.2g

## Simple Cheesecake

Servings: 3
Cooking Time: 20 Minutes

**Ingredients:**

- ½ egg
- 2 tablespoons sugar
- ⅛ teaspoon vanilla extract
- ¼ cup honey graham cracker crumbs
- ½ tablespoon unsalted butter, softened
- ¼ pound cream cheese, softened

**Directions:**

1. Line a round baking dish with parchment paper.
2. For crust: In a bowl, add the graham cracker crumbs and butter.
3. Place the crust into baking dish and press to smooth.
4. Press "Zone 1" and "Zone 2" and then rotate the knob for each zone to select "Bake".
5. Set the temperature to 350 degrees F/ 175 degrees C for both zones and then set the time for 5 minutes to preheat.
6. After preheating, arrange the baking dish into the basket of each zone.

7. Slide each basket into Air Fryer and set the time for 4 minutes.
8. Remove the crust from the oven and set aside to cool slightly.
9. Meanwhile, take a bowl, add the cream cheese and sugar. Whisk until smooth.
10. Now, place the eggs, one at a time and whisk until mixture becomes creamy.
11. Add the vanilla extract and mix well.
12. Place the cream cheese mixture evenly over the crust.
13. Arrange the baking dish into the Air-Fryer basket.
14. Remove from the oven and set aside to cool.
15. Serve and enjoy!

## Berry Crumble And S' mores

Servings: 8
Cooking Time: 15 Minutes
**Ingredients:**

- Berry Crumble:
- For the Filling:
- 300 g mixed berries
- 2 tablespoons sugar
- 1 tablespoon cornflour
- 1 tablespoon fresh lemon juice
- For the Topping:
- 30 g plain flour
- 20 g rolled oats
- 1 tablespoon granulated sugar
- 2 tablespoons cold unsalted butter, cut into small cubes
- Whipped cream or ice cream (optional)
- S'mores:
- Coconut, or avocado oil, for spraying
- 8 digestive biscuits
- 2 (45 g) chocolate bars
- 4 large marshmallows

**Directions:**

1. Make the Berry Crumble :
2. 1. Preheat the air fryer to 204ºC. For the filling: In a round baking pan, gently mix the berries, sugar, cornflour, and lemon juice until thoroughly combined. 3. For the topping: In a small bowl, combine the flour, oats, and sugar. Stir the butter into the flour mixture until the mixture has the consistency of breadcrumbs. 4. Sprinkle the topping over the berries. 5. Put the pan in the zone 1 air fryer drawer and air fry for 15 minutes. Let cool for 5 minutes on a wire rack. 6. Serve topped with whipped cream or ice cream, if desired.
3. Make the S'mores :
4. Line the zone 2 air fryer drawer with baking paper and spray lightly with oil.
5. Place 4 biscuits into the prepared drawer.
6. Break the chocolate bars in half, and place 1/2 on top of each biscuit. Top with 1 marshmallow.
7. Air fry at 188ºC for 30 seconds, or until the marshmallows are puffed, golden brown and slightly melted.
8. Top with the remaining biscuits and serve.

## Oreo Rolls

Servings: 9
Cooking Time: 8 Minutes.
**Ingredients:**

- 1 crescent sheet roll
- 9 Oreo cookies
- Cinnamon powder, to serve
- Powdered sugar, to serve

**Directions:**

1. Spread the crescent sheet roll and cut it into 9 equal squares.
2. Place one cookie at the center of each square.
3. Wrap each square around the cookies and press the ends to seal.
4. Place half of the wrapped cookies in each crisper plate.
5. Return the crisper plates to the Ninja Foodi Dual Zone Air Fryer.
6. Select the Bake mode for Zone 1 and set the temperature to 360 degrees F(180°C) and the time to 4-6 minutes.
7. Select the "MATCH" button to copy the settings for Zone 2.
8. Initiate cooking by pressing the START/STOP button.
9. Check for the doneness of the cookie rolls if they are golden brown, else cook 1-2 minutes more.
10. Garnish the rolls with sugar and cinnamon.
11. Serve.

**Nutrition:**

- (Per serving) Calories 175 | Fat 13.1g |Sodium 154mg | Carbs 14g | Fiber 0.8g | Sugar 8.9g | Protein 0.7g

## Bourbon Bread Pudding And Ricotta Lemon Poppy Seed Cake

Servings: 8
Cooking Time: 55 Minutes
**Ingredients:**

- Bourbon Bread Pudding :
- 3 slices whole grain bread, cubed
- 1 large egg
- 240 ml whole milk
- 2 tablespoons bourbon, or peach juice
- ½ teaspoons vanilla extract
- 4 tablespoons maple syrup, divided
- ½ teaspoons ground cinnamon
- 2 teaspoons sparkling sugar
- Ricotta Lemon Poppy Seed Cake:
- Unsalted butter, at room temperature
- 110 g almond flour
- 100 g granulated sugar
- 3 large eggs
- 55 g heavy cream
- 60 g full-fat ricotta cheese
- 55 g coconut oil, melted
- 2 tablespoons poppy seeds
- 1 teaspoon baking powder
- 1 teaspoon pure lemon extract
- Grated zest and juice of 1 lemon, plus more zest for garnish

**Directions:**

1. Make the Bourbon Bread Pudding :
2. Preheat the zone 1 air fryer drawer to 135ºC.
3. Spray a baking pan with nonstick cooking spray, then place the bread cubes in the pan.
4. In a medium bowl, whisk together the egg, milk, bourbon, vanilla extract, 3 tablespoons of maple syrup, and cinnamon. Pour the egg mixture over the bread and press down with a spatula to coat all the bread, then sprinkle the sparkling sugar on top and bake for 20 minutes in the zone 1 drawer.
5. Remove the pudding from the air fryer and allow to cool in the pan on a wire rack for 10 minutes. Drizzle the remaining 1 tablespoon of maple syrup on top. Slice and serve warm.
6. Make the Ricotta Lemon Poppy Seed Cake :
7. Generously butter a baking pan. Line the bottom of the pan with baking paper cut to fit.
8. In a large bowl, combine the almond flour, sugar, eggs, cream, ricotta, coconut oil, poppy seeds, baking powder, lemon

extract, lemon zest, and lemon juice. Beat with a hand mixer on medium speed, until well blended and fluffy.
9. Pour the batter into the prepared pan. Cover the pan tightly with aluminum foil. Set the pan in the zone 2 air fryer drawer. Set the temperature to 164ºC and cook for 45 minutes. Remove the foil and cook for 10 to 15 minutes more, until a knife inserted into the center of the cake comes out clean.
10. Let the cake cool in the pan on a wire rack for 10 minutes. Remove the cake from pan and let it cool on the rack for 15 minutes before slicing.
11. Top with additional lemon zest, slice and serve.

## Cake In The Air Fryer

Servings:2
Cooking Time:30
**Ingredients:**
- 90 grams all-purpose flour
- Pinch of salt
- 1/2 teaspoon of baking powder
- ½ cup of tutti fruitti mix
- 2 eggs
- 1 teaspoon of vanilla extract
- 10 tablespoons of white sugar

**Directions:**
1. Take a bowl and add all-purpose flour, salt, and baking powder.
2. Stir it in a large bowl.
3. Whisk two eggs in a separate bowl and add vanilla extract, sugar and blend it with a hand beater.
4. Now combine wet ingredients with the dry ones.
5. Mix it well and pour it between two round pan that fits inside baskets.
6. Place the pans in both the baskets.
7. Now set the zone 1 basket to BAKE function at 310 for 30 minutes.
8. Select MATCH for zone two baskets.
9. Once it's done, serve and enjoy.

**Nutrition:**
- (Per serving) Calories 711| Fat4.8g| Sodium 143mg | Carbs 161g | Fiber 1.3g | Sugar 105g | Protein 10.2g

## Pecan And Cherry Stuffed Apples

Servings: 4
Cooking Time: 20 Minutes
**Ingredients:**
- 4 apples (about 565 g)
- 40 g chopped pecans
- 50 g dried tart cherries
- 1 tablespoon melted butter
- 3 tablespoons brown sugar
- ¼ teaspoon allspice
- Pinch salt
- Ice cream, for serving

**Directions:**
1. Cut off top ½ inch from each apple; reserve tops. With a melon baller, core through stem ends without breaking through the bottom.
2. Preheat the air fryer to 175ºC. Combine pecans, cherries, butter, brown sugar, allspice, and a pinch of salt. Stuff mixture into the hollow centers of the apples. Cover with apple tops. Put in the air fryer basket, using tongs. Air fry for 20 to 25 minutes, or just until tender.
3. Serve warm with ice cream.

## Peanut Butter, Honey & Banana Toast

Servings: 4
Cooking Time: 9 Minutes
**Ingredients:**
- 2 tablespoons unsalted butter, softened
- 4 slices white bread
- 4 tablespoons peanut butter
- 2 bananas, peeled and thinly sliced
- 4 tablespoons honey
- 1 teaspoon ground cinnamon

**Directions:**
1. Spread butter on one side of each slice of bread, then peanut butter on the other side. Arrange the banana slices on top of the peanut butter sides of each slice . Drizzle honey on top of the banana and sprinkle with cinnamon.
2. Cut each slice in half lengthwise so that it will better fit into the air fryer basket. Arrange the bread slices, butter sides down, in the two air fryer baskets. Set the air fryer to 190ºC cooking for 5 minutes. Then set the air fryer to 205ºC and cook for an additional 4 minutes, or until the bananas have started to brown. Serve hot.

## Bread Pudding

Servings: 4
Cooking Time: 15 Minutes
**Ingredients:**
- 2 cups bread cubes
- 1 egg
- ⅔ cup heavy cream
- ½ teaspoon vanilla extract
- ¼ cup sugar
- ¼ cup chocolate chips

**Directions:**
1. Grease two 4 inches baking dish with a cooking spray.
2. Divide the bread cubes in the baking dishes and sprinkle chocolate chips on top.
3. Beat egg with cream, sugar and vanilla in a bowl.
4. Divide this mixture in the baking dishes.
5. Place one pan in each air fryer basket.
6. Return the air fryer basket 1 to Zone 1, and basket 2 to Zone 2 of the Ninja Foodi 2-Basket Air Fryer.
7. Choose the "Air Fry" mode for Zone 1 at 350 degrees F(175°C) and 15 minutes of cooking time.
8. Select the "MATCH COOK" option to copy the settings for Zone 2.
9. Initiate cooking by pressing the START/PAUSE BUTTON.
10. Allow the pudding to cool and serve.

**Nutrition:**
- (Per serving) Calories 149 | Fat 1.2g |Sodium 3mg | Carbs 37.6g | Fiber 5.8g | Sugar 29g | Protein 1.1g

## Monkey Bread

Servings: 12
Cooking Time: 10 Minutes
**Ingredients:**
- Bread
- 12 Rhodes white dinner rolls
- ½ cup brown sugar
- 1 teaspoon cinnamon
- 4 tablespoons butter melted
- Glaze
- ½ cup powdered sugar
- 1-2 tablespoons milk
- ½ teaspoon vanilla

**Directions:**

1. Mix brown sugar, cinnamon and butter in a bowl.
2. Cut the dinner rolls in half and dip them in the sugar mixture.
3. Place these buns in a greased baking pan and pour the remaining butter on top.
4. Place the buns in the air fryer baskets.
5. Return the air fryer basket 1 to Zone 1, and basket 2 to Zone 2 of the Ninja Foodi 2-Basket Air Fryer.
6. Choose the "Air Fry" mode for Zone 1 at 350 degrees F(175°C) and 10 minutes of cooking time.
7. Initiate cooking by pressing the START/PAUSE BUTTON.
8. Flip the rolls once cooked halfway through.
9. Meanwhile, mix milk, vanilla and sugar in a bowl.
10. Pour the glaze over the air fried rolls.
11. Serve.

**Nutrition:**

- (Per serving) Calories 192 | Fat 9.3g |Sodium 133mg | Carbs 27.1g | Fiber 1.4g | Sugar 19g | Protein 3.2g

## Mini Strawberry And Cream Pies

Servings:2
Cooking Time:10

**Ingredients:**

- 1 box Store-Bought Pie Dough, Trader Joe's
- 1 cup strawberries, cubed
- 3 tablespoons of cream, heavy
- 2 tablespoons of almonds
- 1 egg white, for brushing

**Directions:**

1. Take the store brought pie dough and flatten it on a surface.
2. Use a round cutter to cut it into 3-inch circles.
3. Brush the dough with egg white all around the parameters.
4. Now add almonds, strawberries, and cream in a very little amount in the center of the dough, and top it with another circular.
5. Press the edges with the fork to seal it.
6. Make a slit in the middle of the dough and divide it into the baskets.
7. Set zone 1 to AIR FRY mode 360 degrees F(180°C) for 10 minutes.
8. Select MATCH for zone 2 basket.
9. Once done, serve.

**Nutrition:**

- (Per serving) Calories 203| Fat12.7g| Sodium 193mg | Carbs20 g | Fiber 2.2g | Sugar 5.8g | Protein 3.7g

## Dessert Empanadas

Servings: 12
Cooking Time: 10 Minutes

**Ingredients:**

- 12 empanada wrappers thawed
- 2 apples, chopped
- 2 tablespoons raw honey
- 1 teaspoon vanilla extract
- 1 teaspoon cinnamon
- ⅛ teaspoon nutmeg
- 2 teaspoons cornstarch
- 1 teaspoon water
- 1 egg beaten

**Directions:**

1. Mix apples with vanilla, honey, nutmeg, and cinnamon in a saucepan.
2. Cook for 3 minutes then mix cornstarch with water and pour into the pan.
3. Cook for 30 seconds.
4. Allow this filling to cool and keep it aside.
5. Spread the wrappers on the working surface.
6. Divide the apple filling on top of the wrappers.
7. Fold the wrappers in half and seal the edges by pressing them.
8. Brush the empanadas with the beaten egg and place them in the air fryer basket 1.
9. Return the air fryer basket 1 to Zone 1 of the Ninja Foodi 2-Basket Air Fryer.
10. Choose the "Air Fry" mode for Zone 1 at 400 degrees F(205°C) and 10 minutes of cooking time.
11. Initiate cooking by pressing the START/PAUSE BUTTON.
12. Flip the empanadas once cooked halfway through.
13. Serve.

**Nutrition:**

- (Per serving) Calories 204 | Fat 9g |Sodium 91mg | Carbs 27g | Fiber 2.4g | Sugar 15g | Protein 1.3g

## Simple Pineapple Sticks And Crispy Pineapple Rings

Servings: 9
Cooking Time: 10 Minutes

**Ingredients:**

- Simple Pineapple Sticks:
- ½ fresh pineapple, cut into sticks
- 25 g desiccated coconut
- Crispy Pineapple Rings:
- 240 ml rice milk
- 85 g plain flour
- 120 ml water
- 25 g unsweetened flaked coconut
- 4 tablespoons granulated sugar
- ½ teaspoon baking soda
- ½ teaspoon baking powder
- ½ teaspoon vanilla essence
- ½ teaspoon ground cinnamon
- ¼ teaspoon ground star anise
- Pinch of kosher, or coarse sea salt
- 1 medium pineapple, peeled and sliced

**Directions:**

1. Simple Pineapple Sticks :
2. Preheat the air fryer to 204ºC.
3. Coat the pineapple sticks in the desiccated coconut and put in the zone 1 air fryer drawer.
4. Air fry for 10 minutes.
5. Serve immediately
6. Crispy Pineapple Rings :
7. Preheat the air fryer to 204ºC.
8. In a large bowl, stir together all the ingredients except the pineapple.
9. Dip each pineapple slice into the batter until evenly coated.
10. Arrange the pineapple slices in the zone 2 drawer and air fry for 6 to 8 minutes until golden brown.
11. Remove from the drawer to a plate and cool for 5 minutes before serving warm

## Apple Fritters

Servings: 14
Cooking Time: 10 Minutes

**Ingredients:**

- 2 large apples
- 2 cups all-purpose flour
- ½ cup granulated sugar
- 1 tablespoon baking powder
- 1 teaspoon salt

- 1 teaspoon ground cinnamon
- ½ teaspoon ground nutmeg
- ¼ teaspoon ground cloves
- ¾ cup apple cider or apple juice
- 2 eggs
- 3 tablespoons butter, melted
- 1 teaspoon vanilla extract
- For the apple cider glaze:
- 2 cups powdered sugar
- ¼ cup apple cider or apple juice
- ½ teaspoon ground cinnamon
- ¼ teaspoon ground nutmeg

**Directions:**

1. Peel and core the apples, then cut them into ¼-inch cubes. Spread the apple chunks out on a kitchen towel to absorb any excess moisture.
2. In a mixing bowl, combine the flour, sugar, baking powder, salt, and spices.
3. Add the apple chunks and combine well.
4. Whisk together the apple cider, eggs, melted butter, and vanilla in a small bowl.
5. Combine the wet and dry ingredients in a large mixing bowl.
6. Install a crisper plate in both drawers. Use an ice cream scoop to scoop 3 to 4 dollops of fritter dough into the zone 1 drawer and 3 to 4 dollops into the zone 2 drawer. Insert the drawers into the unit. You may need to cook in batches.
7. Select zone 1, select BAKE, set temperature to 390 degrees F/ 200 degrees C, and set time to 10 minutes. Select MATCH to match zone 2 settings to zone 1. Press the START/STOP button to begin cooking.
8. Meanwhile, make the glaze: Whisk the powdered sugar, apple cider, and spices together until smooth.
9. When the fritters are cooked, drizzle the glaze over them. Let sit for 10 minutes until the glaze sets.

**Nutrition:**

- (Per serving) Calories 221 | Fat 3g | Sodium 288mg | Carbs 46g | Fiber 2g | Sugar 29g | Protein 3g

## Lemony Sweet Twists

Servings:2

Cooking Time:9

**Ingredients:**

- 1 box store-bought puff pastry
- ½ teaspoon lemon zest
- 1 tablespoon of lemon juice
- 2 teaspoons brown sugar
- Salt, pinch
- 2 tablespoons Parmesan cheese, freshly grated

**Directions:**

1. Put the puff pastry dough on a clean work area.
2. In a bowl, combine Parmesan cheese, brown sugar, salt, lemon zest, and lemon juice.
3. Press this mixture on both sides of the dough.
4. Now, cut the pastry into 1" x 4" strips.
5. Twist each of the strips.
6. Transfer to both the air fryer baskets.
7. Select zone 1 to air fry mode at 400 degrees F(205°C) for 9-10 minutes.
8. Select match for zone 2 basket.
9. Once cooked, serve and enjoy.

**Nutrition:**

- (Per serving) Calories 156| Fat10g| Sodium 215mg | Carbs 14g | Fiber 0.4g | Sugar3.3 g | Protein 2.8g

## Apple Crisp

Servings: 8

Cooking Time: 14 Minutes.

**Ingredients:**

- 3 cups apples, chopped
- 1 tablespoon pure maple syrup
- 2 teaspoons lemon juice
- 3 tablespoons all-purpose flour
- ⅓ cup quick oats
- ¼ cup brown sugar
- 2 tablespoons light butter, melted
- ½ teaspoon cinnamon

**Directions:**

1. Toss the chopped apples with 1 tablespoon of all-purpose flour, cinnamon, maple syrup, and lemon juice in a suitable bowl.
2. Divide the apples in the two air fryer baskets with their crisper plates.
3. Whisk oats, brown sugar, and remaining all-purpose flour in a small bowl.
4. Stir in melted butter, then divide this mixture over the apples.
5. Return the crisper plate to the Ninja Foodi Dual Zone Air Fryer.
6. Select the Bake mode for Zone 1 and set the temperature to 375 degrees F(190°C) and the time to 14 minutes.
7. Select the "MATCH" button to copy the settings for Zone 2.
8. Initiate cooking by pressing the START/STOP button.
9. Enjoy fresh.

**Nutrition:**

- (Per serving) Calories 258 | Fat 12.4g |Sodium 79mg | Carbs 34.3g | Fiber 1g | Sugar 17g | Protein 3.2g

## Strawberry Nutella Hand Pies

Servings: 8

Cooking Time: 10 Minutes

**Ingredients:**

- 1 tube pie crust dough
- 3–4 strawberries, finely chopped
- Nutella
- Sugar
- Coconut oil cooking spray

**Directions:**

1. Roll out the pie dough and place it on a baking sheet. Cut out hearts using a 3-inch heart-shaped cookie cutter as precisely as possible.
2. Gather the leftover dough into a ball and roll it out thinly to make a few more heart shapes. For 8 hand pies, I was able to get 16 hearts from one tube of pie crust.
3. Set aside a baking tray lined with parchment paper.
4. Spread a dollop of Nutella (approximately 1 teaspoon) on one of the hearts. Add a few strawberry pieces to the mix. Add a pinch of sugar to the top.
5. Place another heart on top and use a fork to tightly crimp the edges. Gently poke holes in the top of the pie with a fork. Place on a baking sheet. Repeat for all the pies.
6. All of the pies on the tray should be sprayed with coconut oil.
7. Install a crisper plate in both drawers. Place half the pies in the zone 1 drawer and half in zone 2's, then insert the drawers into the unit.
8. Select zone 1, select BAKE, set temperature to 390 degrees F/ 200 degrees C, and set time to 10 minutes. Select MATCH to match zone 2 settings to zone 1. Press the START/STOP button to begin cooking.

**Nutrition:**

- (Per serving) Calories 41 | Fat 2.1g | Sodium 18mg | Carbs 5.5g | Fiber 0.4g | Sugar 4.1g | Protein 0.4g

## Mini Peanut Butter Tarts

Servings: 8
Cooking Time: 12 To 15 Minutes
**Ingredients:**

- 125 g pecans
- 110 g finely ground blanched almond flour
- 2 tablespoons unsalted butter, at room temperature
- 50 g powdered sweetener, plus 2 tablespoons, divided
- 120 g heavy (whipping) cream
- 2 tablespoons mascarpone cheese
- 110 g cream cheese
- 140 g sugar-free peanut butter
- 1 teaspoon pure vanilla extract
- ⅛ teaspoon sea salt
- 85 g organic chocolate chips
- 1 tablespoon coconut oil
- 40 g chopped peanuts or pecans

**Directions:**

1. Place the pecans in the bowl of a food processor; process until they are finely ground.
2. Transfer the ground pecans to a medium bowl and stir in the almond flour. Add the butter and 2 tablespoons of sweetener and stir until the mixture becomes wet and crumbly.
3. Divide the mixture among 8 silicone muffin cups, pressing the crust firmly with your fingers into the bottom and part way up the sides of each cup.
4. Arrange the muffin cups in the two air fryer drawers. Set the air fryer to 148°C and bake for 12 to 15 minutes, until the crusts begin to brown. Remove the cups from the air fryer and set them aside to cool.
5. In the bowl of a stand mixer, combine the heavy cream and mascarpone cheese. Beat until peaks form. Transfer to a large bowl.
6. In the same stand mixer bowl, combine the cream cheese, peanut butter, remaining 50 g sweetener, vanilla, and salt. Beat at medium-high speed until smooth.
7. Reduce the speed to low and add the heavy cream mixture back a spoonful at a time, beating after each addition.
8. Spoon the peanut butter mixture over the crusts and freeze the tarts for 30 minutes.
9. Place the chocolate chips and coconut oil in the top of a double boiler over high heat. Stir until melted, then remove from the heat.
10. Drizzle the melted chocolate over the peanut butter tarts. Top with the chopped nuts and freeze the tarts for another 15 minutes, until set.
11. Store the peanut butter tarts in an airtight container in the refrigerator for up to 1 week or in the freezer for up to 1 month.

## Apple Pie Rolls

Servings: 8
Cooking Time: 12 Minutes
**Ingredients:**

- 3 cups tart apples, peeled, cored and chopped
- ½ cup light brown sugar
- 2½ teaspoon ground cinnamon, divided
- 1 teaspoon corn starch
- 8 egg roll wrappers
- ½ cup cream cheese, softened
- Non-stick cooking spray
- 2 tablespoons sugar

**Directions:**

1. In a small bowl, mix together the apples, brown sugar, 1 teaspoon of cinnamon and corn starch.
2. Arrange 1 egg roll wrapper onto a smooth surface.
3. Spread about 1 tablespoon of cream cheese over roll, leaving 1-inch of edges.
4. Place ⅓ cup of apple mixture over one corner of a wrapper, just below the center.
5. Fold the bottom corner over filling.
6. With wet fingers, moisten the remaining wrapper edges.
7. Fold side corners toward center over the filling.
8. Roll egg roll up tightly and with your fingers, press at tip to seal.
9. Repeat with the remaining wrappers, cream cheese and filling.
10. Spray the rolls with cooking spray evenly.
11. Press "Zone 1" and "Zone 2" and then rotate the knob for each zone to select "Air Fry".
12. Set the temperature to 400 degrees F/ 205 degrees C for both zones and then set the time for 5 minutes to preheat.
13. After preheating, arrange 4 rolls into the basket of each zone.
14. Slide each basket into Air Fryer and set the time for 12 minutes.
15. While cooking, flip the rolls once halfway through and spray with the cooking spray.
16. Meanwhile, in a shallow dish, mix together the sugar and remaining cinnamon.
17. After cooking time is completed, remove the rolls from Air Fryer.
18. Coat the rolls with sugar mixture and serve.

## Mini Blueberry Pies

Servings:2
Cooking Time:10
**Ingredients:**

- 1 box Store-Bought Pie Dough, Trader Joe's
- ¼ cup blueberry jam
- 1 teaspoon of lemon zest
- 1 egg white, for brushing

**Directions:**

1. Take the store brought pie dough and cut it into 3-inch circles.
2. Brush the dough with egg white all around the parameters.
3. Now add blueberry jam and zest in the middle and top it with another circular.
4. Press the edges with the fork to seal it.
5. Make a slit in the middle of the dough and divide it between the baskets.
6. Set zone 1 to AIR FRY mode 360 degrees F(180°C) for 10 minutes.
7. Select the MATCH button for zone 2.
8. Once cooked, serve.

**Nutrition:**

- (Per serving) Calories 234| Fat8.6g| Sodium187 mg | Carbs 38.2 g | Fiber 0.1g | Sugar13.7 g | Protein 2g

## Lemon Sugar Cookie Bars Monster Sugar Cookie Bars

Servings:12
Cooking Time: 18 Minutes
**Ingredients:**

- FOR THE LEMON COOKIE BARS
- Grated zest and juice of 1 lemon
- ½ cup granulated sugar
- 4 tablespoons (½ stick) unsalted butter, at room temperature
- 1 large egg yolk
- 1 teaspoon vanilla extract
- ⅛ teaspoon baking powder
- ½ cup plus 2 tablespoons all-purpose flour

- FOR THE MONSTER COOKIE BARS
- ½ cup granulated sugar
- 4 tablespoons (½ stick) unsalted butter, at room temperature
- 1 large egg yolk
- 1 teaspoon vanilla extract
- ⅛ teaspoon baking powder
- ½ cup plus 2 tablespoons all-purpose flour
- ¼ cup rolled oats
- ¼ cup M&M's
- ¼ cup peanut butter chips

**Directions:**

1. To prep the lemon cookie bars: In a large bowl, rub together the lemon zest and sugar. Add the butter and use a hand mixer to beat until light and fluffy.
2. Beat in the egg yolk, vanilla, and lemon juice. Mix in the baking powder and flour.
3. To prep the monster cookie bars: In a large bowl, with a hand mixer, beat the sugar and butter until light and fluffy.
4. Beat in the egg yolk and vanilla. Mix in the baking powder and flour. Stir in the oats, M&M's, and peanut butter chips.
5. To cook the cookie bars: Line both baskets with aluminum foil. Press the lemon cookie dough into the Zone 1 basket and insert the basket in the unit. Press the monster cookie dough into the Zone 2 basket and insert the basket in the unit.
6. Select Zone 1, select BAKE, set the temperature to 330°F (165°C), and set the timer to 18 minutes. Press MATCH COOK to match Zone 2 settings to Zone 1.
7. Press START/PAUSE to begin cooking.
8. When cooking is complete, the cookies should be set in the middle and have begun to pull away from the sides of the basket.
9. Let the cookies cool completely, about 1 hour. Cut each basket into 6 bars for a total of 12 bars.

**Nutrition:**

- (Per serving) Calories: 191; Total fat: 8.5g; Saturated fat: 5g; Carbohydrates: 27g; Fiber: 0.5g; Protein: 2g; Sodium: 3mg

## Banana Spring Rolls With Hot Fudge Dip

Servings:4

Cooking Time: 10 Minutes

**Ingredients:**

- FOR THE BANANA SPRING ROLLS
- 1 large banana
- 4 egg roll wrappers
- 4 teaspoons light brown sugar
- Nonstick cooking spray
- FOR THE HOT FUDGE DIP
- ¼ cup sweetened condensed milk
- 2 tablespoons semisweet chocolate chips
- 1 tablespoon unsweetened cocoa powder
- 1 tablespoon unsalted butter
- ⅛ teaspoon kosher salt
- ⅛ teaspoon vanilla extract

**Directions:**

1. To prep the banana spring rolls: Peel the banana and halve it crosswise. Cut each piece in half lengthwise, for a total of 4 pieces.
2. Place one piece of banana diagonally across an egg roll wrapper. Sprinkle with 1 teaspoon of brown sugar. Fold the edges of the egg roll wrapper over the ends of the banana, then roll to enclose the banana inside. Brush the edge of the wrapper with water and press to seal. Spritz with cooking spray. Repeat with the remaining bananas, egg roll wrappers, and brown sugar.
3. To prep the hot fudge dip: In an ovenproof ramekin or bowl, combine the condensed milk, chocolate chips, cocoa powder, butter, salt, and vanilla.
4. To cook the spring rolls and hot fudge dip: Install a crisper plate in each of the two baskets. Place the banana spring rolls seam-side down in the Zone 1 basket and insert the basket in the unit. Place the ramekin in the Zone 2 basket and insert the basket in the unit.
5. Select Zone 1, select AIR FRY, set the temperature to 390°F (200°C), and set the timer to 10 minutes.
6. Select Zone 2, select BAKE, set the temperature to 330°F (165°C), and set the timer to 8 minutes. Select SMART FINISH.
7. Press START/PAUSE to begin cooking.
8. When the Zone 2 timer reads 3 minutes, press START/PAUSE. Remove the basket and stir the hot fudge until smooth. Reinsert the basket and press START/PAUSE to resume cooking.
9. When cooking is complete, the spring rolls should be crisp.
10. Let the hot fudge cool for 2 to 3 minutes. Serve the banana spring rolls with hot fudge for dipping.

**Nutrition:**

- (Per serving) Calories: 268; Total fat: 10g; Saturated fat: 4g; Carbohydrates: 42g; Fiber: 2g; Protein: 5g; Sodium: 245mg

## Pineapple Wontons

Servings: 5

Cooking Time: 15 To 18 Minutes

**Ingredients:**

- 225 g cream cheese
- 170 g finely chopped fresh pineapple
- 20 wonton wrappers
- Cooking oil spray

**Directions:**

1. In a small microwave-safe bowl, heat the cream cheese in the microwave on high power for 20 seconds to soften.
2. In a medium bowl, stir together the cream cheese and pineapple until mixed well.
3. Lay out the wonton wrappers on a work surface. A clean table or large cutting board works well.
4. Spoon 1½ teaspoons of the cream cheese mixture onto each wrapper. Be careful not to overfill.
5. Fold each wrapper diagonally across to form a triangle. Bring the 2 bottom corners up toward each other. Do not close the wrapper yet. Bring up the 2 open sides and push out any air. Squeeze the open edges together to seal.
6. Preheat the air fryer to 200ºC.
7. Place the wontons into the two drawers. Spray the wontons with the cooking oil.
8. Cook wontons for 10 minutes, then remove the drawers, flip each wonton, and spray them with more oil. Reinsert the drawers to resume cooking for 5 to 8 minutes more until the wontons are light golden brown and crisp.
9. When the cooking is complete, cool for 5 minutes before serving.

## Crispy Pineapple Rings

Servings: 6

Cooking Time: 6 To 8 Minutes

**Ingredients:**

- 240 ml rice milk
- 85 g plain flour
- 120 ml water
- 25 g unsweetened flaked coconut
- 4 tablespoons granulated sugar
- ½ teaspoon baking soda
- ½ teaspoon baking powder

- ½ teaspoon vanilla essence
- ½ teaspoon ground cinnamon
- ¼ teaspoon ground star anise
- Pinch of kosher, or coarse sea salt
- 1 medium pineapple, peeled and sliced

**Directions:**

1. Preheat the air fryer to 190ºC.
2. In a large bowl, stir together all the ingredients except the pineapple.
3. Dip each pineapple slice into the batter until evenly coated.
4. Arrange the pineapple slices in the zone 1 basket and air fry for 6 to 8 minutes until golden brown.
5. Remove from the basket to a plate and cool for 5 minutes before serving warm

## Fluffy Layered Peanut Butter Cheesecake Brownies

Servings: 6
Cooking Time: 35 Minutes

**Ingredients:**

- ½ cup blanched finely ground almond flour
- 1 cup powdered erythritol, divided
- 2 tablespoons unsweetened cocoa powder
- ½ teaspoon baking powder
- ¼ cup unsalted butter, softened
- 2 large eggs, divided
- 8 ounces full-fat cream cheese, softened
- ¼ cup heavy whipping cream
- 1 teaspoon vanilla extract
- 2 tablespoons no-sugar-added peanut butter

**Directions:**

1. In a large bowl, combine ½ cup erythritol, almond flour, baking powder and cocoa powder. Add in butter and one egg, stir well.
2. Spoon mixture into 6&quot| round baking pan. Put pan into the air fryer basket.
3. Set the temperature to 300°F (150°C), then set the timer for 20 minutes.
4. A toothpick inserted in center will come out clean when fully cooked. Allow to completely cool for 20 minutes and firm up.
5. In a large bowl, beat heavy cream, cream cheese, remaining ½ cup erythritol, peanut butter, remaining egg, and vanilla until turns fluffy.
6. Spoon mixture over cooled brownies. Return the pan into the air fryer basket.
7. Set the temperature to 300°F (150°C), then set the timer for 15 minutes.
8. When fully done, cheesecake will be slightly browned and mostly firm with
9. a slight jiggle. Let it rest and refrigerate for at least 2 hours before serving.

## Maple-pecan Tart With Sea Salt

Servings: 8
Cooking Time: 25 Minutes

**Ingredients:**

- Tart Crust:
- Vegetable oil spray
- 75 g unsalted butter, softened
- 50 g firmly packed brown sugar
- 125 g plain flour
- ¼ teaspoon kosher, or coarse sea salt
- Filling:
- 4 tablespoons unsalted butter, diced
- 95 g packed brown sugar
- 60 ml pure maple syrup
- 60 ml whole milk
- ¼ teaspoon pure vanilla extract
- 190 g finely chopped pecans
- ¼ teaspoon flaked sea salt

**Directions:**

1. For the crust: Line a baking pan with foil, leaving a couple of inches of overhang. Spray the foil with vegetable oil spray. 2. In a medium bowl, combine the butter and brown sugar. Beat with an electric mixer on medium-low speed until light and fluffy. Add the flour and kosher salt and beat until the ingredients are well blended. Transfer the mixture to the prepared pan. Press it evenly into the bottom of the pan. 3. Place the pan in the zone 1 air fryer drawer. Set the temperature to 176ºC and cook for 13 minutes. When the crust has 5 minutes left to cook, start the filling. 4. For the filling: In a medium saucepan, combine the butter, brown sugar, maple syrup, and milk. Bring to a simmer, stirring occasionally. When it begins simmering, cook for 1 minute. Remove from the heat and stir in the vanilla and pecans. 5. Carefully pour the filling evenly over the crust, gently spreading with a rubber spatula so the nuts and liquid are evenly distributed. Keep the air fryer at 176ºC and cook for 12 minutes, or until mixture is bubbling. 6. Remove the pan from the air fryer and sprinkle the tart with the sea salt. Cool completely on a wire rack until room temperature. 7. Transfer the pan to the refrigerator to chill. When cold , use the foil overhang to remove the tart from the pan and cut into 8 wedges. Serve at room temperature.

# RECIPE INDEX

Printed in Great Britain
by Amazon

23041435R00064